THE COMPLETE BOOK
OF HOUSEPLANTS

THE COMPLETE

Photographs by the author unless otherwise noted

BOOK OF HOUSEPLANTS

by Charles Marden Fitch

A Helen Van Pelt Wilson Book

Hawthorn Books, Inc.
Publishers · New York

*For my friends around the world.
I hope we will cultivate an understanding
interest in each other and learn to
live in peace. Let's begin with our
mutual love of nature's beauty.*

THE COMPLETE BOOK OF HOUSEPLANTS

TYPOGRAPHY BY STAN DRATE

4   5   6   7   8   9   10

Acknowledgments

To my horticultural friends in many countries who helped me to learn about tropical plants in varied habitats I send heartfelt thanks. *Mil gracias* to biologist Ines Triana Gary for her assistance in exploring Colombian natural history. For providing special information and helping with photographs, thank you Albert and Diantha Buell, gesneriad specialists, and Joy Logee Martin, of Logee's Greenhouses.

Thank you to Fred Bender, Harold Epstein, Margaret Ryan, and Julius Weber for opening your homes and hearts to help me. To fellow members of tropical-plant societies, thank you for horticultural suggestions and your collective enthusiasm. To my friends Alex D. Hawkes, who first helped me to learn about orchids, Elizabeth C. Hall, an enthusiastic source of information, and Alfred Byrd Graf, an encouraging influence through personal correspondence and his extraordinary book *Exotica*, thank you. For early encouragement and advice on gesneriads, thank you, Elvin McDonald. I am especially grateful to Helen Van Pelt Wilson for her advice. A thank-you that begins the day I was born, to my parents, Dr. and Mrs. W. P. Fitch, who first encouraged their son in his exploration of nature's world.

C. M. F.

Contents

Introduction: My Travels
in the Tropics

WHEN I WAS GROWING UP IN NEW YORK CITY, I thought of the tropics as mysterious regions where my favorite radio heroes fought savage natives and risked their lives struggling through creature-infested jungles. In school I learned to locate the tropics at the globe's waist, and I imagined these regions to be unbearably hot places inhabited by farmers growing coconuts and bananas. Such was the information that my early stay-at-home teachers managed to convey.

One Saturday in June my parents took my brother Don and me to visit the greenhouses of the New York Botanical Garden. These greenhouses are flanked by spacious fish pools where, each summer, water lilies, lotuses, and papyruses create an exotic scene. This was my introduction to tropical plants, and it has led me into a succession of fascinating explorations.

It must have been the landscape inside a steamy glasshouse that made the greatest impression on a boy accustomed only to privet hedges and ailanthus trees growing through holes in a sidewalk. The luxuriant rain-forest plants were a dramatic change. Every breath I drew was heavy with the perfumes of passion flowers, twining jasmines, humus, and other unfamiliar scents. I recall a pool surrounded by philodendrons and palms which grew much larger than any I had ever seen in a store window or movie-house lobby. It was hot, but the plants were so intriguing that I didn't realize how uncomfortable it was.

On our birthdays my brother and I were permitted to do anything we thought would be fun. Previous years we had gone to movies, visited the Museum of Natural History, or eaten in a foreign restaurant, but this year was different: On July 30 I announced that we would go to my newly discovered tropical paradise at the New York Botanical Garden.

The temperature outside was 96°, a standard New York heat wave and thus a unique phenomenon unrivaled in discomfort anywhere in the tropics. Inside the giant greenhouse a relative humidity close to 100 percent combined with heat to push our "comfort index" off its scale. Mother and Dad were sincerely abetting my interest, but I remember that they both chose to give up the greenhouse visit for a longer look at the water lilies outdoors. (I later learned that the tropical plants were thriving in spite of the stifling summer greenhouse temperature rather than because of it.)

When we moved out of the city, the tropics were pushed aside to make room for studies in local natural history. For years ecology, conservation projects, and native wild animals occupied my after-school hours. By running a small game farm I came to know all manner of wild creatures, including an array of domestic birds and assorted mammals. Soon hardy plants— rhododendrons, *Hemerocallis*, hostas, and wild flowers—caught my interest. For a time I felt the conflict between wanting my animals to run free and hoping they would not trample or eat up the garden.

While driving through Florida years after my visit to the botanical garden, I began to recall the happy hours of exploring those big greenhouses. Palms, Spanish moss, and the jungle ambience of the Florida woods triggered anew my interest in the tropics. In time I found that the Everglades in southern Florida are only semitropical, but for a New Yorker that was close enough, at least as a start, and so I chose to live in Coral Gables just on the edge of the Everglades.

For two years I studied at the University of Miami. Every late afternoon and early evening I worked with a friend on a Miami television program. Weekends we drove out to the wild areas, studying nature and collecting an occasional snake, turtle, or plant for use on the television program. In parts of southern Florida, cypress and buttonwood trees are draped with red-flowered air plants (tillandsias) and delicate honey-scented epidendrum orchids. If I had not been addicted to tropical plants before, I was certainly hooked by these sprays of yellow orchids swaying in a warm breeze against an electric-blue sky.

After transferring to New York University for a B.S. degree, I re-created the tropics in my home by filling every window with exotic warm-climate plants. One year I concentrated on bromeliads, the next on gesneriads, a season for begonias, another for succulents, and then on orchids. My primary pleasure is in teaching others about the world of nature, so for an M.A. degree I specialized in communications.

As a television director I had difficulty at first in getting fellow students to work on the studio crew. They came to expect a bag full of snakes, a pot of thorny cacti, or a station wagon of toothy opossums and raccoons for each of my productions. Fortunately everyone ended up fascinated by his introduction to living plants and animals. Later, as talent-producer for a New York television station a series of features I created taught me that almost everyone enjoys programs concerned with the world of nature when presented with enthusiasm and honesty.

When the Peace Corps began a pilot educational television project in Colombia, I was made director-producer of natural science programming. My duties included the creation of documentary films and field research for nationally broadcast science programs. In this work I traveled from chilly Andean peaks to sweltering Amazonian jungles, exploring, talking with the people, and studying a great variety of plants.

Other explorations have taken me to Africa, Europe, and the Caribbean. Later, as an executive director-producer with a United States Department of State ETV project I lived in Central America. These journeys enhanced for me the fascination of tropical ecology and botany. Even more, they have made me want to share my discoveries and the treasures that I now grow at home: Mediterranean bulbs, South African succulents, Australian euca-lypti, and my first favorites, the true tropicals from gesneriads to orchids.

1

Habitats of Houseplants

M ANY ATTRACTIVE PLANTS from tropical countries can adapt themselves to the average home. This is one excellent reason for selecting them as your houseplants, and they are widely available from mail-order nurseries. Plant explorers are still finding new treasures, and plant breeders are developing and selecting hybrids for introduction around the world.

This book is concerned with modern techniques for growing houseplants, most of them adaptable tropicals, unusual plants that come from many varied regions, from cloud forests to dry deserts. You will have success with houseplants when the species are suited to the conditions you can provide. What we loosely label the tropics actually encompasses several types of climate with variations in moisture and temperature. I base cultural recommendations on the original habitat of each species.

Light and Temperature in the Tropics

In tropical areas plants receive an almost equal duration of light hours daily throughout the year. Since there is little difference in the twelve-hour day length from one month to the next, most plants from the tropics can be grown in our homes with little concern for day length. Some will respond to longer-than-normal days by increased growth and often more abundant bloom, as orchid seedlings growing to maturity or as African-violets and rex begonias which, by extended light hours, can often be kept from dormancy or resting.

A few species, usually from the margins of the tropics, farther away from the equator, need twelve hours of daylight or somewhat less every twenty-four hours to initiate flowering, as the poinsettia, of Central Mexico and usually *Phalaenopsis schilleriana*, a pink-toned moth orchid of the Philippines. The majority, however, will come to flower without concern for short days.

The temperature range is close to that normally preferred in our homes. Variations in altitude do create habitats with lower temperatures, but even plants from eight thousand to nine thousand feet will still do well, especially if they are grown where night temperatures are at least 5° to 10° lower than daytime highs. Even nights indoors that are slightly cooler than normal, down to 60°, for example, are beneficial to most plants from mountains or high plains. The tropical plants that prefer stuffy overly hot conditions are very few. Plants that come from areas where temperatures rise into the 90's by day and fall into the 60's by night become adapted to variable conditions in capitivity, as many flowering shrubs and philodendrons, if humidity remains above 40 percent, and succulents, too, even without high humidity.

Where there is little variation between day and night temperature, you can succeed with plants from lowland rain forests so long as the humidity can be maintained above 40 percent and minimum night temperature approximately 65°. Under such conditions episcias, anthuriums, and *Phalaenopsis* orchids do well.

Where Plants Live

Within the true tropical regions—mainly between the tropic of Cancer and the tropic of Capricorn—there are four recognized climates classified by ecologists as *equatorial, tropical, tropical desert*, and *tropical mountain*. This simplifies our investigation, although in nature the basic types blend throughout the tropical world.

In my travels I have seldom encountered a distinct and abrupt change from the dry steppe or desert and the wet rain forest. Some microclimates with distinct demarcation do exist, but the transition from one clime to the next is most often gradual, as is the temperature variation in altitude. Most of the tropicals we grow in our northern homes come from such blending habitats rather than from small specialized microclimates, and this accounts for their general adaptability. In cultivation it is practical to group tropical plants according to their preferred habitats and exposures. Some species do range through several merging habitats, and such plants can be grown under otherwise poor conditions, as several bromeliads, philodendrons, sansevierias, and certain vigorous hybrids in numerous genera.

Tropical

The majority of warm-preference houseplants come from areas classified as tropical, according to the four basic climate types. The characteristics of this climate are constant temperatures of 68° to 84° by day and 65° to 70° by night, with altitude variations, a relatively high humidity even during rain-free months, and a yearly pattern of rainfall that is constant except for defined dry seasons.

Dry seasons in the tropics vary from one to two months in areas near the equator to six to eight months for some countries closer to the latitude limits of the true tropics' such as Guatemala and Mexico. Some places may have one long dry season and then later in the year a shorter one, so plants from these regions grow best with a variation in moisture, determined by their activity.

Equatorial

The equatorial climate with temperatures of 80° to 90° by day and 68° to 70° by night is warmer than the average tropical climate. Here the rainfall is evenly dispersed throughout the year. When I was taking motion pictures in the Choco jungles on the Pacific coast of Colombia, where up to four hundred inches of rain falls each year, there was a heavy shower every day. This caused a real problem with my equipment, but the rain is the main reason for exploring this jungle.

Downpours are followed by burning sun that evaporates the fallen rain. This water cycle maintains the humidity above 85 percent. The Choco jungle is not on the equator, yet it has a typical equatorial climate. Plants from the Choco, such as some columneas and anthuriums, thrive, in cultivation, under the same conditions as do plants of other genera from comparable wet regions in Asian and African tropics, like the Congo basin of Central Africa.

Such heavy rainfall is not the rule throughout the tropics, and many equatorial areas gradually blend into the drier habitats where many species stop growing during the dry months. Outside of equatorial climates rain may not fall in drops for months, yet there is a night dew that maintains resting plants in plump condition.

Mountains in the Tropics

In a single tropical country like Venezuela or Tanzania I have explored hot, muggy rain forests in coastal regions or along sea-level riverbeds, brisker habitats with lower humidity at four thousand to six thousand feet, and then chilly, often misty cloud forests in mountains above eight thousand feet. Vegetation and rainfall are distinct in the heart of each region.

Plants from the cloudy mountains usually require cool (45° to 55°) nights and high relative humidity. Certain succulents, such as the popular red-flowered *Mamillopsis senilis* cactus from Mexico, require winter temperatures below 50° but can endure low humidity, since they come from dry regions. Shrubs of *Lantana* and *Malpighia* genera will grow with these succulents indoors.

Moist high-mountain conditions are diffcult to create in a centrally heated house, so cloud-forest species should not be attempted as houseplants. Some may be successfully flowered in a cool greenhouse, but these are challenges for the specialists. Most tuberous begonias and odontoglossum orchids are cool growers and may languish with normal home temperatures. The plants from dry mountains, mainly succulents, are easier, since they need only low temperatures, not high humidity. A cool window or sun porch is good for them.

Fortunately there are so many easy-to-grow tropicals from the lowlands and medium-altitude or dry mountain slopes that you need not struggle with difficult species in order to fill your home or office with flowering and foliage beauty.

Night Temperatures

Most of the plants you grow will thrive with a drop of 8° to 15° at night. African-violets seem to prosper with no difference between day and night, but most orchids, succulents, and foliage plants do best with a night minimum at least 8° to 10° lower than their daytime highs. Under no circumstances is it advisable to have higher temperatures during dark hours.

The minimum night temperature is the most important to determine so that each individual can be placed according to preference. Plants from the higher altitudes (a few begonias, some orchids) and those from desert regions (many succulents, geraniums) prefer lower minimum night temperatures than do plants from low altitudes—steppes, grasslands, rain forests, or tropical jungles—such as columneas, anthuriums, and gloxinias. Optimum temperatures for various tropicals and other plants are given in later chapters.

Tropical Desert

Tropical-desert plants come from comparatively arid regions with an annual rainfall of under sixteen inches, often less. This isn't the classic Sahara Desert where rain may not fall for years on end. The succulent plants found in cultivation come from dry regions which are sunny and hot by day, often above 90°, but cool into the low 50's at night, since the desert retains less heat at night than does a moist woodland.

Many available desert plants, like euphorbias, come from subtropical regions in South Africa, and many favorite cacti come from subtropical as well as tropical Mexico. They require a rest from water rather than a cold dormant period, so we classify them, practically, as tropicals. Other lovely plants, like *Edithcolea* from Kenya and Tanzania, are actually accustomed to warmer temperatures but need very little water.

Plants from the arid tropics survive with minimum rainfall. Some have deep roots that tap underground water, but most often the aboveground parts are formed to conserve the slight amount of moisture that does fall in these places. A waxy cuticle coating over stem and leaves holds in moisture.

Cacti, stapelias, and other succulents have a green thickened stem that functions as leaves in the manufacture of food. The succulent wax-coated green parts store water and prevent the loss of quantities of moisture through transpiration that is common in thin leaves. Some euphorbias from the desert do have a few small true leaves, but there is less loss of plant moisture than with fully thin-leaved species. The crown of thorns, *Euphorbia splendens*, shows this modification. Other tropical desert plants survive by having thick succulent leaves that transpire little water through their leaf openings or stomates. Species of *Crassula, Aloe*, and *Kalanchoe* are examples. Similarly adapted from our own arid Southwest are agaves, opuntias, and some sedums.

You can illustrate this adaptation by an easy experiment. On a dry sunny windowsill place three different plants from the same genus, *Euphorbia*. Choose *Euphorbia splendens* or its hybrid *E. X keysii*, a true succulent species like *E. lactea* from India, and a poinsettia, *E. pulcherrima*. The crown of thorns, *E. splendens*, comes from the hot semidesert regions of western Madagascar. The poinsettia is native to southern Mexico, where it receives more moisture and lower temperatures than prevail in the habitat of *E. splendens*. The succulent thick-stemmed *E. lactea* is from a region where it must live for long periods with little water. Which one of these three euphorbias will be the first to wilt when you withhold water for several weeks?

Cloud Forest

As you go up in altitude through the tropics, the temperature drops an average of $1°$ for every 300 feet. I needed a thick wool blanket on my bed during the two years I lived in Bogotá, Colombia. This cloudy capital city sprawls out in a verdant savannah at 8,600 feet, where the mean temperature is $57°$. Since my apartment was a few hundred feet higher, on a hill, the actual altitude was greater. The night temperature dropped into the 50's, even lower at times. Although I was technically living in the tropics, I sometimes wished for central heating when mist and Andean winds blew through the mountain gaps.

On top of Meru Mountain in Tanzania I got wet while photographing native plants, but the moisture was from thick mists rather than rain. In your rooms you might be able to provide the 40° to 65° temperatures for plants from such a region, but the constant 98- to 100-percent relative humidity would be difficult to duplicate and unpleasant to live in.

We find tropical plants suitable for growing in our homes and warm greenhouses if we choose the adaptable varieties, usually those from lower elevations but in any case not from the cloud forests. Culture depends upon the altitude and climate of each plant's habitat. Fortunately, for those of us who enjoy growing plants the vast majority of tropicals are adaptable to minor variations in temperature and humidity. This is especially true if they are in their preferred potting medium, grown with proper exposure to light, and given careful watering.

Designed Adaptability

Hybrids tend to be especially adaptable, and by creating them plant breeders can design plants for this useful trait. A hybrid is produced by crossing two species of plants, usually of the same genus. The resulting off-spring are often easier to grow than one or both parents because of inherited hybrid vigor. This does not hold true for crosses between plants that vary greatly in their genetic compatibility, but it is well known that most hybrids of ornamental plants are easier to grow than pure species.

Popular African-violets have three or four species in their backgrounds, some from regions where nights are quite warm, some from altitudes of cooler night temperatures. The hybrids combining these different genetic backgrounds adapt themselves to a wide range of temperature. The number of flowers, frequency of bloom, growth habit, and ability to withstand fluctua-tions in temperature, watering, and light are characteristics that can be im-proved by creating hybrids from selected species.

Clones

When you buy a plant with a name like *Dieffenbachia* 'Rudolph Roehrs' or *Hoya carnosa* 'Exotica', you acquire a select clone. Vegetatively propa-gated ornamental plants are given a clone name to distinguish them from unselected species or hybrids that can differ appreciably, although they are classified botanically under the same species name. Clones are reproduced by vegetative (asexual) propagation and are genetically identical to the original selected plant.

For example, you can order a plant of the variegated *Hoya carnosa* 'Exotica' and be sure of getting the attractive multicolored leaf, but if you request only *Hoya carnosa*, you will not be sure of getting the clone 'Exotica'. *Hoya carnosa* can be reproduced from seed, as can any other pure species, and dealers often grow ornamental plants in this way. A selected clone, however, is propagated from cuttings or some form of tissue culture (as in meristems of orchids) in order to preserve the unique characteristics of the original individual plant.

Cultivars and Strains

A cultivar is a plant that in cultivation has developed and retains distinct features, such as of size, color, leaf pattern, habit of growth, and chemical-genetic makeup. A cultivar group transmits these characteristics when reproduced by seed (sexually) as well as by division cuttings (asexually). A cultivar label includes a broader range of characteristics than the clone.

An assemblage that retains exact features when propagated from seed has traditionally been called a strain. Even today many catalogs list select strains of begonias, coleuses, lilies, and other ornamentals. However, the internationally accepted term is now "cultivar," although "strain" is still widely used. There is an important exception in such nomenclature with orchids, where cultivar refers to an individual plant with its subsequent divisions (a clone).

Commercial versus Botanical Usage

There is some confusion between what is correct according to the international code of botanical nomenclature for cultivated plants and what is used in catalogs or on plant labels. Since you must deal with what is, I present this detail to help you translate the various styles of listing plants.

Seed-propagated cultivars (strains), although varying more than vegetatively propagated plants, are still more uniform than randomly seed-propagated species. Coleus is a good example. In this genus of multicolored foliage plants you will find clones, plain species seed, and select seed offered as a specific strain. The Rainbow Strain (cultivar) is created by gathering seed from parents selected for desirable plant habit and leaf color. You can get a good idea of what the Rainbow Strain seedlings will look like by reading catalog descriptions or looking at a color photo.

The characteristics of strains will normally be more predictable than those of nonselected seed. Strains are chosen not only for leaf or flower beauty but also for adaptability and disease resistance. Selected strains of species orchids, philodendrons, or bromeliads are superior to collected or randomly propagated plants. For example, an especially fine individual *Laelia anceps* (a Mexican orchid) can be bred onto itself or with another superior clone of the same species. The resulting seedlings (there may be thousands from a single seedpod) are then offered as a select strain of this easy-to-grow species.

Sometimes a single individual may be selected from hundreds of seedlings to be propagated vegetatively, as *Aglaonema commutatum* 'The Queen'. Growers selected 'The Queen' from many seedlings of the common Chinese evergreen, *Aglaonema commutatum*. Now this beauty is available to you as a clone, correctly named 'The Queen'.

A similar process of selection is used by most plant breeders. They grow thousands of seedlings but usually introduce only those individuals that are markedly different from, or an improvement over, existing types.

Choose Carefully

My own plants are pot grown and set in window boxes throughout the house, in containers on the wall, in a greenhouse, in the cellar, and of course outdoors during the warm months. By understanding the requirements of each species I am able to succeed with most of the plants I want. Your own pleasure will increase with your success when you choose wisely. In this book I concentrate on the more adaptable species and cultivars. You can have a euphorbia from the tropical desert steppe growing on a windowsill next to a rain-forest philodendron if you provide the potting mediums I recommend and supply water in keeping with the needs of each plant.

Amazon rain forest from a low-flying airplane

The Choco jungle along Colombia's Pacific coast receives more than four hundred inches of rain per year. Conspicuous in these few square feet, struggling for air and light, are a bromeliad, gesneriads, philodendrons, and a palm seedling.

At ten thousand feet on Meru Mountain in Tanzania constant clouds provide mist for epiphytic ferns, orchids, moss, and lichens.

The pendent roots of *Ficus thonningii* are eaten away by elephants, yet the plant lives on. The elephant damage provides room for a patrol road to go through in Mount Meru Park, Tanzania.

2

The Environment—Light, Heat, and Humidity

Y<small>OU CAN GROW</small> an attractive plant in any exposure, dim light to full sun, if you select a species appropriate to the exposure. With fluorescent lights to supplement or replace daylight you can control light duration and intensity. Humidity can be increased by setting plants on trays filled with moist pebbles or perlite. Temperatures can be controlled and microclimates of varying temperature found in every building. How light, heat, humidity, and air circulation interrelate determines the environment in each location.

Light

Light intensity can be measured in scientifically calibrated footcandles with a small General Electric footcandle meter or a photographic light meter, like the Lunasix or Weston, which come with directions for converting readings into footcandles. Some texts give light-intensity requirements only in footcandles, but I prefer to put these recommendations into more easily understood terms. If you wish to translate general-brightness terms into footcandle measurements, you will find that strong light required for cattleya orchids is two thousand to three thousand footcandles; bright-diffuse light under which many orchids, begonias, and gesneriads thrive is one thousand to two thousand; and bright or direct reflected light, six hundred to one thousand footcandles.

Dim light may be as low as one hundred footcandles, adequate for some foliage plants, but ranges up to five hundred footcandles indoors near windows or fifteen to eighteen inches under forty-watt fluorescent tubes. Research reveals that light quality (color) is equal in importance to light intensity. Day length or period of brightness is also a factor.

To measure bright sun, the sort required for most orchids and many other flowering plants, hold your hand between the light source and foliage. If a soft-edged shadow is projected, the light is sufficient. A hard-edged shadow indicates that light is strong and may burn some foliage unless plants have a high light-tolerance and gradual exposure. No shadow indicates insufficient intensity for active flowering plants.

Recommendations for fluorescent lights are based upon the distance between tubes and foliage, so footcandle measurements are not generally given, assuming bright, clean reflectors and new growth tubes at least every twelve months.

Variables

When deciduous trees grow nearby, window light may vary during the year, from bright to dim. Winter sun comes directly through with no foliage to lessen its strength, but new spring leaves soon shade the glass. If you can move plants outside for the summer, it doesn't matter that a once-sunny window becomes dim. Otherwise, provide supplemental light with fluorescents, or move plants to a brighter window.

How Much?

Plants that don't need direct sun are no problem, even when deciduous trees cast shade. Sunlight is weaker in winter than in spring or summer. On that account, shade from trees may turn out to be a blessing, since it can prevent burning of houseplants, which sometimes occurs when direct summer sun comes through glass. By late November, leaves fall, but the sun is far enough away to be safe again.

A saintpaulia plant may burn in direct sun between March and October, but during the winter it will flower freely in direct light. To bloom well, flowering plants should receive as much light as they can take, short of burning or turning yellow.

Foliage plants require less light. Since you grow them for attractive leaves, the bright light that induces bloom is not essential. Sunlight is harder on plants than are fluroescent lamps because it can be too hot at midday. Reduce too-bright sun with a thin curtain, slat blinds, or a fiber-glass drapery.

From Shade to Sun

When you move plants from a shady location to brighter light, do it gradually. Allow ten to fifteen days for them to adjust. This is also the procedure for moving houseplants outdoors in the summer, when even cacti are given high shade for the first few days.

From Sun to Shade

It isn't harmful to move plants from strong to dim light for decoration if you eventually return them to their preferred exposure. For example, orchids grow in strong light, and in bloom can be kept for weeks on a dim coffee table. Foliage plants that require diffused light can decorate a hall for several months, then be rejuvenated in a brighter location. Plants that don't need bright sun should be protected from it or they may develop poor foliage. Rex begonias and episcias look washed out if they get too much sun.

Sun is reflected into windows from water, from white buildings, or from nearby white or pastel terraces. A north window in your house, opposite a white wall, may have more light than a neighbor's east window near a dark driveway or many trees. Grow your plants according to the strength of light that actually reaches them, not just by points of the compass.

Low Light (Twelve to Eighteen Hours per Twenty-four)

Low light is the illumination found toward the middle of rooms with west or south windows, near north windows, in lobbies with large glass fronts, and under forty- to ninety-watt fluorescent ceiling fixtures. Few plants actually prefer such low levels of light, but many tropicals will tolerate it for months, especially if they are not in a period of active growth.

Some foliage plants, such as aucubas, ferns, *Ficus*, and various philodendrons, may stay attractive for a year or more with low light, but aralias, dieffenbachias, podocarpuses, and yuccas are likely to need brighter light after several months. When plants provide decoration under low light, they need less water, little or no fertilizer, monthly cleaning of foliage with a gentle shower in dusty places, and of course suitable temperatures. Most of these low-light plants are intermediate growers that thrive with nights at 60° to 65°. Daytime temperatures of 5° to 10° higher are satisfactory.

Moving these tolerant plants into bright-diffuse light, even for one week in six, helps them make sturdier growth; and spotlights and banks of fluorescents are useful to increase light intensity and day length, thus prolonging the plants' attractiveness.

Here are listed some plants that will grow in low light. Descriptive comment and cultural information for these subjects and for those in subsequent lists for other light levels are given later in the chapters on each group of plants.

Aechmea fasciata	Ficus diversifolia
Aglaonema	F. elastica
Anthurium	F. 'Exotica'
Araucaria heterophylla	Fittonia
Asparagus	Maranta
Aspidistra	Pandanus veitchii
Calathea	Peperomia
Crassula argentea	Philodendron
Cryptanthus species	Rhapidophora aurea
Dracaena	Sansevieria
Fatshedera	Spathiphyllum

These ferns will tolerate low light:

Adiantum	Nephrolepis
Asplenium nidus	Platycerium
A. viviparum	Pteris
Davallia	

Bright-Diffuse Light, Indirect Sunlight

Bright-diffuse light occurs just inside of east windows or beyond the direct rays in south and west windows, where rooms will normally be bright enough for plants in this section. Some early morning sun will benefit them. Minimum night temperature of 65° is generally best. Also, most of these plants must be turned slightly every week to prevent all their growth leaning toward the light. Plants in bloom can be moved temporarily to low-light areas and soon returned to their preferred bright-light windows. The plants in my low-light list, especially those for flowers, will grow better in bright-diffuse light.

A few plants well suited to this degree of light are:

Alocasia	Codiaeum
Aphelandra squarrosa	Columnea hybrids
Aralia	Cryptanthus fosterianus hybrids
Begonia boweri hybrids	Dieffenbachia cultivars
B. rex	Episcia cultivars
Cissus	Hoya
Clivia miniata	Paphiopedilum hybrids

Phalaenopsis hybrids
Philodendron
Pilea
Plectranthus
Rechsteineria

Saintpaulia hybrids (light-colored)
Sinningia
Streptocarpus
Veltheimia
Zebrina

Morning Sun, East to South Exposure

The east to south exposure is one that receives three to five hours of bright sun with direct rays every morning and sometimes by late afternoon as well. The location receives bright-diffuse light when the sun is not streaming directly in. Light gauze drapes will temper sun that is too hot from spring into fall, but the plants listed will take direct sun from late fall into early spring.

Abutilon
Acalypha
Aeschynanthus
Allamanda cathartica
Amaryllis (Hippeastrum)
Begonia (all but rex hybrids)
Beloperone
Bromeliads (most)
Cacti (Christmas and Easter cacti need cooler fall rest)
Chlorophytum
Citrus
Coleus blumei
Crossandra
Euphorbia X keysii
E. splendens
Gasteria

Geranium (Pelargonium)
Gynura
Haemanthus
Haworthia
Ixora
Kohleria
Neomarica
Orchids (many)
Oxalis
Passiflora
Petrea
Punica
Ruellia
Saintpaulia (dark-leaved and dark-flowered hybrids)
Smithiantha
Tradescantia sillamontana

South to Southwest, Direct Sun

A window facing south to southwest will usually receive at least six hours of direct sun each day. With such intense light coming through glass many tropicals will burn, but a few thrive and bloom well because of the bright light, especially succulents. Here is a reliable selection:

Agave
Aloe
Ananas comosus 'Nanus'

Ananas comosus variegatus
Bougainvillaea cultivars
Dyckia

Euphorbia (succulent species)

Geranium (thick-stemmed succulent sorts)

Hibiscus rosa-sinensis

Kalanchoe tomentosa

Mammillaria species and hybrids

Notocactus

Orchids:

Ascocenda

Brassavola

Dendrobium nobile hybrids

D. phalaenopsis hybrids

Epidendrum ibaguense

Laelia anceps; L. rubescens

Renanthera hybrids

Setcreasea purpurea

Tradescantia blossfeldiana

Vallota speciosa

Artificial Light

In the last decade thousands of gardeners have been growing houseplants under fluorescent lights. Modern interior design sometimes incorporates planted wells, lit by ceiling or panel lights, where foliage plants requiring only low light will last for a year or more. Flowering plants can be grown to perfection under fluorescent tubes.

Although research on the effects of artificial light by the United States Department of Agriculture, various universities, and the Indoor Light Society indicates that many tropicals will bloom well under fluorescent lamps, the field is still new and open to more detailed observation and development. In my own collection I have found how to succeed with a wide range of genera under fluorescent growth lamps, so my personal experience and conclusions, coupled with research findings, are presented here.

Types of Lamps

Are all fluorescent lamps the same? Certainly not; even standard home-lighting bulbs come in warm white, cool white, daylight, and color combinations varying among manufacturers. Now we have several tubes formulated specifically for horticultural use. Sylvania offers a Gro-Lux and Gro-Lux Wide Spectrum tube; Westinghouse, Plant-Gro; General Electric, Plant-Light; and the Duro-Test Corporation, sunlight-matched Vita-Lite and Natur-escent. Each tube differs in the proportions of red, blue, green, and other spectrum colors that determine light quality.

Since fluorescent tubes give off much less heat than incandescent bulbs, they reduce the chance of leaf burn or excessive drying. You can get plant-growth fluorescent lamps in hardware stores or from the supply firms listed at the end of this book.

My longest experience is with Gro-Lux tubes, which I have successfully used for a wide variety of plants, including amaryllises, gesneriads, orchids, and many foliage plants. I favor tubes designed for plants rather than household tubes combined with incandescent bulbs. Fluorescents, like the Gro-Lux Wide Spectrum, are designed for high-energy requirement plants, such as succulents and orchids.

Color of Tubes

Standard Gro-Lux and Plant-Gro tubes, in contrast to whiter-glowing Gro-Lux Wide Spectrum or Duro-Test lamps, have a warm red-violet light that enhances color. If you don't like the light hue of these tubes, switch to the sunlight-colored Duro-Test lamps, Gro-Lux Wide Spectrum, or even standard white fluorescents. I find Gro-Lux Wide Spectrum the best combination of a near natural color with a good plant-growth spectrum.

Some growers still add incandescent bulbs to fluorescent fixtures to increase the amount of far-red light required by high light-energy plants. However, with wide-spectrum plant tubes, far-red output has been increased to the point where there is no need for incandescent bulbs.

The plants I grow under standard Gro-Lux include begonias, foliage plants, gesneriads, and even some orchid seedlings where there is adequate light, as from four to six forty-watt tubes. Many seedlings grow well under standard growth fluorescents. The increased far-red light of wide-spectrum tubes is important, for plants approaching maturity, to promote good blooming achieved only with this wavelength.

Indoor Light Gardens

Grow tropicals under fluorescents anywhere that you can maintain the required temperature and humidity. Some of my plants spend the winter in the basement; friends have year-round gardens in dim rooms and in cellars. Closets, dark halls, bookcases, shelves under workbenches, and corners of living rooms are all potential locations for fixtures.

Where it is not important to have decorative reflectors, a basic aluminum fixture hung with adjustable chains or incorporated into a plant stand of several tiers is practical. But obviously in living areas attractive fixtures that complement a room or conceal lamps with a valance or molding look best. When fluorescents provide only supplemental illumination, they can be set behind plastic panels, in wall pockets, above or under hung shelves, or beside windows where the lights are concealed by frosted panels or a valance.

Types of Fixtures

Several styles of fixtures are illustrated in the catalogs of supply firms. The light carts have two to four tiers of adjustable shelves, built-in fixtures, and a timer. The sort that is designed for starting seeds has shelves set close to the lights, but with insufficient space for mature plants. One design with adjustable shelves and lamps is good for begonias, bromeliads, orchids, and other mature flowering plants. Shorter plants can be brought closer to the lights by placing them on inverted pots.

A simple arrangement for windowsill or table consists of a single two-bulb fixture above a tray. Still another is a miniature Wardian case or large glass box fitted with lamps and sliding glass doors. More elaborate cases come with built-in fans, timers, and heaters. My favorite simple fixtures, designed to be hung or otherwise used in your own custom-built fashion, have a one-piece metal top with aluminum reflectors—a construction that prevents water dripping from above into the wiring.

To increase my greenhouse space, I hang fixtures under benches where humidity and temperature encourage healthy growth. I prefer fixtures with two to four forty-watt tubes. Without this arrangement there would be a great deal of wasted space, and even with glass-to-ground construction the supplemental light extends the range of plants that can be grown. A sheet of heavy building-grade plastic protects fixtures from water that drips through the bench. Industrial aluminum foil on the floor reflects light back to plants.

Materials and Controls

Fixtures and stands designed for plants generally withstand humidity, spilled water, and high temperatures, so if you build fixtures yourself, be sure to get outdoor-grade materials. Plywood should be exterior grade and metal parts coated with rust-resistant paint.

Aluminum reflectors are excellent for light transmission and portability. Easy-to-adjust galvanized chain is good for hanging fixtures. Bookshelf or window fixtures are attached to a fixed wood base or metal shelf strips with adjustable clips. Cypress, redwood, or other woods well treated with Cuprinol are preferred for longevity. If care is taken about spilling water, plain untreated wood can be covered with clear Contact paper or waterproof materials in simulated wood grain.

Light Hours

Use an automatic timer when lamps are the major source of light. When fluorescents are only for decorative or supplemental light, you may prefer to control them with a standard manual switch. In my greenhouse and basement I have automatic timers, but fixtures for decorative lighting above windows and near display areas are on manual switches.

A total of sixteen hours of light for each twenty-four-hour period is a reasonable average for most plants. When used as a supplement, fluorescents extend daylight hours or increase the intensity of light available. Anthuriums, begonias, bromeliads, gesneriads, foliage plants, and orchid seedlings benefit from at least fourteen hours of light—with sixteen hours the ideal. Up to eighteen hours can help make up for low light with *Saintpaulia* and most foliage plants.

Grow plants under at least two forty-watt tubes. Three or four forty-watt tubes are even better for those plants, such as orchids, that require strong light to bloom well. I find Gro-Lux Wide Spectrum better than standard Gro-Lux for such plants. Foliage plants thrive under standard growth tubes, and for those in dim places even an incandescent spotlight or table lamp as auxiliary light is beneficial.

Your fixtures may have outlets between the fluorescent tubes for incandescent lamps. It is claimed that African-violets grown under standard Gro-Lux tubes produce more flowers and sturdier foliage when incandescent light at fifteen watts per square foot supplements the fluorescents. I don't think incandescents are required for maximum growth if wide-spectrum tubes are used. If you wish to create a special spectrum, you could begin by adding two incandescent bulbs, twenty-five to forty watts each, to each two-tube fluorescent fixture. The idea is to add 10 to 20 percent of the total wattage in incandescent bulbs and thus provide more far-red energy. Buy 130-volt incandescent bulbs because they give off less heat and last longer than standard 120-volt bulbs.

Distance from Tubes

For a mixed collection hang adjustable fixtures so that tubes are eight inches above foliage. Low plants and those with high light requirements can be set closer on inverted flowerpots. Because the strength of fluorescents decreases toward the ends of the tubes, place plants that need the most light directly under the center.

Check your plants every week or so to be sure all growth is several inches below the tubes. This is important for orchids that are likely to send up an inflorescence far above the leaves. Although fluorescents are cooler than incandescents, they will burn foliage and buds that touch them for several hours.

Tube Life

With age, fluorescent tubes decrease in strength, so when tubes are the major source of light, replace them when the ends darken, or once every eight to ten months, with a fourteen- to sixteen-hour day. When lamps are used only as a supplement or for decoration, they will serve up to seven thousand hours. If your budget is limited, you may prefer to keep tubes a longer time, but remember that the plants may not grow as well, especially those having a high light requirement.

Total Environment

The environment for plants under lights must be in keeping with their required humidity, temperature, and air circulation. In a basement, humidity and temperature are often easier to control than in a greenhouse or at a window, where you must contend with variables of sun and climate. Trays filled with moist gravel, and clear plastic curtains drawn around light carts offer two practical ways of maintaining humidity above 50 percent. In a basement you can also install a misting humidifier, which might produce too much spray for a living room. A small fan blowing anywhere except directly on plants keeps air in healthy circulation.

Arrange fixtures and plant trays so as to protect electrical parts from moisture. Water plants with a controlled device like the Fogg-It pot waterer, or use an all-purpose nozzle to control the stream and avoid the shock of sloppy overhead watering. It is good to wash off foliage with a gentle stream of water every few weeks, but take care not to soak electrical parts.

Rotation

Fluorescent light stands in a basement or other out-of-the-way place make useful revival stations for decorative plants that may have been displayed elsewhere. Keep a bromeliad, coleus, or gesneriad under low light while enjoying blooms or foliage, then after a few weeks return to a fluorescent stand for sturdy growth. I grow many plants to perfection under artificial light and then bring them into a prominent location for display.

Summer Care

Plants grown at windows or under fluorescents will be the better for an outdoor summer, with the exception of a few delicate downy-leaved gesneriads like *Saintpaulia*. When night temperatures stay above 55° to 60°, gradually move the plants outside, first to shade, then to as much light as the species can take. Sink the pots up to the rim into beds of peat moss or peat-lite mix, or set them on inverted pots in an outdoor bed.

Long-lived expensive plants are best cared for outdoors on raised tables or plant shelves of metal or redwood. I put some orchids outside on tables and hang others under tall oaks, which provide shade from noonday sun. Amaryllises go out in plastic flats; smaller pots are sunk into moist peat moss; larger ceramic pots are supported just above the ground or paving so that excess water will drain off. Many coleuses and begonias are planted directly in garden beds. In late summer or early fall I take cuttings for vigorous new plants, leaving the old plants to provide color into October before they are ruined by frost.

Temperature

In summer, outdoor temperatures into the 90's won't harm even cool-preference plants if humidity remains above 60 percent, but in the winter, when plants must endure drying artificial heat, cooler temperatures must prevail and plants be placed according to their desired minimum night temperature.

A cool bright porch with temperatures in the low 50's at night but climbing into the high 60's with warming rays of the sun is excellent for the cooler-growing plants listed at the end of this book.

Temperatures, Night and Day

During dark periods green plants utilize food manufactured in photosynthesis while they were exposed to light. When night temperatures are no lower than those of daytime, plants can seldom assimilate stored food efficiently. Without a night drop most of your plants will not grow or bloom to full potential. One of the few exceptions is the African-violet, which often thrives with constant temperatures.

How much temperature drop is required depends upon the type. Most plants adjust satisfactorily to a drop of 8° to 10°. Some lowland rain-forest gesneriads, such as gloxinias, do well for me with a 5° drop, whereas begonias, cattleya hybrids, and succulents do their best with a minimum drop of 10°.

If you find the temperature in a given area does not fall at least 5° during the night, put plants like African-violets or episcias in that location. You can create cooler areas by enclosing a bay window with clear plastic shades, shutting out much of the warmer air from the heated room. Normally colder outside air will cool off the enclosed section.

A maximum-minimum thermometer, available for less than thirteen dollars, has two sides with red indicators clearly showing highest and lowest temperatures. Put it in a kitchen window with indicators set against each mercury column. Both sides might read 73° in the morning. By early afternoon the high side will have pushed the red marker up to 78°. That night the low side indicates 65° as the mercury reverses its course. The following day, indicators may show a minimum night temperature of 65°, the maximum daytime 78°, an excellent range for tropical plants. Now, with the magnet supplied on each thermometer, draw the red indicators back to the current temperature, and you are ready to measure another location.

Seasonal Variation

Throughout the temperate zone, night temperatures near windows will be lower during winter, and these microclimates can be of value to you in helping geraniums, high-altitude orchids, succulents, and other cool-growing plants to do well in our often overheated rooms. Arrange plants that prefer cooler nights close to windows; inside the room put warm growers— anthuriums, for example. This grouping often corresponds to light preferences as well, so sun-loving geraniums and cacti are near the glass where sun is direct and they get their required low night temperature. Below and farther away from the glass would be saintpaulias, anthuriums, a few bromeliads, and perhaps a rex begonia—plants that require warmer nights and somewhat less light.

During the summer houseplants can be put out in the garden or on a balcony where temperature naturally drops at night. Even inside air-conditioned buildings, where plants may stay all year, temperatures at night are lower than by day.

Special Cases

Alocasias, calatheas, and episcias do prosper with a night temperature of 65° to 68°. Such tropical growers are special only in lack of tolerance for low temperatures—to 55°, a night minimum which does not harm most other houseplants. The ultimate test for any subject is how well it does under the conditions you can provide. Use my recommendations as a guide until experience proves that a given plant will tolerate other extremes when grown under your own conditions.

Flower Buds and Temperature

A few tropicals require a month or more of quite cool nights to produce flowers. Large cymbidiums must have thirty to sixty days with nights at 45° to 50°, but miniature cymbidium hybrids, bred with warm-growing species, don't require so much cold and are more suited to home culture. They are also successful in warm climates as in southern Florida.

High-altitude cacti, like *Mamillopsis senilis*, bloom best when subjected to a three-month winter rest with nights of 40° to 50°. Even Christmas and Easter cacti flower poorly unless they also have a cool rest of six to eight weeks after their summer growing season. *Dendrobium nobile* orchids need a dry rest, below 60°, to bloom freely. Such plants can be enjoyed in a mixed collection if you give them cool fall-winter nights, perhaps outside until frost, then against a cool indoor window.

Poinsettias during their budding period do best with night temperatures in the low 60's, in addition to needing days of fewer than twelve hours. Keep them in a cool window or on a sun porch in fall, or leave them outdoors until just before the first frost (usually late September or early October in southern New York). I find this works for dendrobiums and Christmas cacti, which I keep on the dry side during the same cool period.

The other plants recommended in this book should do well without a low-temperature treatment. If you can't provide a cool period for Christmas cacti or *Dendrobium nobile*, grow plants that bloom without a chilly rest.

Humidity—Moisture in the Air

As temperature rises, humidity drops. Warm air holds more vaporized moisture than cool, so a given room will have lower relative humidity through warm daylight hours than during cooler nights, a major reason that tropicals in the same house may grow satisfactorily in a cool room but not in a warm one. Physicians report that humidity above 40 percent is better for us than the common 20 percent or less. Low humidity is bad for the human respiratory tract and also damaging to furniture and paintings. So for your own sake, even if you grow only cacti, try to provide humidity of at least 40 percent in all living and working areas.

It is moisture in the air that constitutes humidity, and lack of this vaporized water cannot be compensated for by additional water on roots. Epiphytes such as cattleyas illustrate this when they are grown under too dry conditions. Beginners frequently water orchids when they see leaves and pseudobulbs shrinking, without checking to see if the medium is wet or not. More often than not, the plants have had sufficient water, but humidity below 30 percent causes more water loss through transpiration than the orchids can replace through their roots. These unfortunate effects of low humidity are more quickly seen in warm growing areas or when roots have been recently disturbed.

A few xerophytic tropicals (native to arid regions) will endure humidity down to 10 or 15 percent, but they thrive where humidity is 60 percent so long as they are not overwatered. Most cacti and other succulents are true xerophytes, which is why they can thrive in hot sunny windows. A few Caribbean orchids are almost as adaptable, but in general they tolerate low humidity only if misted every day. In their growing areas at a window or in a greenhouse a humidity of 40 to 60 percent is better.

Epiphytes normally need greater air circulation around their roots than do soil dwellers, but an imbalance between water and humidity can also occur for terrestrials. An example is a leafy philodendron growing in a bright living room or office where humidity is below 30 percent. Leaves will wilt, and the plant will cease to grow vigorously even when roots are constantly moist, since this soil moisture does not make up for required humidity around foliage. An epiphytic orchid will lose its roots from too much water before the terrestrial philodendron, but the end will be the same for both— dead rotted roots that can't absorb moisture—so the whole plant dies.

How to Raise Humidity

You can increase humidity by putting pots on moist gravel, pebbles, or perlite in a fiber-glass plant tray or metal cooking pan. Fill the tray with two to six inches of gravel, pebbles, or coarse perlite, then keep the water level at least one inch below the surface so that the bottom of each pot will stand clear of water. It is essential to maintain the water level below the pots unless you are growing a bog plant like the papyrus.

Humidifiers

Central-heating units can be equipped with a humidifier. My home has a forced hot-air heating system fueled by natural gas, a poor sort of central heating for tropicals because the hot air tends to be dry (but natural gas is much cleaner than oil). To avoid the harmful effects of dry air, the heater-blower has a device with water-soaked pads that add moisture to the hot air as it is distributed to vents. You will feel warmer when humidity increases, so it is possible to set daytime thermostats at 68° and still feel comfortable in the winter.

Portable humidifiers come in a range of styles and prices from less than fifteen dollars to more than one hundred dollars. Some models are suitable for a living room; they look like a small air conditioner and don't give off a soaking spray. According to the manufacturer, a unit sold as a "heavy-duty automatic humidifier" for about sixty dollars, can supply up to 7 gallons of water per day. Since the tank holds only 3¾ gallons, you would have to fill it twice a day in a dry room. These portable units are powered by household current and are little more than vaporizers such as you might use in a sick room.

Larger units that connect directly to a waterline are fine for stone or cement porches, greenhouse, cellar, garage, or large lobby planting, but are not recommended for living rooms. I have two of these humidifiers in my greenhouses. The Frisco Fog has a continuously running fan in front of a water nozzle that blows out mist when activated by a humistat. This automatic device is effective in the greenhouse and gives a fine circulation of air by means of the fan, but in a house it would soak the furniture.

The Herrmidifier brand has no moving fan but throws out a fog by centrifugal force when triggered by its humistat. I find this humidifier excellent above orchid seedlings in my warmer greenhouse, but this too would not be practical in a living room. It just might serve if mounted about ten feet above a large lobby or waiting-room planting.

Misting

If even a small humidifier seems unnecessary, you may find misting with warm water effective. On sunny mornings humidity will drop as temperature goes up, so that's a good time to mist lightly with water in an old perfume bottle or one of the more efficient foggers sold for plants. Inexpensive plastic misters, like the Fluoralite or Syfonex plastic hand sprayer, have lasted longer for me than costly metal models.

Apply only a light fog that will evaporate by late afternoon. Don't soak foliage, especially of hairy gesneriads, when you are misting to raise humidity. Mist orchids on sunny mornings, but don't let water accumulate in new growths or leaf centers of *Phalaenopsis* or other vanda-type orchids where water may trigger rot if it remains overnight. Use a twisted paper towel to draw up any water that remains in orchid growths. Plants under bright light in a free circulation of air can accept more mist without risk of rot.

In full sun, water drops may cause burns, although any plant that burned in my collection was damaged by sun alone, coming through glass. It is cold water that causes foliage damage, expecially on hairy gesneriads. Plants under fluorescent lights in the basement will usually need less misting but much more soil watering, compared with window plants in similar temperatures. African-violets, growers report, need from two to three times more water and fertilizer under fluorescent lamps than when grown at a window.

Water in the Soil

Even the toughest heat-resistant sun-loving cacti must have water to live. No nutrients can be absorbed unless they are dissolved in water, and new growth depends on a supply of water in excess of the maintenance quantity. When to water is a question that must be answered on location. "Water geraniums every three days" may work for geraniums in your neighbor's house but not for those at your window. The rule must be indefinite; to water only when each plant requires moisture at the roots. Coleuses, gardenias, and geraniums are some tropicals that signal a need for water by drooping slightly. Epiphytes, like most orchids, show shrinking of new stems when they are low on moisture, but their signals are given after the plant has gone beyond its initial need.

Shrinking or wilting plants will revive if given a deep watering, but thin-leaved terrestrial plants, permitted to wilt frequently, will slow down, perhaps lose some lower leaves, and not make a maximum display of flowers. Water should be applied just before soil dries out, but it is better for most tropicals to go a day drier than to be kept constantly soggy. When you do water, soak the soil until water runs out the drainage hole, but very dry peat-lite mediums may not absorb enough moisture unless the pot stands in water for thirty minutes; after that time remove any remaining water.

Quality of Water

Apply lukewarm or room-temperature water. Don't use cold water, since it shocks warm growers and often causes foliage spots. Some people use ice to water cool-growing cymbidiums in hopes that this will substitute for the cool nights these plants require to set buds, but I have seen no evidence that this technique works. (Grow warm-preference miniature cymbidiums!) My own tropicals are kept healthy with mildly warm water.

The quality of most public water supplies is good, but in a few cases there may be enough chlorine present to stunt sensitive individual plants. If you suspect that some of your tropicals are suffering from chlorine damage, let the water stand overnight so the gas can escape. Rainwater is excellent unless you live in an area with polluted air. Rain and snow carry down atmospheric pollutants, so the purity of rain depends on the quality of the air through which it falls. Tap water that contains a high mineral content may contribute to chemical buildup in potting mixes. Sulfur, for example, can build up in orchid compost to the point where roots are killed. The cure is to use rainwater and repot every two years. Rain washing through the pots outside for the summer also helps.

Double Pots

To slow down the drying out of soil in clay pots, you can put a smaller clay pot inside a larger one, the space between filled with moist peat moss, sphagnum moss, coarse perlite, or vermiculite. To retard drying even more, select glazed clay or plastic for the outer container. Then put an inch or two of pebbles in the bottom of the outside pot to allow for drainage from the inner pot, or be sure the larger pot has a drainage hole.

Plastic, glazed clay, and plastic-foam pots (Styrofoam) dry out more slowly than plain clay; they are good for plants that require two- to three-inch containers, like seedlings, which grow best when they are not subjected to the rapid drying common in small clay pots. Planting several small specimens in a single larger pot is another good technique for maintaining an even moisture level.

Plastic Bags

Before you go on vacation, water plants well, set them in a slightly dimmer area than is usual, and the day after watering, cover them loosely with plastic bags. Insert thin bamboo stakes or cut coat hangers to hold the plastic just above the foliage. This protection will sustain them without additional water for up to two weeks. If the temperature can be set at 65°, with the plants kept out of strong light, they will do better while you are away. Remember that with higher temperatures and bright light, plants will need more water.

Root Check

If an established plant droops or looks as though it requires water, even when the potting medium is moist, do a root check. Put your fingers over the pot, hold it upside down, and tap the rim lightly with a hammer or against a table. The root ball should drop out in a solid lump. Healthy roots are usually white to yellow. Rotted roots, usually from overwatering, will be dark brown or black and mushy. This is a valid check for plants that have been growing in their containers long enough to make extensive roots. Unestablished plants, even with healthy roots, will not yet have a root system to hold all the soil together.

Roots kept constantly wet will rot and can no longer transfer water to the rest of the plant. If you catch this condition early, a plant may usually be saved by letting it dry out at the roots. Cut it back, or with tropicals like African-violets, remove some larger leaves, then cut away all rotted roots, and repot in a fresh peat-lite or similar soil-free mix. I have done this with root-rotted saintpaulias and had good results when I dipped the base in rooting powder (Rootone with fungicide) to spark new roots and stop rot.

Most tropicals are beyond saving if all their roots have rotted. Some orchids may later sprout a dormant eye and make new roots, but they will be years making enough healthy growth to bloom again. If all roots are gone, you must amputate back to sound tissue, dust the wound with Rootone, tap off excess powder, and root the healthy top in a mix of perlite and milled sphagnum moss or, for terrestrial species, in a propagating or peat-lite mix.

This operation works with begonias and many gesneriads and succulents and has saved, for me, a few rootless half-rotted amaryllis. Partly rotted epiphytes are best covered with a plastic bag while they re-form a good root system in fir bark or perlite with unmilled sphagnum moss. Rot troubles can usually be prevented by careful watering.

Normally, different species dry out at their own speeds. My cacti in winter may go six to eight weeks before they require water, whereas a coleus in the same-size pot will need daily watering. Set aside some time each day to check individual plants. By caring for them as individuals you will have healthier plants than if you force them to an arbitrary schedule of "water every Monday" or some such arrangement. Even a given plant will dry out faster during sunny warm spring and summer weather than it will under cool dull days of winter.

Self-watering Pots

Some self-watering pots function with wicks, others with tubes of water, still others by simple capillary action between roots and water. Your experiments will indicate which type suits your method of cultivation. African-violet growers report good results with plastic wick pots, but in my own collection I prefer to grow plants in plain plastic pots with standard bottom drainage, and I water from the top. (See Chapter 4 for details on self-watering containers.)

Since watering does depend on the individual plant and the conditions under which it is grown, you have to make your own decisions about when to water. However, the following suggestions may make such decisions easier:

Guide for Watering

Water More Frequently If:

Pot is completely filled with roots.
Large plant is in a small pot.
Humidity is low.
It is sunny and windy.
Plant has wide thin leaves.
Stems are thin or woody.
Container is unglazed clay.
Plant is grown on a slab of bark or tree fern.
Plant is in active growth with good light.

Water Less Frequently If:

Plant has few roots in a large pot.
Small plant is in a large pot.
Humidity is high or it is raining.
It is cloudy; air is still.
Weather is cool, below 65°.
Growth is succulent as in agaves, aloes, and cacti.
Plant is just getting established.
Bulbs have just been potted.
Plant is resting or dormant.
Pot is plastic, glazed, or painted.

Asplenium nidus (right), *Cordyline terminalis* (left background), *Dizygotheca elegantissima* (left center), trailing variegated peperomia (bottom), and *Hedera canariensis variegata* (against top of *Asplenium*) all thrive in a bright humid location.

A wall of mirrors in my dining room doubles an orchid and African-violet display and reflects light on foliage plants, *Syngonium* (left), *Polypodium* (right). Below the wood valance is a forty-watt fluorescent lamp to light blooms and supplement daylight for growth and bud development.

Hoya carnosa varieties trained around a window provide decorative foliage and if they receive enough light, fragrant blooms in spring to summer. On the window ledge grows *Chlorophytum elatum vittatum*.

A west window of Helen Van Pelt Wilson's plant room provides adequate light for assorted houseplants, including *Philodendron scandens oxycardium* (lower left), *Hedera helix* cultivar in wall bracket (top right), *Asparagus sprengeri* in brass pot (lower right), fragrant-flowered *Murraea exotica* (on middle shelf), and numerous African-violets. Plants on the top shelf receive supplemental light from growth lamps hidden by valance. (*George C. Bradbury*)

Bright overhead spotlights give dramatic effect and supplemental light to *Ficus elastica decora, Monstera deliciosa*, and narrow-leaved *Dracaena marginata*. Dieffenbachia cultivars (lower left) would grow better with brighter light, but even with spots alone they remain attractive for many months. (*General Electric Company*)

Fluorescent Tube Craft plant stand on wheels is easily moved. Here the kitchen is brightened with African-violets and *Aucuba japonica* set on white gravel. Water in the trays is kept below the base of the pots; a timer turns lights on and off. (*General Electric Company*)

A bookshelf fitted with a water-proof tray and fluorescent lamps creates a suitable indoor display garden. *Paphiopedilum* doesn't require as much light as most orchids, but for best performance have growth lamps set four to six inches above the foliage. A greater distance is required for flowering plants on display.

This basement was turned into an indoor greenhouse by Fred Bender, of New Rochelle, New York, when he constructed two glass walls, installed fluorescent fixtures, fans, humidifiers, hot and cold running water, and sturdy wire plant shelves set above water-filled trays. Lights are on timers; fans and heating are controlled automatically.

The Shaffer Garden Case makes it possible to provide a warm, humid atmosphere anywhere. Fluorescent lamps can be arranged to give adequate light for display or enough for the growth of some tropicals. Switches on front control light, heat, and ventilation. (*Shaffer's Tropical Gardens*)

An automatic timer controls lights; maximum-minimum thermometer indicates just how warm or cold it is in specific area. This plastic-lined redwood bench is filled with moist perlite; lamps one to twelve inches above plants give adequate light for display or growth of cuttings.

Orchids under fluorescent lights in a basement receive extra humidity from water-filled trays under wire grids on which pots rest. Hygrometer shows relative humidity. Thermostat controls heater and vent fans.

Plastic tray filled with coarse perlite kept lightly moist will furnish extra humidity for plants. Coleus cutting is growing in a reused Styrofoam coffee cup.

A lean-to greenhouse is viewed from the living room in the home of Mrs. Edward Eagan. Plants can be enjoyed but are still in an ideal environment with bright light and high humidity.

3

Soils and Fertilizers

M OST PLANTS ARE EARTH DWELLING with roots that require soil or something similar for physical support and mineral nutrition. If fertilizer is regularly supplied, many tropicals can also live in water or in soil-free mediums that alone provide no nutrients.

Soils

Packaged soils are sold in garden stores, in some supermarkets and flower shops, and by most nursery and seed firms. Reliable brands are pasteurized to kill weed seeds, fungi, and insect pests. They are formulated for house-plants in general and specifically for most begonias, foliage plants, geraniums, and cacti. The humus-rich mixtures, sometimes labeled African-violet mix, are good for caladiums, ferns, gesneriads, and rex begonias—all adapted to the humus accumulations of their habitats.

The prepared soil labeled Cactus Mix is generally right for other succulents, including agaves, aloes, euphorbias, living stones, and stapelias. These thrive in a combination of leaf mold and sand. For them too much clay contributes to root rot. For a few succulents the addition of a little more leaf mold is desirable. And the epiphytic cacti, less succulent than desert cacti, need an Epiphyte Mix—a further modification of Cactus Mix (Chapter 15). In any case, no matter what you grow, I recommend pasteurized pre-

33

packaged soils to save trouble. They can always be modified to suit special requirements.

With sterilized commercial mixes you can avoid the pests and diseases frequently found in unpasteurized outdoor soil. If you must use outdoor soils, they can be pasteurized at home by baking them in an oven. Have the soil or compost from garden or woods slightly moist. Bake the covered material in an oven at 180° for one hour, timed from the moment your oven reaches 180°. Cool with the cover still intact. This treatment is smelly but effective. If garden soils are not pasteurized, be on guard for pests and diseases.

Sterilizers and Soil Insecticides

Liquid soil sterilizers are a partial substitute for baking, but they can harm certain delicate plants, so follow manufacturer's directions precisely. Each product will control specific troubles—fungi, insects, or nematodes— but no single chemical, for home use, controls all possible harmful organisms as effectively as moist heat. Panodrench (Panogen Company, Ringwood, Illinois) controls fungi that attack seedlings. Use it as a soil drench before you plant or as an emergency treatment for damping off. Dr. "V" (Summit Chemical Company, Baltimore, Maryland) is a soil insecticide safe for most gesneriads. I find it also safe for bulbs. But proceed with caution on plants not listed in any product leaflet.

Some soil-treatment chemicals have the power to kill certain insects, but the active ingredients in these chemical products are often dangerous. Several commercial compounds have recently been taken off the market by law. Chemicals can be used to treat unpasteurized soils, but I do not recommend this procedure. It is far more effective and much safer to use a clean medium made from prepackaged soils or your own mix composed of clean ingredients like packaged peat moss, perlite, whole or milled sphagnum moss, and vermiculite, perhaps combined with a pasteurized commercial soil suited to the specific plants.

Modifications

To lighten standard soils for humus-requiring alocasias, caladiums, ferns, and orchid-cacti (hybrids of *Epiphyllum*), mix in oak leaf mold or coarse sphagnum peat moss, both available in plastic bags. If you have space, you can get peat moss by the bale. Geraniums and citrus trees need a somewhat heavier soil, so you can combine coarse builder's sand (not beach sand) with a standard mix, or select a packaged soil that contains more clay loam than organic matter. Some mixes come in transparent bags so you can see what the mixes look like.

Additives

Nonnutritive additives are useful in preparing potting soils. You can use them to modify prepackaged soils or as with the peat-lite mediums, to create a soil-free mix. With any potting soil, hardwood charcoal helps to absorb excess salts and harmful gases. Place the large chunks in the bottom of pots; combine chips and granulated bits with soil.

Perlite, a white sterile volcanic rock with a neutral pH, comes in fine, medium, and super-coarse grinds. It makes soils lighter, helps to prevent packing, and thus gives roots a greater oxygen supply. A disadvantage of perlite is its light weight, which makes it an unsuitable substitute for builder's sand in mixtures for top-heavy plants. (A gravel mulch can help to give weight.) Mixed with peat moss or milled sphagnum moss, perlite is a good medium in which to root cuttings or sow seeds. For epiphytes, coarse perlite (Sponge-Rok) is added to fir bark and tree-fern fiber.

Vermiculite, mica rock which has been exploded by heating to 1,800°, is lightweight when dry but will hold a quantity of water. The pH for domestic horticultural vermiculite ranges from 6.5 to 7.2. Nutrients are held captive between the silvery-gold vermiculite layers until water washes them into solution. This same power to absorb helps to buffer mediums from rapid changes in moisture content, pH value, and temperature. Combined with perlite and peat moss or sphagnum, vermiculite is also a good medium for cuttings, seeds, and growing some plants to maturity. It is marketed in fine grade for seeds, medium for soil mixes, and coarse for packing bulbs or delicate plants in shipping.

Sphagnum moss is a bog plant with antibiotic qualities that protect seedlings from disease. Sow seed directly on the moist milled sphagnum, then feed young plants with one-quarter to one-half strength water-soluble fertilizer. Unmilled or natural sphagnum strands, sold in small bags to large bales, are useful to cover drainage material in pots. Plants will grow in pure sphagnum if they are fertilized. The Geo. W. Park Seed Company offers milled and unmilled sphagnum alone and also in mixtures with other materials. (See Sources of Plants and Supplies at the back of this book.)

Unmilled sphagnum (or chopped strands) is incorporated in bark mixes for orchids like *Phalaenopsis* that require constant moisture. I set newly imported jungle orchids on slightly moist sphagnum spread over charcoal chunks until plants recover from the journey and fumigation. Chopped sphagnum mixed with fir bark and coarse perlite makes a porous compost good for anthuriums, bromeliads, and cloud-forest orchids like odontoglossums.

Sphagnum peat moss, from bogs where it has formed for centuries, is sphagnum in a state of partial decay. The less decayed, coarse, light-brown peat, not the dark-brown to black velvety type, is best for plants that need humus. The acid peat is excellent for azaleas, gardenias, and most gesneriads that require an acid soil.

Basic or Standard Mix

Here is a good general potting mix if you wish to make your own:

> 1 part clean builder's sand (not beach or extra fine)
> 1 part rich humus or leaf-mold compost
> 1 part topsoil ("good garden loam")

Lighten heavy clay soils with an equal volume of rough sphagnum peat moss, and unless your soil is very alkaline, work in ten tablespoons of powdered dolomite limestone per two bushels of soil. But do not use this for high-acid-requirement plants. In my recommendations I consider the average commercially prepared houseplant soils to be comparable to this standard mix. Modify either sort to fit specific plants.

Humus Mix

Some of the best humus-rich mediums contain no soil. For example, nationally available Black Magic Planter Mix is humus, peat moss, leaf mold, and perlite, a good mixture for various tropicals, but it is expensive if you have many to pot, and it may be too light for certain tall plants. I like to mix it half and half with a standard packaged pasteurized soil. Other soil-free humus mixes available locally or through mail-order firms include New Era Formula #5, Laviga Mix, and Panonex Planter Mix by Hyponex Company. If these are not available, you can prepare soil-free humus mix.

Soil-Free Humus Mix

> 1 part coarse perlite
> 1 part rough sphagnum peat moss
> 1 part leaf mold (half redwood, half oak is best)
> 1 part rotted humus
> 1 cup granulated hardwood charcoal per two quarts of mix
> Light dusting of dolomite limestone mixed in

This makes a porous medium that provides air circulation for roots without drying them out, but it contains little nutrients, so feed with a dilute balanced fertilizer. Moisten this mixture with a half-strength fertilizer solution before using it. Soak, then squeeze out excess water before potting. Such mixtures are hard to overwater in drained containers; they remain sweet and do not pack down. Most tropicals thrive in them when properly fertilized. Commercially prepared humus mixes may already contain some fertilizer; make sure to read the directions on the bag.

Packaged humus-rich mixes are convenient to use, just as they come from the bag, and of course are labor-saving. When possible, start with a packaged mix as a base and modify it if required. Redwood fiber or fir bark chips are good additives for some gesneriads, ferns, and foliage plants that need a loose medium. Under average home conditions the humus mix and the peat-lite mix (see below) may be too loose for geraniums, *Begonia semperflorens*, and succulents, so these plants are potted in the standard mix or a succulent medium.

Peat-lite Mix

Mixtures of sphagnum peat moss with perlite and vermiculite will grow many plants if balanced fertilizer is applied regularly. Cornell University has developed several recipes for easy-to-prepare peat-lite mixes that do not require sterilization. The original Cornell formulas are based upon commercial plant-growing techniques, and I find a modified peat-lite mix better for houseplants. In the recipe below you can double the quantity of peat moss for gesneriads and plants that require lots of humus.

> 1 bushel coarse sphagnum peat moss
> 1 bushel medium-grade vermiculite
> 1 bushel medium to coarse perlite
> 5 tablespoons dolomite limestone

For starting cuttings or sowing seeds substitute fine-grade vermiculite and perlite, and cover mixture with a one-inch layer of milled sphagnum moss. Before sowing seeds I wet the medium with a weak fertilizer solution—one-quarter teaspoon of Hyponex in two quarts of warm water. Seedlings are treated with this same solution at least every other watering. Adult plants receive a dilute balanced fertilizer in keeping with their rate of growth, usually every other watering.

I don't mix dry chemical fertilizers with peat-lite, although the original Cornell formulas include superphosphate and a balanced chemical fertilizer like 10-10-10 or 5-10-5. I prefer to add granulated charcoal and a sprinkle of steamed bone meal in mixtures for mature plants, especially for bulbs and tubers. The Park's "Sure-Fire" Sowing and Gro Mixes are commercially available versions of peat-lite, prepared with peat moss and vermiculite plus nutrients.

Organic additives—fish or bone meal and seaweed powder—are sometimes mixed into peat-lite with little danger of root burn, especially when the organic products are kept below the roots of freshly potted plants. Put one-quarter to one-half teaspoon of meal (bone, fish, seaweed, or all combined) in the medium under the roots, cover with unfertilized peat-lite, set the plant, and fill the pot to within an inch of the rim. Eventually the roots will reach down into the richer bottom soil.

To feed established plants, stir the organic products into the surface of the mix. Bone and seaweed meals have little unpleasant odor, but fish meal will smell for a week unless it's well covered.

Keep soil-free peat-lite mediums lightly moist because peat moss, once it dries out, is difficult to get wet. Potted plants in peat-lite benefit from a mulch of attractive fir or redwood bark chips, washed stream pebbles, or white gravel chips. A mulch prevents splashing, root exposure, and excessive evaporation, and it looks better than bare soil.

If you find soil-free mediums too light for heavy plants, especially those in plastic pots, combine coarse builder's sand with the mix, and mulch with heavy gravel. Washed seashells make a nice mulch. I place chunks of coral around the base of my amaryllis to steady the bulbs as the tall flower stalks develop.

Epiphyte Mix

Plants that perch on trees and rocks are not potted in standard soil mixtures. Epiphytic bromeliads and orchids require special airy, quickly drained mediums. I discuss these mixes for epiphytes in the chapters on bromeliads and orchids.

Semiterrestrial Mix

Some bromeliads, orchids, and a few other tropicals thrive in a medium halfway between soil and the loose mix for epiphytes. These can be successfully grown in the bromeliad mixture (Chapter 8) if there is enough water to keep roots evenly moist. Even better are commercially prepared mixes: Lager & Hurrell's, Rivermont terrestrial orchid formula, Stewart's Cymbidium Mix, McLellan Super Orchid Mix, and Wonderbark Mix. (See Sources of Plants and Supplies for addresses.) Pot with these prepared mixes as they come, but water them less frequently than pure bark or fern-root mediums. Fertilize according to manufacturer's recommendations, or see my notes in Chapters 8 and 12. Among the gesneriads and cacti are a few species that live on moss-covered branches or in pockets of accumulated leaf mold. Aeschynanthuses, columneas, epiphytic jungle cacti, and similar semiterrestrial tropicals thrive in a humus-rich soil mixture diluted with 50 percent

commercial terrestrial orchid mix or, second best, with 25 percent medium-
to fine-grade bark chips.

Succulent Mix

For spiny terrestrial succulents, such as desert cacti, use:

    1 part sharp coarse builder's sand
    1 part leaf mold (oak is best)
    1 part standard potting soil (packaged houseplant mix)

For a six-inch pot stir in one-half teaspoon of powdered dolomite limestone, a sprinkle of granulated hardwood charcoal, and a dusting of steamed
bone meal. The medium should be porous and drain quickly. For cacti with
many white hairs or spines provide double the lime, or mix in crushed
oyster shells, which may be available at a local feedstore. (Poultry use
oyster shells.) The old-man cactus (*Cephalocereus senilis*) and other hairy or
white-spined species thrive in a slightly alkaline medium, so additional
dolomite limestone or shells is required to balance acid leaf mold.

For desert cacti that require very sharp drainage, like *Cephalocereus* and
Astrophytum, the succulent mix can be further modified with an additional
one part small gravel or very coarse perlite, a safeguard against having a
medium that remains wet too long. This additional gravel is usually required
for succulents in nonporous containers like plastic or completely glazed
pots. When relatively small clay pots are used, the original soil formula
without extra gravel is satisfactory.

Acid and Alkaline

Chemists use a precise pH scale to express relative concentrations of
hydrogen and hydroxide ions in a solution. With soil-testing kits your soil is
suspended in a test tube of plain or distilled water. Chemical indicator dyes
are added, and the resulting color, matched to a color scale, indicates the
relative acid-alkaline balance.

The pH scale expresses both acidity and alkalinity with values that run
from 0 to 14. At 7 pH as neutral, concentrations of acid hydrogen ions and
alkaline hydroxide ions are balanced. You don't have to understand chemistry to test a medium with a kit sold for home gardeners.

On the pH scale any number above 7 indicates alkalinity; below 7
represents an acid condition. African-violets and episcias, for example, grow
best in a slightly acid medium, a pH of 6.5 to 6.8.

A change of one number on the pH scale represents a big difference. Thus a change from pH 5 to pH 4 is a tenfold change in actual acidity. If a soil has a reading of pH 9, it is one hundred times as alkaline as the neutral pH 7 soil. (It is a geometric progression on a logarithm base of 10.) This is why a small difference between pH numbers may indicate a significant change in the suitability of a medium for a specific plant.

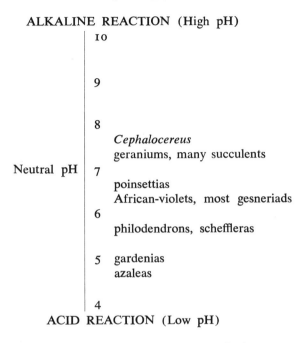

ALKALINE REACTION (High pH)

10

9

8

Cephalocereus
geraniums, many succulents

Neutral pH   7

poinsettias
African-violets, most gesneriads

6

philodendrons, scheffleras

5   gardenias
azaleas

4

ACID REACTION (Low pH)

This section of the pH scale shows that the tropicals we most often grow thrive in a range between pH 6 and pH 7, with fewer species needing very acid or very alkaline soil.

Why pH Matters

When soil is too alkaline or too acid, some of the required elements like phosphorus are chemically compounded or tied up in forms that cannot be absorbed by root hairs. A soil that contains enough phosphorus for African violets would still not be suitable if its pH were above 7.3 or below 5.

The phosphorus would be available to saintpaulias in a soil with a pH between 6.5 and 6.8, the proper range for this genus. Most tropicals thrive in slightly acid to neutral soil, 5.5 to 7 on the scale. Prepared potting mediums conform to these preferences.

Soil bacteria must decompose the organic matter in organic fertilizer before plants can benefit from the feeding. The bacteria function efficiently in a medium with a 6 to 6.9 pH.

How to Check the pH

You can test the pH with an inexpensive soil test kit. The Sudbury Model D has given me good results. Some botanical gardens and state agricultural extension labs offer soil-testing services without charge or for a small fee. The Robert B. Peters Company offers a soil analysis service. Manufacturers of fertilizers and potting mediums sometimes state the pH on the package.

To obtain a soil sample for testing, dig with a clean tool, and put soil in a tight well-washed bottle or plastic container. Any trace of fertilizer or lime on tools or in container will cause an erroneous reading.

It is well to take about eight samples of soil from the area you expect later to use. Mix the samples, then send one cupful to the testing laboratory.

If you follow my recommendations for growing mediums, you should never have to bother with soil testing. However, you may enjoy the scientific aspect of growing plants and wish to make a precise pH test. Remember to pasteurize garden soil before using it for indoor plants.

Fertilizers

Green plants require certain minerals in adequate amounts for healthy growth. Fortunately you don't have to understand the chemistry of plant growth to provide the correct fertilizers, for scientists have been able to determine which elements and combinations are needed for maximum health. By growing plants under controlled conditions they discover more and more about the functions of various plants.

Green plants also have the ability to make their food by turning light energy into simple sugar (glucose). For this photosynthesis, or food manufacturing, they must have enough water and air to supply carbon, hydrogen, and oxygen. This is a simplified explanation of an involved and as yet incompletely understood process, but it is sufficient background to understand the reasons behind horticultural recommendations. Fertilizers supply the other elements required for growth, in addition to carbon, hydrogen, and oxygen furnished by water and air.

Lightly Does It

Don't assume that any sickly plant needs fertilizer. Foliage plants in rich loam will grow well for a year or two without any extra fertilizer. Most ailing houseplants are suffering from inhospitable environment or improper watering (too much, too little, or too infrequently) rather than from lack of sufficient nutrients.

Check the light, potting medium, drainage, watering schedule, and temperature. If then you are certain that all basic conditions have been met, consider fertilizer as an aid. If leaves are light green, nitrogen is usually required. Should an otherwise healthy plant fail to bloom, it may be lacking phosphorus.

Guidelines

When you receive healthy soil-grown plants from a nursery or florist, it is safe to withhold fertilizer for at least a month or two. A dish garden of slow-growing succulents or a foliage plant kept under low light should go without fertilizer for six months unless the plant comes with directions to the contrary.

Resting or inactive specimens do not require fertilizer. Any environmental change that slows down plant growth will also decrease the amount of required water and food. Consider fertilizers as an aid for active plants growing under optimum conditions rather than as a cure-all for assorted plant maladies.

Ingredients

Nitrogen, phosphorus, and potassium (potash) are the three major ingredients in fertilizers. These elements are used by the plant to create new cells and are thus building blocks for the basic matter of life, protoplasm. It is not enough for a green plant to have light and water. You can try growing a rooted Chinese evergreen (*Aglaonema*) or a coleus in a glass of distilled water. The plant will soon deteriorate unless the water is enriched with minute amounts of the mineral salts needed for growth.

Besides these three major ingredients, other elements are required in very small quantities. These micronutrients, or trace elements, include boron, copper, manganese, molybdenum, and zinc. Needed in somewhat greater concentrations but still available in most growing mediums are calcium, iron, sulfur, and magnesium. Complete fertilizers usually contain these elements, and organic products from the sea are rich in them.

The Label

Numbers on a fertilizer label designate, in this order, nitrogen (N), phosphorus (P), and potassium (K). The relative percentage of each can be read from the numbers as can the ratio between the three components. For example, the standard formula for a water-soluble fertilizer for orchids growing in fir bark mixtures is 30-10-10—that is, 30 percent nitrogen, 10 percent phosphorus, and 10 percent potassium, usually as potash. The ratio between the elements is 3-1-1.

A 6-2-2 fertilizer would have the same ratio as the 30-10-10 but would be less concentrated. "High-analysis" fertilizers have a high content of available primary plant food, and they go further but are not necessarily more expensive.

How Much?

No fertilizer is good if applied too strong. An excess of mineral salts will cause root hairs to lose moisture, with resulting local tissue damage called burn. Fertilizers, especially high-analysis chemical sorts, are to be used strictly according to manufacturer's directions. If there is any doubt, mix at a weaker concentration than listed, never higher. Sea-Born liquid seaweed .4-.2-.3 is the weakest fertilizer I use, but it contains numerous valuable trace elements, so I like to apply it in combination with other fertilizers. Fertilizers can be combined so long as the total solution is not overstrength.

Which Formula?

Know the correct names of the plants you wish to fertilize so you can obtain fertilizers balanced specifically for them. Manufacturers often label fertilizers with the names of the plants for which they are primarily formulated, for example, "Foliage plant food," "Bloom stimulant for African-violets," or "Orchid formula for plants in bark." Growing foliage plants require a higher proportion of nitrogen than do plants cultivated mainly for flowers. A preparation labeled as bloom producer will contain comparatively high percentages of phosphorus and potassium but not too much nitrogen. An excess of nitrogen encourages vegetative growth, usually at the expense of flower production.

Read labels carefully. If you are feeding a plant that requires an acid soil—such as citrus, epiphyllum cactus, or gardenia—use an acid-reaction fertilizer. Stern's Miracid (30-10-10) and Peters' Acid Special (21-7-7) are two such products. Most companies offer folders that tell in detail how to use their fertilizers. In the parts of this book that deal with specific plants, the best formulas for certain plants are designated. Where no designation is given, the use of a general balanced formula for houseplants is implied. Fertilizers made for garden application are often too strong for indoor plants.

To get good leaf growth, a high-nitrogen formula is best; for blooming or for slowing down a plant before its rest, a formula low in nitrogen.

What Form?

Water-soluble chemical fertilizers are easy to store, measure, and apply. Examples are Hyponex, Miracle-Gro, Peters' formulas, and Wonderlizer, which come in convenient boxes, often with a measuring spoon. Liquid fertilizers are bulky to ship and store but are often concentrated, so they are still practical. Many of the best organic products come as liquids: Atlas Fish Emulsion, Mer-Made, and Sea-Born liquid seaweed formulas.

Mix dry fertilizers, designed to be used directly, with potting soils, or work around established plants. Certain dry organic fertilizers, bone or blood meal, for example, can be sprinkled on fir bark or tree fern around orchids. Most dry types become available to roots only as they break down with bacterial action, but the chemical sorts, often in tablet form for house-plants, can be absorbed as soon as they dissolve in water around the roots. Some good tablet types are Black Magic (2-3-2) and Plantabs (11-15-20).

The slow-release products like Poracell and Q.U.E. Fertil Pearls let out minute amounts with each watering. A semiporous plastic coating permits this gradual dissolving. Such chemical fertilizers work best when your culture includes heavy watering to flush away residual salts. I like slow-release fertilizers for my orchids before I put them outdoors for the summer or go away on a long trip.

Organic or Chemical?

Every fertilizer must be dissolved in water before it can be absorbed by a plant. Root hairs take in minute quantities of minerals but only when the salts are in solution. Chemical fertilizers are concentrated salts. Organic fertilizers are forms of once living matter (fish, bones, leaves, manure) that have nutrient value when they have been decomposed by bacteria. Organic fertilizers offer little risk of root burn but may cause unpleasant odors indoors.

Chemical and organic fertilizers can be used together. I alternate organic emulsions (fish, seaweed) with a water-soluble chemical compound. Sometimes I mix chemical with organic, each at half-strength or less. The chemicals act rapidly, and the gradually available organics contain trace elements sometimes missing in chemical formulas. And organics help to form humus.

Potting materials. Left row, top to bottom: white marble chips, medium-grade fir bark, chunks of hardwood charcoal, crocks—all for drainage with terrestrial plants. Middle row, top to bottom: medium-grade vermiculite, natural sphagnum moss, medium-grade perlite, sphagnum peat moss. Right row, top to bottom: granulated hardwood charcoal, peat-lite mixture, Baccto potting soil.

Redwood bark products (of Dimmick Forest Company) are useful in growing mediums for bromeliads, gesneriads, and orchids, and provide a good mulch material for soil. I'm holding the coarse grind of redwood bark chips; at top center is medium grind; top right is medium mixed with extra fine; at bottom right, a fine grind for seedling epiphytes or mixing in gesneriad soils.

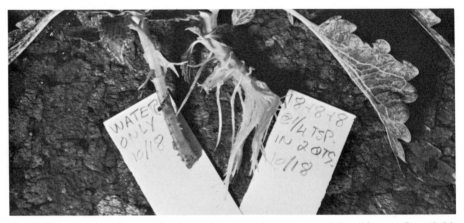

Two coleus cuttings of equal size from the same plant were used for this test. One (left) was placed in plain tap water; the other in a solution of a quarter teaspoon 18-18-18 balanced water-soluble fertilizer per two quarts water. Roots formed faster and were thicker on the cutting in the weak fertilizer solution. Cuttings grew side by side in a bright location, 65° night to 75° daytime temperatures.

46

4

Pots, Potting, and Repotting

IN ONE GARDEN SHOP THAT I KNOW, containers are available in many materials, styles, and prices, from fifty-cent clay pots to a hundred-dollar antique Italian urn. What you choose depends not only on your taste and your budget but on the plant that is to grow in each container. Colored containers, plain or ornamented, are best used with plants whose foliage or flower colors will harmonize or agreeably contrast. A deep-purple cattleya in a pale-yellow container looks fine, but the same flower in a red pot is hardly attractive.

The shape of a plant is also to be considered. Tall subjects, like some of the tropical figs, require a sturdy floor pot. Delicate miniatures can be charming in small ceramics. As a rule, select a simple container for an ornate plant, like a flowering orchid or flamboyant coleus. Use ornamented containers, like those of multicolored tiles, for plants bold in mass, in leaf forms, or in silhouette.

Materials

Plastic and Clay

Plastic pots are favored for their light weight, assorted colors, ease of cleaning (usually in a dishwasher), varied shapes, and low cost. Plastic loses no water except through drainage holes, so plants need less watering than in porous clay pots. The disadvantages of plastic are the brittleness of some types, little weight to support top-heavy plants, and no evaporation through the pot wall, causing certain plants to stay wet too long. Epiphytes like *Oncidium* or *Brassavola* orchids thrive in quick-drying clay pots but sometimes rot if potted in plastic, regardless of the medium they are grown in.

If clay pots can be bought near a pottery, they are inexpensive; otherwise, heavy shipping weight brings their price up to or above plastics. However, weight is an advantage for potting tall plants, which may topple in light containers. Quick-drying clay pots are to be preferred in humid regions and for those plants that grow better if the medium dries out well between waterings. If you tend to overwater, by all means pot in clay.

Clay pots, by evaporating water, build up an unsightly crust of minerals on the rim, which burn any leaves or petioles that touch them. This condition is rare on plastic pots. Tuberous plants, like caladiums and gloxinias, that stay potted during dormancy keep in better condition in plastic pots.

Glazed

Glazed pots evaporate little or no water and are more attractive than either plain clay or plastic. On a terrace or patio a slow-drying pot is an advantage, and glazed containers have enough weight to prevent tall plants from toppling. If you don't wish to pot in glazed or plastic pots but still want to slow down drying of the soil, put a smaller pot inside a larger one (with drainage holes), and stuff the space between with sphagnum or peat moss. If the outside container has no drainage hole, raise the inside pot on a brick or block of wood above collecting water. Outdoors, however, it is important to have drainage holes in both containers so that rain cannot drown the roots.

Terra-cotta

Also slower-drying, and much heavier than standard clay, are ornamental terra-cotta containers from Mexico and Italy. A favorite of mine is a sturdy green terra-cotta jar with impressions of caladium leaves. Others come with anything from simple line designs to embossed cherubs and swags of fruit.

Wood

Redwood and cypress are popular long-lasting woods for baskets, window boxes, and square metal-banded tubs. If you pot an orchid in a wooden container, the roots will grow into the wood as it rots. More suitable and always charming is a summer display of tuberous begonias in a redwood basket.

To make these expensive natural-wood containers last longer, I sink a clay pot into a basket filled with moist sphagnum, which avoids letting the soil come into contact with the wood. I hang the basket from a terrace bracket or low branch until cold weather, then bring in the whole display or sometimes break it down into individual pots again. This way each basket remains in good condition for years.

New Materials

Besides the thin rather brittle plastic pots we all know, there are some types that do permit a slight exchange of air through the sides. These are made from Styrofoam and related lightweight plastic foams. I am finding white Tufflite pots (Geo. W. Park Seed Company) satisfactory for amaryllises, begonias, and gesneriads so far. Even succulents are thriving in these lightweight foam pots, when I add enough bottom drainage and don't overwater or overpot. Another plastic-foam pot comes in a reddish terra-cotta color, a somewhat liverish hue that actually blends well with most plants. I'm growing *Phalaenopsis* orchids in them with good results. Foam pots are too light for tall plants, and they don't accept the pot-gripping stakes sometimes used in orchid growing but otherwise are durable and attractive. Seed flats are now made in white foam; perhaps hanging baskets will be next.

Self-watering Pots

Self-watering wick pots are good if you must leave your begonias or gesneriads for weeks at a time. They are not, in my experience, suitable for some drier-growing begonias, bromeliads, geraniums, orchids, and mature succulents. They are handy for plants that require lightly moist growing conditions, including many begonias, most gesneriads and foliage plants, and seedlings in general. For plants under fluorescent lights, where reaching all pots for daily watering may be difficult, self-watering wick pots are a godsend.

The Plantender (Plantamation, Inc.) is a container designed to water automatically through the action of a sensor embedded in the growing medium. The sensor controls the water flow, which is permitted to enter the soil from a reservoir. One form of Plantender includes a "beautiful vinyl figurine" in the form of a grinning Chinese Hotai. It is supposed to bring good luck, but I don't find such decorative touches necessary with naturally beautiful plants.

A nicer design of the same sensor system is a plastic pole reservoir to hold water behind the wooden slab or log so often used in philodendron or monstera pots. Another Plantender model, the Plantender Pot, is designed to hold a regular pot, while you go on vacation perhaps, but with the sensor inserted in the growing medium. It will keep the plant evenly moist for a week or more.

The simpler Aquamatic Planter (Bermas Plastic Company) is a rectangular white or green hollow-walled styrene container seven by four by three inches. The hollow walls hold up to thirty days' water supply. Water feeds into roots through a hole between the hollow wall and container inner base. You fill the reservoir through a top hole, normally plugged with a rubber stopper. This container will grow nice saintpaulia plants if you follow the supplied directions about planting.

Plain wick-fed pots, like the Hyponex Panonex design, are plastic pots with a fiber-glass wick running out of the bottom. Each pot rests on a saucer base which accepts about one-half to one cup of water. If you find that soil stays too wet, you can let the saucer stay dry for a day or two between waterings.

You can get fiber-glass wick material and cut it into three- or four-inch lengths to devise your own kind of wick pots. Sometimes a plant that is growing over a water tray will turn one of its roots into a wick. Several of my *Phalaenopsis* are growing in pots on top of a metal grid. Below the grid is a fiber-glass window box filled with water, for extra humidity. The orchids have sent several roots into the water and appear to thrive on the added moisture. I had expected the roots to rot, yet they are sound after many months. Of course the majority of the roots are in well-drained fir bark.

Improvised Containers

A delightful complement to your cultivation of houseplants is collecting containers when traveling. Everywhere in the world you can discover some small mug, saucer, bracket, jar, or similar memento that will add richness and interest to your plant collection.

Some of my favorites are a coconut-fiber pot cover from El Salvador, a Masai snuff holder from Kenya, an Indian yucca flour scoop made in Brazil, miniature hayforks from Spain, seashells from Cape Cod, cholla cactus wood from Texas, water-polished stones and driftwood collected everywhere. In tropical countries look for objects of light wood or straw. These can be utilized as pot covers or decorative stakes.

I look for usable pots in everyday containers, especially in those we would otherwise discard. By reusing materials you will save money and do your part in conserving natural resources. Reducing the amount of garbage we produce is a responsibility we all share.

Save plastic spray-can tops and coffee measures to hold miniatures like *Sinningia pusilla*. All improvised containers function best with drainage holes, unless you plan to use them as holders for small conventional pots.

Crystal-clear plastic cups are good containers if you want to watch root growth, useful when you are learning how to water certain plants.

Drainage

Few plants thrive if their roots stand in water, so drainage material is put in the bottom of each container. Pots without a drainage hole are suitable as holders for drained pots, to display flowering plants, for example, but often they accumulate excess water if used for direct potting. In nondrained containers you may wish to use a device that helps to prevent stagnation and encourages evaporation of excess water. The Syfonex Plant Protector (Hyponex Company) is a wide green plastic rod that comes six to fifteen inches long. It is inserted at the bottom of a container with the wick-containing top protruding about two inches above the soil line. Excess water, transferred from the bottom, evaporates through air slits at the top. It is a nice idea for plants that have to be in closed containers, but a better idea is to use pots with drainage.

The drainage hole should be covered with crocks, gravel, and coarse sphagnum to keep it open. My plants are always grown in drained pots except for the rare miniature that I may keep in an ornamental cup or dish for temporary display. Plantsman Alfred Byrd Graf reports that undrained containers should be left without any pebbles or crocking so that the excess water will be drawn efficiently up to the soil surface by capillary action. I find that this practice works. Even with such natural evaporation you will have to be extremely careful in watering plants in undrained pots.

Fortunately most pots come with a drainage hole. If not, you can drill holes in clay, burn them in plastic. I use a knife heated over a gas flame to put extra holes in plastic pots for orchids, and this also works on disposable drinking cups, tops from aerosol cans, and other recycled containers of plastic. These otherwise discarded items make fine pots for small plants, seedlings, or divisions for gifts.

Pot Size

Container size is primarily determined by plant dimensions. It is best to limit root run on most indoor plants. Too much soil leads to root rot. Select a pot that provides enough root room for about a year of growth. It is better to repot than to overpot and risk poor growth from soggy soils.

Cleaning

If you are potting in used containers, they must be thoroughly washed. I use hot water and a soap with germicidal action, like Safeguard, and a Brillo pad for any accumulated salts or sticking roots as with used orchid pots. Then, after a general wash, I put the pots in a dishwasher for their final cleaning. I discard any containers from plants that were suspected of carrying a virus. Plastic pots with a single crack can be repaired by burning a small hole or two in each side of the crack, then holding the pot together with a green plastic plant wire. The plastic-coated metal wire is sold on spools in garden stores and is much better than the paper-coated twist-ties.

Potting

Select an appropriate-size container, prepare a batch of slightly moist soil suited to the plant you wish to pot, gather required material for drainage, mix a transplanting solution of quarter-strength balanced fertilizer with Transplantone powder, and then begin. Terra-cotta and clay pots are soaked in plain water before being used.

The crock is placed to form a curved dome over the drainage hole. Water will drain, but with enough crocking and some pebbles and charcoal covered with a thin layer of sphagnum moss, soil won't wash down to block the exit. Procedures for drainage may vary with the plant being potted. Plastic pots require more pebbles for all but plants that like to remain very moist. Clay pots will need less drainage, since they transpire water. Epiphytes and succulents need the most drainage.

To settle soil evenly around the roots, knock a container on a table or bench several times as you add soil around the root ball. Geraniums and other plants that require firm potting should have soil pushed in around the root ball. Firm in the potting mix with your thumbs or a small wooden tamper. Gesneriads and plants that don't need tight potting can be lightly firmed in without much pressure. Water newly potted plants with the transplanting solution. Keep them away from direct sun until leaves are firm, usually seven to ten days. Under fluorescent lights my transplants don't wilt when I put them eight to twelve inches under the tubes until new roots take hold.

Repotting

When a plant reaches maturity, you can keep it in the same-size container for many years, but it will still need repotting to renew the soil. At repotting time most houseplants can have some side and top roots lightly pruned and top growth proportionately cut back. Do this if you are trying to keep a specimen compact. Otherwise just shift it to a larger container when the present pot becomes filled with roots.

Constant root pruning and top cutting is not practical on standard-size shrubs or any naturally tall plant that you might wish to keep in a four- to five-inch pot, unless you use classic bonsai techniques. The alternative is to select species and hybrids that are genetically compact, dwarf, or miniature.

To remove a plant from its pot, slip the stem between your fingers, invert the pot, and strike its rim with a trowel handle or against anything hard. A firm root ball should drop out cleanly. A pencil eraser can be pushed through drainage holes for stubborn cases. If roots have come through the bottom of the pot and you don't plan to prune back top growth, gently fold the dangling roots around the root ball, or spread them out in the new container. It is root tips that are most important in absorbing dissolved nutrients and water, so cutting them off, if overdone, will naturally shock a plant.

Select a container one to two inches wider than the old root ball. Gently loosen the old tangled roots, pull out any drainage material, and set the plant in the new container at the same level as it was previously growing. Don't plant it any deeper unless it was too shallow to begin with or, like philodendron, has active aboveground roots that can establish themselves in soil.

Clay pots must be wet before potting or they will steal water from the soil. Should you wish to limit growth on a mature plant, cut back one third of the side roots and lightly prune foliage on top. Then don't overfertilize, for too much feeding just causes more rapid growth. Begonias, coleuses, geraniums, and leggy philodendrons are better started anew from cuttings. Even with African-violets that are several years old, better growth comes from new plants started from leaves or side shoots.

When shifting plants to a larger container without disturbing the root ball, it may be useful to make a mold in the packed new medium. With saintpaulia plants that have many leaves extending several inches beyond the correct-size container, you will find the mold technique very helpful. Otherwise, it is difficult to add soil around the plant. To make a mold, fill the new container three-quarters full, then press in the pot that held the plant to be transplanted or a similar pot of the same outside dimensions. This makes a neat hole slightly larger than the root ball, and the plant will drop neatly into the cavity. Now tap the container on the table while holding the plant down gently; soil will settle in around the root ball. Should you still have to add more medium, a small spoon or improvised paper funnel may prove helpful. Even with fuzzy-leaved saintpaulias you can wash off any soil with warm water, but do let plants dry off away from sun in a warm airy place.

Transplanting Solutions

Inevitably some roots will be damaged when you transplant seedlings or repot. Since the upper part of the plant gets the bulk of its moisture and food through the fine root hairs, any extensive damage to roots should be balanced with a light pruning of top growth. Exceptions here are most epiphytic species (bromeliads, orchids) and water-storing succulents, which recover well without a fuss if they are kept in a somewhat cooler, shadier, humid location until new roots take hold.

For other tropicals I recommend a transplanting solution, in addition to light pinching or top pruning. A solution that will reduce shock and stimulate new roots is made by mixing water-soluble fertilizer at quarter to half strength with a small amount of hormone root stimulant like naptylacetamide or indolebutyric acid.

Transplantone is one such hormone product. Water-soluble fertilizers that contain some vitamin B_1, like standard Hyponex, are excellent when combined at quarter strength with Transplantone. Put a quarter teaspoon of fertilizer in two quarts of warm water along with a slight pinch (less than one-eighth teaspoon) of Transplantone, then wet the soil around transplants.

If roots have been unusually damaged or the plant is sensitive, you may also have to cover the top portion with clear plastic, or mist foliage several times each day to prevent excessive wilting, until root hairs grow. Finish off potting with a mulch like gravel or some medium to large redwood bark chips.

Attractive containers add to the charm of plants. Some are best as holders for clay pots. Others, with drainage holes, are suitable for direct planting. Plastic bottles (upper left) are "misters" and help to raise humidity around plants or cleanse foliage with warm-water fog. (*George C. Bradbury*)

Porous clay containers include a strawberry jar (rear center) and saucers (left) drilled with holes to hold chains for hanging.

Attractive pottery container (left) is suitable for ferns or large foliage plants. Hanging baskets can be lined with sheet moss or a pressed-paper pot (bottom right). Plastic pot with attached saucer (top right) is convenient where dripping water might be a problem.

Plastic wick pot ready to receive a propagated gesneriad. Charcoal (right) is for maintaining sweet condition in bottom of pot, sphagnum moss (left) to put over the charcoal, and peat-lite mix for the potting.

This Plantender, with an automatic sensor device, keeps soil of these plants lightly moist. Sensor-tipped tubes reach from water reservoir in Plantender to pots, at left of Jerusalem cherry, to center pot of paperwhite narcissus. *Dracaena marginata* receives water from green Plantender jar; center bromeliad holds water for itself in leaf vase; crassula, philodendron, and dieffenbachia at right are kept moist through tubes drawing in water from reservoirs in Hotai figurine, plastic "pole," and Plantender jar. (*Paulus Leeser for Plantamation, Inc.*)

Improvised containers from plastic spray-can tops, coffee measures, Chinese mustard containers, Styrofoam drinking cups, and clear plastic cups reuse otherwise discarded products of modern living. Cuttings of begonias, coleuses, and African-violets are for gifts.

When roots have filled pot and are in danger of strangling themselves, as with this *Murraea exotica*, a plant must be moved to a larger pot.

Pot is knocked hard against a table to remove root ball with soil as a solid unit.

Begonia 'Corallina de Lucerna', cut back prior to repotting in a larger container. Drainage materials in the background include charcoal, pebbles, crocks, and sphagnum moss to cover them.

Newly potted coleus with white marble mulch looks at home in a graceful clay pot.

5

Propagating Houseplants

To PROPAGATE CHOICE PLANTS is to increase and perpetuate beauty. It is a special joy to propagate favorite plants as gifts for friends. What other possession can be so easily shared? You can hardly give a piece of a painting or an antique to an admiring friend, yet when someone appreciates your coleus, cattleya, or zebrina, you can indeed say, "I'll give you a piece."

If you want to duplicate a plant exactly, propagate it by vegetative means —cutting, offshoot, division, or runner. If you want a sizable number of similar plants, grow them from seed. Self-pollinated plants or plants pollinated by another clone of the same species produce seeds that come reasonably true. Pollination by a plant of another species produces hybrids, which may differ widely.

When you do plant seed, be sure it is fresh and correctly labeled. Proper growing conditons can be determined if you have the correct name.

Some of the firms listed at the end of this book offer seed flats, miniature greenhouses, and pots designed for growing seedlings efficiently. These containers provide drainage, transparent covers, and often some form of wick-watering. Other vessels for seed sowing may be clay or plastic pots or improvised flats made from ice trays, from plastic refrigerator food holders, from clothes boxes. Choose the container that will be most convenient but still maintain even moisture and permit some air circulation without excessive drying or temperature variations.

My favorite containers for sowing fine seed are miniature plastic greenhouses, and for larger seeds that don't have to be covered, the light-green plastic flats available in several sizes. These durable plastic trays, usually about two inches deep, must have drainage holes burned through them with a hot knife. It is a good idea to do the same for any miniature plastic greenhouses that don't already have drainage holes in the bottom tray.

Preparing the Medium and Sowing Seed

1. Cover the container floor with a half inch of medium to fine pebbles or fine fir bark.

2. Fill the container to within a half inch of the top with your favorite seed-sowing mixture. I like equal parts of medium-grade perlite, medium vermiculite, and milled sphagnum moss. I cover this with a half- to one-inch layer of plain milled sphagnum moss for fine seeds. Larger seeds can be planted without the sphagnum topping. Pour boiling water over sphagnum moss if you have any trouble getting it wet. Alternative mixtures that have given me good results include Park's "Sure-Fire" Sowing Mix and nationally distributed New Era Starter Mix, both packaged in small plastic bags.

3. Soak the mix with a solution of a quarter teaspoon Hyponex or similar balanced chemical fertilizer in two quarts of warm water. Don't increase the strength of this solution. If you are planting on a commercially prepared mixture, check the bag label to see if it already includes fertilizer; if so, eliminate the initial soaking with fertilizer solution.

4. Press down the mix with a flat section of wood to make the surface even. I often prepare flats the day before sowing seed and let them settle and drain. Sow the seed.

Fine Dustlike Seed

The seed of begonias, gesneriads, and some other tropicals is extremely small. Sow these fine seeds on top of the moist mix, then gently settle them with a mist of warm water. Cover the flat with clear glass, plastic, an upturned clear plastic pot, or a plastic bag supported by stakes. Since seed is sown on a moist mix and the covering will help retain moisture, you usually won't have to uncover the container for watering until all seeds have germinated. If you do have to water, use a gentle warm mist. Slight condensation on the cover is proper, but water covering the whole inner surface indicates that some ventilation is needed.

After seed germinates, gradually increase air circulation. Fern spores are sown just as suggested for fine seed, only they are kept moister.

Medium to Large Seeds

Quite a few plants produce seeds large enough to handle individually. Seeds of amaryllis, many bromeliads, geraniums, and succulents can be sown one by one, using fingers, tweezers, or a lightly moist probe to pick up and space each seed in the sowing mix. Space seeds twice their size in distance. Thus a half-inch amaryllis seed is spaced with one inch between each seed. This gives seedlings room to grow and avoids the necessity of early thinning or transplanting.

Another technique for larger seeds is to fill half of the container with a pasteurized soil mix and the upper half with a nonnutritive sowing mix. When seedlings begin to grow, roots will reach into the soil for sustenance, yet the seed has the protection of a sterile surrounding medium.

Cover medium to large seeds with a sprinkle of sowing mix to bury them twice their size in depth. I cover amaryllis, coleus, geranium, and similar seed with a quarter inch of mix, then gently water the flat and firm the medium with a wood block. In dry locations cover the container with clear plastic or glass, adjusted to avoid heavy condensation. In the greenhouse or other humid place a cover can be eliminated for larger seeds.

Temperature

Germination is best for most tropicals at 65° to 75°. Seed packets usually note the desired germination temperature. Gentle bottom heat fosters uniform germination. On a windowsill above a radiator, bottom heat is simple to arrange, but make sure to put seed containers in a large tray of moist perlite or gravel to prevent rapid drying.

A soil heating cable with built-in thermostat (under five dollars) can be set down in the bottom of a plastic tray to provide evenly controlled bottom heat anywhere. In the greenhouse or plant room keep seed flats on a bench over the warm heating pipes or stove. Shelves above fixtures in fluorescent light stands will receive heat automatically from the ballasts below.

Air temperature of 70° to 75° is a good average for tropical seeds. Some optimum germination temperatures for popular tropicals are:

Amaryllis. 75° to 80°, germination in two to four weeks.
Anthuriums. 75° to 80°, seed must be very fresh.
Begonias. 65° to 75°, warmest for rex cultivars.
Bromeliads. 65° to 70°.
Coleuses. 65° to 75°, germination within a week.
Fern spores. 75° to 80°, evenly moist, wetter than for seeds.
Geraniums. 55° to 60°, germination in twenty days, sometimes longer.

Gesneriads. 75° to 85°, may sprout unevenly over four to six weeks.
Palms. 75° to 80°, germination in two months for many species.

Light

Fine seed sown on top of the medium germinates best with bright-diffuse
light from fluorescent growth lamps. Standard horticultural growth lamps
like Gro-Lux are excellent light sources for germinating seeds. If your fixtures are equipped with the wide-spectrum tubes, keep flats covered with one
layer of white paper towel or twelve to fifteen inches away from the lamps
until germination occurs. A fixture with two twenty-watt Gro-Lux lamps hung
six to eight inches above the seeds is an excellent arrangement for strong
growth. Seed flats are checked daily to be sure they don't dry out.

Larger seeds covered with mix are kept in bright-diffuse light, although
illumination is not so important until germination occurs. Giving seedlings
fifteen to eighteen hours of fluorescent light per twenty-four-hour period will
shorten the time until bloom. This is a great advantage for long-term projects
like growing amaryllis bulbs from seed, since they usually take three to
five years to bloom under standard natural days. Fluorescent light supplements daylight and increases day length, so amaryllis bloom for me in two
to three years.

After Germination

Reduce temperatures about 5° after germination is complete. Be sure
sprouted seed has bright-diffuse light, or young plants may get weak and
leggy. Fertilize seedlings with quarter-strength water-soluble nutrients (I·
use Hyponex and Peters) after the first true leaves have expanded. Seed
sown on mixes that contain nutrients can go longer before they receive supplemental feeding; check directions sent with the mix.

I sow most seeds on the sphagnum-perlite-vermiculite mix and so must
fertilize three out of four waterings. Seeds sown on a mixture over standard
soil require less attention to fertilizing once the roots have grown down into
the nutrition-rich soil below. Tiny seedlings are watered with a gentle
drenching mist from a plastic sprayer. To avoid disturbing seedlings, some
people set flats or pots in a saucer of water and let them soak up water from
below. Plantlets in wick-watered flats are in no danger of being washed up
by strong overhead watering.

Transplanting

Thin out seedlings when large enough to handle. All overcrowded plants
should be thinned so they have room to grow. If you have sown larger seeds

with care, you may not have to transplant seedlings until they are ready for individual pots. If you have many more plants than required, pull up extras to leave room for the largest seedlings. This is a quick procedure and works well except for mixed rex begonias and other hybrids in which smaller plants may eventually turn out to be the most desirable for dwarfness or color.

Seedlings to be grown on are transplanted into community containers (compots), usually at least as large as a six-inch pot. Space them one to two inches apart, more for fast-growing sorts. Grow them on until they have four or five true leaves, then transplant to individual pots, using the proper soil for the species you are potting.

I pinch begonias, coleuses, geraniums, and similar fast growers when they are transplanted to individual pots. Pinching out the top set of leaves promotes side-shoot growth and creates bushy seedlings. Adequate light is also important in growing compact seedlings. Plants that lean toward the light source or have long nodes between leaves are not receiving enough light. Growing seedlings under fluorescent lamps is better than trying to succeed with variable, sometimes too hot, sun.

Growing On

Continue to shift seedlings to larger pots as the roots fill smaller containers. There is no need to disturb the root ball when transplanting. Follow directions given for potting in Chapter 4. It is usually better to shift seedlings several times during their growing period than to overpot them. Bulbs that require several years before they bloom are spaced in community flats, then can be grown without further transplanting until they begin to produce flowers. Keep amaryllis growing for at least twenty-six to thirty-six months with even moisture, fertilizer, and fluorescent lights; then let them dry out, and lower temperature to 50° or 55° for a month (fall to winter) to induce blooming. Gesneriads, even though they may have to form a tuber or rhizome, usually bloom the first year from seed. Begonias and geraniums also bloom within eighteen months; some in only four to six months. Succulents may take two or more years before flowers show; bromeliads, four to six years.

Asexual or Vegetative Propagation

Vegetative propagation is most successful when the plant is in active growth, usually from early spring into fall. Cuttings of begonias, coleuses, and geraniums that have been growing in the garden are usually taken in early fall before frost.

Propagating from various forms of cutting—stems, leaves, runners, and offsets—has much in common with seed sowing. Bottom heat is an advantage, moisture must be even, humidity high, and light bright but diffuse (no hot strong sun). The simple technique of rooting a stem section or leaf in water requires no elaborate preparation. Just cut the leaf or stem with a razor (take off the lowest set of leaves on stem cuttings), and set the cutting in a glass containing about one inch of pure water or, as I do, in a quarter-strength solution of chemical fertilizer. Plant the cutting before the new roots become tangled, normally as they reach two to three inches.

Propagating Mix

Most often propagations are rooted in a moist mix. I use the same formula as for seed sowing: equal parts of milled sphagnum moss, medium-grade perlite, and vermiculite. Peat-lite (with no fertilizer) and commercially prepared seed-sewing mixtures are also suitable when used according to package directions.

Root-Stimulating Hormone

A light dusting of root-stimulating hormone powder with fungicide helps prevent rot while it encourages cuttings to form roots rapidly. The weakest-strength rooting hormone is safe for houseplants, but stronger No. 2 and No. 3 grades (intended mainly for hardwood cuttings) are likely to injure tissues or retard top growth. The new improved Rootone No. 1 with fungicide has given me excellent results with a wide range of plants. It contains the synthetic plant hormones napthaleneacetimide, methyl-napthaleneacetimide, indole-3-butyric acid, and Thiram fungicide. To stimulate roots and discourage damp-off fungus, I dust medium to large seeds with dry Rootone before planting them.

Transplanting Solutions

Transplanted seedlings and freshly potted propagations establish better when watered in with a quarter-strength balanced fertilizer solution to which a root stimulant has been added. In two quarts of warm water I mix a quarter teaspoon soluble fertilizer and slightly less than one-eighth teaspoon of Transplantone hormone powder. This is a slightly weaker solution than that recommended for transplanting mature plants. I drench the potting medium with this solution and get good results, no harm to any tender subjects.

Moisture

Cuttings kept in an area of 50 to 80 percent humidity, as in a greenhouse or damp basement under fluorescent lights, may not require a moisture-containing cover, but in other conditions thin-leaved cuttings must be kept covered until roots appear. Thick-leaved cuttings, succulents, heavy rhizome sections, or trunk segments need not be covered if humidity is above 50 percent. Cuttings rooted in water or fertilizer solution need not be covered.

Light

Bright light aids growth and thus speeds rooting. I prefer to rely mainly on fluorescent growth tubes for gentle, controlled light without injurious excessive heat. Reflected sun in a north window or behind a thin curtain in brighter exposures is suitable natural illumination. Only succulent cuttings can accept direct sun without wilting. Once roots form, give cuttings exposure preferred by that species, as for mature plants.

Division

Fully grown anthuriums, begonias, some gesneriads, orchids, and many succulents are divided at potting time, and smaller plantlets clustering around the larger stems are potted up individually. This is the easiest sort of vegetative propagation, since the divisions often have their own root systems and thus require only a transplanting solution and a few days of readjustment.

Cut apart overgrown clumps with a sharp knife, or gently break off plantlets, saving as many roots as possible. Wash the knife in soap and water before using it on another plant; do the same for your hands. Pot divisions in soil used for the larger plant, water with transplanting solution, and keep divisions away from strong light for several days. If wilting begins, cover the plants with a clear plastic bag held up by thin stakes. Divisions with small root systems are treated as suggested for stem cuttings.

Layering

Rambling stems, as in episcias and many philodendrons, are layered by pinning or weighting down stems, at a joint when possible, on moist propagating mix. Encourage new roots by cutting half through a stem, dust with hormone powder, and keep the stem down with a stake or stone. I like to cover the cut section with some propagating mix. You can also layer directly in soil around the base of a mature plant by bending down stems, but then you must disturb two root systems when transplanting the layer. Layering is a helpful technique for hard-to-root species because the layered branch receives nutrition from the mature plant until roots form. An easy way with rambling plants like episcias is to set the pot in a large tray of moist propagating mix, then let runners droop down into the tray, where most will form roots without any incision or rooting powder.

Crotons, dieffenbachias, dracaenas, and *Ficus* species are some tall tropicals that can be air-layered in moist sphagnum moss held against a partly cut stem. This is the way to restore leggy plants. Begin by making an upward-slanting cut one third of the way through a stem, several inches below the nearest leaves.

Dust the wound with a light coating of Rootone or the hormone that comes with air-layering kits. Stuff moist unmilled sphagnum moss under the cut stem and form a fist-sized ball completely around the area. Wrap clear plastic around the sphagnum ball, and tie each end snugly with plastic-coated wire. In four to six weeks roots should be seen through the plastic wrap. When roots fill the sphagnum ball, cut off the stem below the new roots, pot the rooted stem, and keep it in a moist shady place until established. The topped base may sprout a new growth, so don't throw it out.

Offsets and Runners

Chlorophytum species and episcias produce small plantlets on the end of runners. These can be layered while still attached to the mature plant or removed and rooted in propagating mix. Offsets are plantlets that form at the side of adult plants as will be seen with agaves, aloes, bromeliads, and *Clivia.* Remove offsets for propagation when the larger plant is repotted. Offsets of bulbs are best left on the main plant for two years until they develop good root systems.

Most amaryllis hybrids make one to three offsets every three years, but some types are more prolific. *A. striata* makes so many vigorous offsets that they can be removed every year or two. To remove offsets from bulbs, shake the soil off to expose the junction between offset and mother bulb. Gently twist the offset first left, then right, until it comes loose. Only rarely will a knife be required to cut tangled roots, and I have never had to cut an offset from the side of a mature bulb. Dust the raw spots with low-strength rooting powder, repot the mature bulb, put offsets in a community pot or in smaller individual pots, and keep them growing as for seedling blubs. Label offsets by color or name.

Offsets bloom in two years if given sixteen- to eighteen-hour days under fluorescent growth lamps. Tubers like caladiums, callas, and gloxinias often form tuberlets that can be removed and potted individually.

Leaf Cuttings

African-violets are famous for their ability to produce plantlets from leaves. Some begonia and kalanchoe species form plantlets on mature leaves without any coaxing from us, and these can be removed and grown on. The classic way to propagate rex begonias and gloxinias is from healthy leaves set in moist propagating mix. Select leaves free from fungus spots and middle-aged, neither very young nor ready to die. With variegated plants choose leaves typical of the pattern you wish to perpetuate.

Cut the petiole (leaf stem) at a 45° angle from the leaf as the top surface faces upward. Leave one to two inches of stem, depending on the size of the leaf. Saintpaulias can be cut shorter, and rex begonias are often left two inches long. If the African-violet is very special and you want a maximum crop of plantlets, leave the leaf stem long so that it can be recut and set down to form plantlets several times. Dust the cut end with rooting hormone powder, tap off excess, make a hole in the rooting mix with finger, pencil, or dowel, insert the cut tip, and firm in the mix to hold each leaf snugly. Put the flat of rooting leaves in a 70° to 75° place with humidity above 50 percent. Light should be bright-diffuse or, even better, fluorescent growth tubes. Some gesneriads may show plantlets at the leaf-petiole junction in five to six weeks, whereas succulents may take much longer, although roots may form quickly.

Pot new cuttings in small pots, or grow them in a compot or flat for later potting when they begin to crowd. Tuberous gesneriads can be left to bloom in the rooting flat, then potted up when they go dormant. African-violets left attached to the mother leaf after they are an inch tall are given half-strength water-soluble fertilizer, since the rooting mix does not have enough nutritional value for healthy growth. You can leave African-violets attached to the leaf until the leaf dies, or you can remove the plantlets and reset the leaf, which will often start more little propagations.

Variations in Leaf Cuttings

The standard method of rooting single leaves will produce a plant or clump of plantlets from the junction between a leaf and the petiole. A way to get more plantlets from rex begonias and gloxinias is to set the whole leaf flat on moist rooting mix. Injure major veins by pushing your fingernail halfway through on the underside, dust the wounds with Rootone, set the leaf bottom-down on moist propagating mix, and weight injured portions with small stones to bring them in contact with the mix. Plantlets form at injured points and at stem end when it is covered with moist mix. Gloxinias may form two tubers at the stem end if it is split before being set. Gentle bottom heat helps roots form quickly.

Rex begonias are frequently cut into wedge-shaped leaf sections, each containing a portion of a major vein. Cut surfaces are lightly dusted with rooting powder (with fungicide), then set a half-inch deep in moist propagating mix. Similar leaf sections of sansevierias and sedums will form plantlets. With most succulents I prefer to set whole leaves or pads of cacti rather than cut them up into smaller segments. Succulent cuttings are left for a day to form a dry scab over the wound before they are set in lightly moist rooting mix. Leave succulent cuttings uncovered, put clear-plastic bags, a glass, or a miniature-greenhouse top over any leaf cuttings that wilt or that must endure a dry atmosphere.

Stem Cuttings

Begonias, coleuses, geraniums, and philodendrons propagate readily from stem cuttings. Soft, rapidly growing stems are cut just at the time when they are starting to become firm. Any thin-leaved sorts that are likely to wilt are covered with clear glass or plastic bags supported by thin stakes while the cuttings form roots. The atmosphere around the cuttings must be very humid, 80 to 90 percent, so a cover for all but succulents or hard woody stems is required. Philodendrons and geraniums usually root in a bright humid place without special moisture-retaining covers, but in dry places they must be covered.

Cut off vigorous active side growths or tops, two to four inches long, with a razor or sharp knife. Remove lowest set of leaves, dip cut stem in hormone powder, tap off excess, and insert cuttings about one inch deep in moist propagating mix. Let succulent stem cuttings sit for a day to form a dry scab before using rooting powder and inserting them into the mix. I do the same for geraniums. Sections of fleshy rhizomes from begonias and leafless stems of dieffenbachias, *Cordyline terminalis*, and dracaenas sprout dormant buds ("eyes") when set horizontally in moist rooting mix, half covered, and provided with gentle bottom heat.

Tuberous plants like gloxinias will sprout more than one stem each season. Extra or secondary shoots are removed and set in propagating mix.

Scaly Rhizomes

Achimenes, kohleria, and smithiantha grow from scaly rhizomes. For sturdy plants, pot the whole rhizome, but if you wish to propagate a variety, break up each rhizome into two or three sections, dust with weak-strength hormone powder, and plant as for medium- to large-size seeds. For an abundance of small plants the rhizomes can be scaled off so that individual scales fall onto a moist propagating mix. Cover the scales with twice their size (depth) of moist propagating mix or pure milled sphagnum moss. With this system a single one-inch rhizome can yield twenty or more plants. Gesneriads with rhizomes will usually double the number of rhizomes per pot each season.

Begonia semperflorens 'Butterfly' seedlings one month after being sown on a commercially prepared seed mixture of peat moss, vermiculite, and perlite

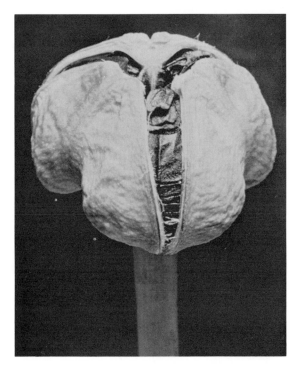

Seedpod of an amaryllis about one month after the cross was made. The pod is ready to be harvested, the seed dried for a day, then planted.

Five-day-old seedlings of cacti, germinated under a cover of clear plastic, can now be left uncovered if room humidity remains above 50 percent. Seedling succulents require more water than mature succulents but still must never get soggy.

Seedlings of *Rhoeo discolor* will soon have to be transplanted if they are to have enough room for sturdy growth.

A miniature plastic greenhouse serves perfectly for rooting African-violet leaves or other propagations that must be covered.

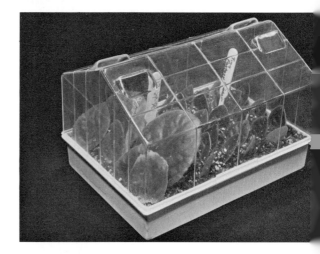

Fleshy rhizome of *Begonia longibarbata* can be cut into two sections and potted in humus-rich soil. Any segments of rhizomes that have no roots are treated with hormone powder and given bottom heat until established.

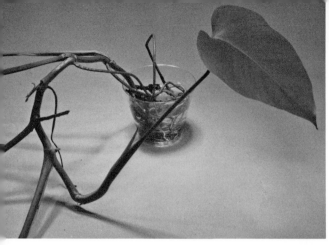

A stem section from *Monstera deliciosa* rooted easily for me in a cup of water. Monstera and philodendron stem sections with root nodes or aerial roots readily form feeder roots in soil or moist propagating mix. Pot them in soil when roots reach several inches.

Calla tuberlets can be removed from the larger tuber at the point shown. Dust the cut with hormone-fungicide powder, and pot individually.

Unusual propagation resulted when I left a cut inflorescence of *Eucomis bicolor alba* in water for several months. Bulblets formed in the small leaves on top of the flowers. These tiny bulbs grew with vigor when I potted them in a propagating mix. In two years they will flower. Normal method of propagating *Eucomis* is by offsets that form in the soil, or by seed.

Propagation of *Saintpaulia* from leaves begins with a dusting of Rootone with fungicide on the cut ends and leaf base (left). Leaves are set in rooting mix, and in a few weeks tiny plants will form at the leaf base (front center). Remove and pot the plantlets when they have four to six good leaves (top center). Miniature 'Tiny Pink' (lower right) is ready to be potted in a 1½-inch pot or plastic coffee measure. I pot miniatures with the leaf attached, then let it die away.

Major veins on the underside of this rex begonia leaf will sprout plantlets if the veins are injured, as indicated by black lines. Leaf is set bottom down on moist propagating mix.

Single leaves of *Graptopetalum paraguayense* produce one or two plantlets each when set on the surface of moist propagating mix and given bright light. Succulent cuttings require good air circulation and bright light, in contrast to other tropicals that must have a more humid atmosphere and diffuse light.

Tall angel-wing begonias can be propagated when they are cut back in spring or early fall. Make a clean cut just below a node. I remove the lower leaf and root the stem in water.

Stem cuttings that root easily in plain water or weak fertilizer solution include coleus (left), *Plectranthus australis* (right), and *Zebrina pendula*, shown in foreground with lower stem leaves removed.

Pellionia pulchra (left) and *Columnea* 'Red Spur' stem-tip cuttings rooting in the propagating mix. I cover the columnea cuttings to keep them in a protected humid atmosphere until roots form. The *Pellionia* rooted without a cover in humidity of 60 percent.

71

This gloxinia tuber has sprouted several shoots, and I am holding the slightly smaller secondary shoots that should be removed for propagation.

With a sharp knife or razor cut each secondary shoot away just at the surface of the main tuber.

Secondary shoots will form sturdy plants that often bloom along with the main tuber that same season. At the left is a secondary shoot with roots already formed; it is in a small pot of standard gloxinia soil, ready to be grown on. The secondary shoots at center are ready for a dusting of rooting powder on the cut stems before they are placed in the small pots of rooting mix (right).

6

Color from Leaves

ONCE I WALKED A NARROW TRAIL, deep into moist Amazonian jungle where occasional flecks of sunlight sparkled on marantas and episcias growing in spongy humus. I could barely see the patches of sky through tangled treetops and rampant vines. Palms, philodendrons, and myriad different plants created a living encyclopedia of leaf forms, colors, and textures. These were plants fighting for light but destined in that dark world only rarely to reach into sunlight. Through the ages they have adapted themselves to survive with the little sun that breaks through the thick canopy of towering trees.

In our homes these same plants may give months of beauty even in dim light and with little care. A few kinds with colorful leaves will also thrive in bright light because their habitats are jungle clearings, bright forest edges, and grasslands.

Tough succulent fans of *Sansevieria ehrenbergii* grew around the dry grassland in Tanzania, where I photographed East African wildlife. In Olduvai Gorge, near Ngorongoro Crater, I found orange-flowered aloes thriving in sandy soil above fossils of earliest man. All over Africa I saw tough euphorbias in full sun, some growing into twenty-foot trees. Indoors we can enjoy young plants of these slow-growing giants and other species of smaller stature.

Foliage tropicals are so varied that I have arranged these sections to help you choose them according to the decorating effect you desire. Single potted specimens make handsome easy-to-move accents; but also consider hanging baskets, raised floor planters, sunken wells, and bookshelf displays. If you are building a house or an addition, consider incorporating a shallow pool surrounded with planting beds.

In a room with lively colored rugs, upholstery, or walls it is usually best to decorate with bold plants of a single color. Green contrasts well with glowing reds, yellows, and many pastels, but leaf texture and overall effect are as important as color. A light feathery plant is lost in a room where everything is already highly detailed or ornate. Conversely, unadorned walls, plain carpet or floor, and emphatic architectural lines may greatly enhance the quality of deeply cut palm leaves or fern fronds.

For boldness in a room with heavy furniture and angular designs pick something like *Monstera deliciosa* or *Ficus elastica.* For grace and yielding lines choose trailing plants with delicate leaves—*Asparagus plumosus* or *Ficus benjamina,* for example.

The green-foliage plants listed below are arranged according to the impression they usually create. Other foliage plants are grouped by their dominant color, concluding with the multicolored crotons, coleuses, and others. Trailers and vines for flowers and foliage are discussed in Chapter 7.

Green—Bold, Ultimately Tall

Aloe arborescens. Treelike succulent, casts dramatic shadows. Gritty succulent mix, grow on dry side in bright-diffuse light to full sun several hours per day.

Amomum cardamon. The Java cardamom ginger. Aromatic, upright, tough lance-shaped leaves from underground rhizome. Pot in humus mix kept moist, provide 60° to 65° nights, diffuse light. Small yellow flowers tucked at base of leaves form seeds for cardamom spice, delightful to chew after an Oriental meal.

Euphorbia lactea. Stiff spiny cactuslike stems, striking silhouette. Culture as for aloes.

Ficus elastica and *F. lyrata* (*F. pandurata*). Both are adaptable trees well suited to indoor decoration in diffuse light and standard slightly moist soil. *F. elastica* is the rubber plant. *F. lyrata* has wavy slightly drooping foliage. Wash foliage with damp cloth for attractive gloss.

Monstera deliciosa. Climbing cut-leaved aroid often sold as a philodendron. Adaptable, long-lived. Stiff aerial roots should have a cork or fern log for support. Seedlings have uncut foliage. Pot in standard soil, keep evenly moist. Tolerates low light, prefers bright-diffuse.

Musa acuminata. A true banana but only two to five feet tall, broad leaves, thick shiny stem. Needs bright light, humus-rich soil kept evenly moist. May be offered as *M. nana* or *M. cavendishii.*

Pandanus veitchii. The screw pine has sword-shaped leaves, thick roots, many aboveground support roots at base. Tolerates low humidity. Grow in standard mix with added gravel for sharp drainage. Keep on dry side when resting in winter. Some plants have white-banded leaves.

Philodendron bipennifolium (P. panduraeforme). Climbing form, good on poles or trailing around pots in large window box. Tolerates low light, requires only even moist standard soil.

Philodendron 'Emerald Queen'. A hybrid especially good for sphagnum-filled totem poles.

Rhaphidophora celatocaulis. Clinging Bornean vine for location with diffuse light, high humidity, support of fern pole or log pole. Pot in humus-rich soil, keep evenly moist, warm, 60° to 65° at night.

Sansevieria nelsonii. Durable stocky upright foliage. Tolerates low light, dry air. Grow in succulent mix or standard soil.

Schefflera actinophylla (Brassaia). Umbrella-shaped tree often used in lobby and office plantings and equally suitable in large living room or plant terrace. Dramatic tropical effect. Pot with standard mix, keep slightly dry between waterings, give bright-diffuse light, although it will tolerate dimmer.

Yucca elephantipes. Upright stem with thin spiny foliage. Culture as for aloes.

Green—Bold, Medium to Dwarf

Agave americana, A. attenuata, A. parrasana. Three excellent symmetrical succulents for full sun, succulent soil mix. These tolerate dry conditions, require little care, and are striking plants. *A. americana* grows to five or six feet eventually and much higher in the wild. *A. attenuata* makes large rosettes of soft gray-green leaves. *A. parrasana* is a dwarf, very similar to *A. potatorum.*

Aglaonema simplex. The Chinese evergreen will thrive in a weak fertilizer solution or standard soil. Needs no direct sun.

Aloe species. Aloes will grow easily in bright locations. Various species are available from dwarf to tall types.

Aspidistra elatior. Cast-iron plant is a good common name for this extra-adaptable species. A variegated form is available. Standard soil kept evenly moist, temperate climate, diffuse to dim light.

Asplenium nidus. Bird's-nest fern. Heavy, shiny, leathery fronds in a neat rosette. Warm moist conditions, diffuse light, standard soil.

Crassula argentea. The jade tree is a succulent shrub but may also be grown as a small dish-garden plant. Pot in succulent mix, permit to dry between waterings. Tolerates low light but needs bright-diffuse light when active.

Fatshedera lizei. A hybrid between English ivy (*Hedera helix*) and *Fatsia japonica.* Large, leathery, glossy three- to five-lobed leaves. Grows well in diffuse light, prefers under 60° at night. Good for cool sun-room or lobby. Variegated variety available.

Fatsia japonica. Cool grower. Makes a large shrub, needs only routine care. Cultivar 'Moseri' is a compact form.

Peperomia maculosa, P. obtusifolia. Low-growing waxy-leaved species good for underplanting, ground cover, table plants, terrarium. Standard soil or humus-rich mix slightly dry between waterings. Bright-diffuse to low light. Other species have glowing metallic-colored foliage and unusual textures; most are excellent houseplants.

Philodendron fragrantissimum (P. melioni). Shiny leaves with lighter veins, self-heading type that forms clump of foliage from a central crown, in contrast to trailing or climbing sorts. Philodendrons are so varied that word descriptions are not adequate, so check illustrated catalogs or visit a nursery. Species and hybrids thrive in diffuse light, grow best in lightly moist standard soil or humus-rich mix mulched with fir bark or rough sphagnum moss. Wash leaves for an attractive shine. Other good types are *P.* 'Lynette', a neat-growing clump; *P. martianum,* slow-growing, glossy foliage from odd inflated petioles; *P. selloum* with dramatic deeply cut leaves; *P. wendlandii* with spatula-shaped foliage in cluster like bird's-nest fern.

Rohdea japonica. A cool-growing lily relative sometimes called sacred lily of China. Makes a low informal rosette of tough smooth green leaves to two feet long, more interesting in the variegated form *R. japonica marginata*. Pot in standard mix well drained, let dry out slightly between waterings, provide filtered light, no hot sun, nights 50° to 60°. Propagates most easily by division of crowns from thick rhizomes. Established clumps sometimes bear white flowers followed by red berries.

Sansevieria ehrenbergii. Tall succulent fan to twenty-eight inches, but compact, sturdy. Standard soil or succulent mix. Tolerates low light, grows best in bright. Endures low humidity. *S. trifasciata* 'Hahnii', the bird's nest sansevieria, is a low and very slow growing rosette, excellent in dish gardens or terrariums.

Green—Feathery, Open, Tall to Medium

Alsophila australis. A tree fern from Australia. May be offered as *A. cooperi*. Needs humus-rich soil, warm moist conditions, diffuse light.

Araucaria heterophylla (A. excelsa). The Norfolk Island pine, a needled-leaved evergreen, makes a delightful Christmas tree. Grow in humus-rich mix kept lightly moist, provide bright light, keep in relatively small pot.

Blechnum brasiliense. This heavy-fronded fern will eventually form a stout trunk up to three feet high but is slower growing than the true tree ferns. *Blechnum* endures low humidity better than most ferns and with occasional misting and bright-diffuse light will grow in warm rooms. Keep the humus-rich soil evenly moist. *B. moorei* is smaller, with fronds to one foot long.

Caryota mitis. The fish-tail palms have broad leaves with shaggy ends. Easy to grow in bright light and humus-rich mix kept evenly moist and warm. Other good species are *C. plumosa* and *C. urens*.

Chamaedorea cataractarum. Bamboo palms need a bright place with humidity above 50 percent to retain their full beauty. Keep the standard soil evenly moist. You can remove older leaves but don't cut growing tip of stem. These tolerate low light but grow best in bright-diffuse. Other good species: *C. costaricana*, to fifteen feet; *C. elegans* (or *Collinia elegans*), sold as *C. bella* in its dwarf form; *C. erumpens*, a cold-tolerant sort; and *C. seifrizii* with tall thin stems, foliage at top.

Chamaerops humilis. The only palm native to southern Europe, and as such is adapted to cool temperatures and thus an excellent choice for chilly rooms. In captivity it is most often a dwarf clump of palmettolike leaves.

Cibotium chamissonii (C. menziesii). A large tree fern from Hawaii but normally under ten feet in cultivation. Does well in a warm humid location, humus-rich mix, filtered sun. *C. schiedei*, from Mexico, is also a good species for humid places, intermediate to warm temperatures.

Coffea arabica. Glossy-leaved coffee trees in my collection were grown from Colombian seeds. You can obtain sturdy seedlings from houseplant nurseries. Humidity above 40 percent, humus-rich soil, and temperatures 50° to 75° are best. Pinching out new shoots results in a bushy shrub with strong trunk. White flowers are followed by green coffee cherries which turn red when ripe. The fruit can be eaten. Inside are the two beans (seeds) which, when washed, dried, roasted, and ground, will make a fine cup of coffee. Fertilize trees every two weeks while they are in active growth. Put outside in shade all summer long, mist foliage to keep away red spiders and dust. Episcias, ferns, and dwarf begonias are attractive around the base; miniature orchids can be grown on the coffee-tree branches, much as they live in the tropics of South America and Africa.

Cyathea arborea. A tree fern for a bright humid greenhouse or warm humid sun-room. In its Caribbean habitat it will reach fifty feet, but under indoor cultivation young plants are usually one to five feet. Keep the root ball constantly moist in humus-rich soil, but provide sharp drainage.

Cycas circinalis. Cycads resemble palms without a tall trunk. If foliage were not so stiff, you might even mistake them for giant ferns. Although slow growing, this *Cycas* will reach six feet. Species *C. revoluta*, called sago palm, is somewhat smaller, the best for indoor culture. Plant *Cycas* in acid humus-rich soil, keep lightly moist while the crown is producing new foliage, but let dry out slightly between waterings when they rest in winter. Bright-diffuse light to direct sun several hours each day, humidity above 40 percent, and temperatures 55° to 65° at night and 70° to 80° by day are preferable. Keep the long-lived foliage clean with damp cloth or warm shower.

Cyperus alternifolius. *Cyperus* thrives with wet roots in standard soil mix. Indoors, all species need bright-diffuse light, but in their African habitat, where humidity is very high, I saw them in full sun. Fertilize every two weeks, keep humidity above 50 percent for best foliage. *C. diffusus* is a bushy species to thirty inches tall, adaptable. *C. papyrus*, the classic papyrus plant, can reach ten feet, has dramatic plumes at top of slender stalks. Grows best in shallow water at edge of a pool or bog garden but will be content in a pot of standard sandy soil kept wet and in bright light.

Dion edule. A Mexican cycad which resembles a dwarf palm. Stiff leaves are finely dissected and have a feathery yet dramatic aspect. This species does best in slightly alkaline standard soil (stir in a tablespoon of dolomite limestone powder per ten-inch pot of soil). *D. purpusi* and *D. spinulosum* do fine in standard mix kept evenly moist. These are slow-growing plants but live for years, and with good culture will outlast most other houseplants.

Dizygotheca elegantissima. Once known as *Aralia*, this feathery adaptable cut-leaved shrub is an excellent decorative accent for bright airy places. Pot in a five- or six-inch container of standard soil kept evenly moist. Fertilize with fish emulsion alternated with a balanced chemical fertilizer every two weeks when active. When not growing new leaves, *Dizygotheca* tolerates low light levels. Keep night temperature above 55°.

Dracaena deremensis 'Janet Craig'. Sturdy appearance rather like a corn plant, the wide foliage halfway between bold and feathery. *D. marginata* (*Cordyline marginata*) has leaves with red edges, but the overall effect is of green swordlike leaves and upright stem, like yuccas. Dracaenas endure low humidity and dim light. Standard soil; keep evenly moist.

Ficus benjamina and cultivar 'Exotica'. Graceful semiweeping small-leaved fig trees adaptable to a wide range of temperature and humidity. Bright-diffuse light is best, but less bright is adequate, especially when plant is not active. Pot in heavy container to prevent tipping. *F. diversifolia*, the mistletoe fig, has small leaves, many yellowish fruits, and more restrained growth. *F. retusa nitida* is lovely as a small upright tree. Let it get slightly dry between waterings.

Howea belmoreana. This kentia palm needs intermediate night temperatures (60° to 50°) for best growth. Pot in relatively small container (to ten-inch diameter) with excellent drainage, standard soil kept evenly moist. Dim light is tolerated, but fronds are sturdier if made in bright-diffuse light. Guard against red spiders with a yearly spray of malathion after the palm spends the summer outside.

Howea fosteriana. This kentia can reach sixty feet in its native Lord Howe Island near Australia, but in captivity is generally five to fifteen feet with fronds to eight feet. *H. belmoreana* is lower, but fronds spread even wider. Either species is lovely in a large room.

Malphighia coccigera. Resembles a miniature holly, with spiny leaves, dwarf growth, red fruit. Standard soil, bright light; water as the soil begins to dry out.

Phoenix roebelenii. A bushy date palm for diffuse light, humus-rich soil kept evenly moist. Tolerates dim light, prefers warm moist conditions but adjusts to cooler places such as air-conditioned rooms.

Pittosporum tobira. Waxy laurel-like foliage on sturdy-trunked shrub actually falls between bold and feathery. Two parts standard soil with one part of sphagnum peat is a good mix. Keep on the dry side, nights to 50°, bright location. Variegated sort is interesting but less tolerant.

Podocarpus macrophylla maki. Semitropical yewlike evergreen for bright-diffuse light and intermediate temperatures, nights into 50's with no harm. Dark-green foliage is long lasting if roots are kept evenly moist. Shear to keep compact, since this shrub can easily reach six to eight feet even under house conditions. Standard soil is good. *P. nagi* has broader leaves, is grown on dry side.

Polyscias filicifolia. A tall shrub with fernlike leaves. Culture as for *Dizygotheca elegantissima.*

Rhapis excelsa, R. humilis. Lady palms. Fronds in graceful fan shape. Prefer bright light, standard soil kept evenly moist. *R. excelsa* reaches six feet; *R. humilis* remains dwarf.

Syngonium podophyllum. Arrow-shaped thin green foliage and sturdy constitution. Comes in several variations of leaf markings and basic color. Grow in standard soil or half-strength Hyponex solution. Will eventually trail or climb.

Green—Low-Growing

Adiantum bellum, A. decorum 'Pacific Maid', *A. tenerum* 'Wrightii'. Maidenhair ferns are delicate in appearance but will grow indoors if you provide humidity above 50 percent, diffuse light, and a humus-rich slightly alkaline soil. Keep them lightly moist and at 50° to 75°.

Agave pumila, A. stricta. Compact agaves of more delicate aspect than the majority. *A. pumila* is almost miniature, a rounded rosette sometimes producing suckers. *A. stricta* has slender spiny foliage, creates a lovely blue-green mound, delightful with back lighting. Succulent culture, bright light to full sun.

Aloe aristata, A. haworthioides. Two similar dwarf aloes, both forming rosettes of fleshy dark-green foliage covered with small white harmless spines and having white hairs at the tip of each leaf. Bright-diffuse light to full sun, succulent culture.

Asparagus densiflorus (A. meyeri). Plumes upright when young, bend in graceful arch with age. Other fluffy asparagus species adaptable indoors are: *A. myriocladus,* a glowing green plant that keeps its bushy shape with pruning, best grown on the dry side; *A. retrofractus* with tuberous roots best in a succulent mix; and *A. sprengeri* from Africa with arching stems and needlelike leaves, thriving in diffuse light. Propagate this genus by seed or division.

Asplenium bulbiferum, A. viviparum. Low-growing fine-fronded ferns which grow new plantlets on mature leaves. Give humus-rich soil, above 50 percent humidity, and keep roots evenly moist. *A. nidus* has a rosette of leathery fronds, is not a feathery sort.

Cryptanthus acaulis. A miniature terrestrial bromeliad for dish garden or terrarium in sandy succulent soil or well-drained semiterrestrial mix. Other species have gray, brown, red-tinged, or patterned leaves, all in rosette form. See Chapter 8.

Cyrtomium falcatum 'Rochefordianum'. The deeply cut fronds of this holly fern will remain attractive for several years if you keep them clean and away from direct sun. Pot in humus-rich mix, keep lightly moist, nights not lower than 50°.

Davallia bullata mariesii, D. fejeensis plumosa, D. trichomanoides (D. canariensis). Davallia ferns have feathery arching fronds, fuzzy creeping rhizomes that lead to the popular names of rabbit's-foot and squirrel's-foot ferns. They look best in baskets but will also thrive in pots of humus-rich soil or in containers carved from tree-fern trunks. Provide moderate light; they need no direct sun. *D. bullata* may lose fronds in the winter if temperatures go below 60° at night.

Doryopteris pedata. The hand fern is low-growing, stiff-fronded. For dim light, a warm humid location, and humus-rich soil kept evenly moist.

Humata tyermannii (Davallia griffithi). Bear's-foot fern. Decorative, fuzzy, and white scaly rhizomes. Culture as for davallias.

Myrsine nummularia. This suggests a dwarf creeping boxwood. Another species, *M. africana,* is called African boxwood. *Myrsine* is valuable where you need a dwarf plant with small shiny foliage for a shady location. *M. nummularia* requires less light than *M. africana,* but both thrive in standard soil mix kept evenly moist.

Neomarica gracilis. Fan of irislike foliage to eighteen inches. Delicate blue flowers last only a day, but several are produced on arching stems in succession. Useful foliage all year. Standard mix with sharp drainage, evenly moist. Bright light. New plants form at tip of the flower stalk; pin down on soil to propagate.

Nephrolepis exaltata 'Fluffy Ruffles', 'Verona'. These compact cultivars of the popular Boston fern do well in humus-rich soil and bright-diffuse light with some direct sun in winter. Keep evenly moist.

Pilea nummulariaefolia, P. prostrata. Of the creeping *Pilea*, most popular are the colored-leaf species *P. cadierei* (aluminum plant) and *P. involucrata* (Panamiga), but these two green-leaved species are useful where you want a low small-leaved quick-growing plant. Give them all humus-rich soil, humidity above 50 percent, bright-diffuse light, and keep evenly moist. *Pilea* roots easily at stem joints or as cuttings in water.

Polyscias fruticosa, P. guilfoylei 'Filigree'. *Polyscias* reminds me of overgrown parsley, but it can be attractive where you need finely cut foliage in bright-diffuse light. Keep night temperatures above 60°, or foliage may drop. Standard soil kept evenly moist is best. Fertilize every three weeks when plants are growing. *P. fruticosa* grows into a shrub five to eight feet tall but can be pruned. *P.* 'Filigree' is smaller and suitable for the window garden.

Polystichum tsus-simense, P. viviparum (P. setiferum proliferum). Dwarf dark-green cut-fronded ferns for dim light and cool conditions, 50° to 70°. Pot in humus-rich soil, keep evenly moist. Good in glass bowl or terrarium.

Pteris ensiformis 'Victoriae'. Sword brake. Dwarf silvery-green finely cut fern for average home conditions, humus-rich soil kept moist, dim to diffuse light. *P. tremula* (Australian brake) grows to two or three feet high under the same indoor culture. Smaller plants are at home in four- to six-inch pots.

Selaginella kraussiana, S. kraussiana 'Brownii', *S. caulescens, S. emmeliana*. Excellent delicate creepers for terrarium ground covers. They require humidity of 60 to 80 percent, humus-rich mix, 60° to 70° temperatures, even moisture, diffuse light. Species with metallic-colored foliage and robust vinelike growth are *S. uncinata* and *S. willdenovii*.

Spathiphyllum floribundum, S. 'Mauna Loa'. Sturdy green foliage, white spathes like anthuriums. Humus-rich mix kept evenly moist, filtered light, warm temperatures. Fertilize when active for best leaves, largest flowers. *S. floribundum* has many small spathes, growth under one foot. *S.* 'Mauna Loa', a hybrid, is robust, to twenty-four or thirty inches tall, has four- to six-inch white spathes and excellent vigor even in air-conditioned rooms (if safe from direct drafts).

Tradescantia multiflora (Gibasis geniculata). Half-inch-long leaves on thin trailing stems, many white flowers when given bright light. Good in baskets, trailing from sunny shelf, or as ground cover around taller plants. Standard soil slightly dry between waterings.

Green Marked White or Gold

Aechmea fasciata. A bromeliad with spikes of pink and blue flowers but worth growing as a vase of green and silver foliage. Keep center filled with water. See Chapter 8.

Aglaonema commutatum cultivars. The Chinese evergreen is an excellent choice for patterned foliage in dim to diffuse light. Pot in standard soil, or grow stems in weak fertilizer solution. If in soil, let dry slightly between waterings. Clean leaves with damp cloth or monthly shower. Bright light means more flower spathes, but direct sun may burn foliage. Good cultivars for silver-gray and cream-on-green patterns are 'Pewter', 'The Queen' or 'Silver Queen', 'The King', and 'Silver King'. A cultivar with cream-flecked foliage is 'White Rajah', which with white and yellow markings may be offered as *A. pseudo-bracteatum*. The species *A. crispum*, sold too as *Schismatoglottis roebelinii*, is green marked light gray and is very tolerant of dim light. *Aglaonema* is slow growing, durable, and propagates easily from stem cuttings or from seed from the reddish berries.

Aucuba japonica variegata. Leathery dark-green foliage heavily spotted bright gold. Small plants in four- to five-inch pots of 50-50 peat with standard soil mix will make nice evergreen specimens that require little care. Cool temperatures are best, down to 40° during winter nights, but warmer rooms are tolerated. Humidity of 40 to 50 percent. Wash the long-lasting foliage for shine. Let soil dry slightly on top between waterings.

Caladium humbodltii, C. 'Candidum', *C.* 'White Queen'. White leaves veined dark green. The first is dwarf, four to six inches; the other two are standard hybrids with broad leaves ten to twelve inches high. See Chapter 14 for complete culture.

Ceropegia woodii. An African succulent vine with silver foliage, thin trailing stems covered with small galls that are actually tubers for forming new plants. Pot in succulent mix, give 55° to 65° temperature, bright-diffuse light. Sometimes sold as string-of-hearts or rosary vine.

Chlorophytum comosum, C. elatum vittatum. The spider plants are lily-family members from South Africa. *C. comosum variegatum* is the largest with foliage to sixteen inches long, edged white. Best for smaller window gardens is adaptable *C. elatum vittatum* with foliage to nine inches. Long stems, which produce exquisite small white flowers and plantlets, may trail to two feet, so the plant is lovely in a hanging basket. Pot in standard soil with enough room for vigorous fleshy roots; let dry slightly between waterings. Propagate by rooting plantlets or by division.

Dieffenbachia amoena. This is a popular three- to five-foot-tall species with foot-long thin leaves banded creamy white. Even more spectacular are cultivars 'Exotica' ('Arvida') with creamy blotches and compact growth and 'Rudolph Roehrs', a *D. picta* selection in delicate shades of chartreuse with ivory markings. Dieffenbachias tolerate low light and high temperatures, grow best in bright-diffuse light, night temperature 60° to 68°. Pot them in standard soil mix, let it dry slightly between waterings, nourish when active with balanced fertilizers alternated with organic fish emulsions. Propagate by rooting top sections or stem sections set in moist propagating mix. Most sorts will easily reach two to three feet under home culture.

Dracaena deremensis warneckei. Grows to fifteen feet but usually sold as much smaller specimen. Other white- or silver-marked selections are *D. fragrans massangeana, D. godseffiana* 'Florida Beauty', and *D. sanderiana*, a tough species with thin white-edged leaves, frequently used in small dish gardens. Pot dracaenas in standard soil with excellent drainage. Keep evenly moist but not soggy when active, slightly dry between waterings when resting. Keep leaves clean of dust.

Ficus elastica variegata, F. elastica 'Doescheri'. These cultivars of the heavy-foliaged rubber plant are nice to bring color to a dim planter, but for the best variegation they should have bright light as new leaves are being made.

Hoya carnosa variegata. Hoyas are twining flowering vines that in variegated cultivars make fine foliage accents. *H.* 'Exotica' and 'Silver Pink' are good ones. See Chapter 7 for culture.

Ligularia tussilaginea 'Aureo-maculata' *(L. kaempferi).* Leopard plant. A low-growing round-leaved plant suitable for dim light and cool temperatures. Leaves are spotted gold. Thrives in standard mix kept evenly moist.

Osmanthus ilicifolius variegatus. Like a variegated holly, to ten feet tall indoors. Prefers nights into 50's. (*O. fragrans* has jasmine-scented small flowers in spring but plain-green foliage.) Pot in relatively small container in standard mix, keep evenly moist, and give bright light.

Pedilanthus tithymaloides variegatus. A relative of the euphorbias with dramatic thin zigzag stems and leaves bordered with white. My plant grows in a bright south window and blushes pink. It thrives in a succulent mix kept lightly moist, tolerates low light when not active.

Peperomia glabella variegata. A dwarf creeper for warm humid places in filtered light. Thrives with standard mix or soil-free medium kept on dry side. Other good white-marked types are *P. obtusifolia variegata* and *P.* 'Sweetheart'.

Philodendron warscewiczii 'Golden Selloum'. A self-heading cultivar selected in Florida for its green-gold foliage. Best with humidity above 50 percent, diffuse light, warm temperature. A golden effect is also made by the climbing *P.* 'Golden Erubescens'.

Plectranthus coleoides 'Marginatus'. A delightful compact white-margined plant. Give standard soil, keep lightly moist, in bright-diffuse light.

Rhapidophora aurea cultivars. Pothos vines are tolerant trailing or twining plants for dim to bright light and standard soil kept lightly moist when plants are growing, at other times dry between waterings. 'Marble Queen', white-flecked, and 'Tricolor', with yellow markings, are sturdy sorts, popular in dish gardens and on poles.

Sansevieria trifasciata cultivars. The ever-popular snake plant has several silver- or gold-marked forms that are adaptable to bright or dim light, high or low humidity, standard or succulent soil. A good dwarf is 'Silver Hahnii'. Taller are 'Bantels Sensation' with golden bands and white stripes and *S. laurentii* with sword-shaped stiff green foliage marked yellow. Optimum growth and health for sansevierias are obtained with standard soil kept on the dry side, bright-diffuse light, warm temperatures, and fertilizer every few weeks in the growing period. Propagate from rhizome cuttings and offsets or even leaf sections.

Veined Leaves

Alocasia 'Amazonica' (*A. sanderiana* X *A. lowii*). This striking hybrid is more vigorous than either parent. White veins on glossy lance-shaped leaf.

Other excellent alocasias are 'Fantasy', a complex dwarf hybrid, and *A. watsoniana*, a Sumatran species with dramatic fifteen- to twenty-four-inch leaves. Pot alocasias in a humus-rich mix with added oak leaf mold or in a mix for terrestrial orchids. Keep night temperature 65° to 68°, humidity above 60 percent, best at 80 percent. Provide diffuse light, and feed when new leaves are growing, alternating organic with chemical fertilizers. If you have trouble with alocasias, try some of the caladium cultivars, which tend to be more tolerant of low humidity and cool temperatures.

Anthurium clarinervum, A. crystallinum, A. forgetii, A. subsignatum 'Wrightii'. Culture as for alocasias except that anthuriums will tolerate slightly cooler temperatures. Add unmilled sphagnum around aerial roots.

Aphelandra chamissoniana. An upright thin-leaved plant for filtered-light areas. Foliage has silver veins, flowers appear from yellow-green pagoda-shaped terminal inflorescence. More compact, and I think even better for foliage-flower combination, are *A. squarrosa* cultivars like 'Louisae' and 'Uniflora Beauty' with shiny dark-green foliage, striking silver-white veins, and glowing-yellow four-sided inflorescence. Pot *Aphelandra* in humus-rich soil, keep evenly moist, humidity above 50 percent, and bright-diffuse light. Fertilize when active. Let them become pot-bound for best flowers, but take care that they don't dry out at roots. Propagate from stem cuttings; the base of older plants will sprout new shoots.

Fittonia verschaffeltii. Creeping Peruvian plant for warm locations, high humidity, good in terrariums with humus-rich soil kept evenly moist, also nice under fluorescent lights. The variety *argyroneura* has green leaves with white veins; *verschaffeltii* itself is green with bright-red veins.

Pellionia daveauana, P. pulchra. Two creeping plants from Vietnam. Nice at base of taller plants like coffee trees or crotons, also excellent in a terrarium. Give warm humid conditions, humus-rich soil. Foliage has brown and silver-green veins; stems root easily.

Plectranthus oertendahlii. Creeping red stems, bronze-green foliage with silver veins, two- to four-inch spires of white flowers. Standard soil kept lightly moist, warm to intermediate temperature, bright-diffuse light. I found it easy from seed.

Sonerila margaritacea. A small jewel-like Javanese herb with bristly foliage tinged dark bronze and heavily colored with silver, especially in cultivar 'Mme. Baextele'. *Sonerila* is best in terrariums or warm moist fluorescent-light gardens. Pot in humus-rich mix, keep evenly moist, night temperature 65° to 68°.

Xanthosoma lindenii 'Magnificum'. A select cultivar of a warm-growing Colombian species. Dark-green foliage veined with creamy white. Pot this aroid in humus-rich soil, keep lightly moist, humidity above 70 percent for lush leaves, night temperature 65° to 68°. Makes a lovely specimen for warm greenhouse or bright plant room, similar to the veined anthuriums in effect and culture.

Silver to White

Cephalocereus senilis. Old-man cactus. One of many silvery or white succulents. Grows to more than fifteen feet with age but in captivity is usually a four- to six-inch pot plant covered with silvery-white hairs. Full sun, succulent mix.

Echeveria elegans. This silver rosette of succulent foliage does not require quite so much light as cacti but thrives in succulent soil mix. Succulent-plant nurseries feature other echeveria species and hybrids that have silver to silver-blue leaves.

Eucalyptus cinerea. Silver-blue foliage, fragrant when crushed, long lasting when cut, durable on the plant. Young foliage is especially attractive, and potted plants are usually cut back each year to encourage vigorous shoots. Many eucalypti will sprout like willows when cut back. Pot this Australian tree in standard mix, provide even moisture, bright light to full sun, especially outside in summer, where it will grow with great vigor. Nights 50° to 60°. Another delightful species, more gray-green than blue or silver, is lemon-scented *E. citriodora*. I grow this as a small tree, kept pinched so it fits on a sunny windowsill. Foliage gives off lemon fragrance even when not cut. Eucalyptus trees will endure very cool temperatures and are therefore excellent subjects for cold sun porches and chilly rooms where sun is bright enough. Most species grow easily from seed.

Kalanchoe tomentosa. From Madagascar with downy silver-toned fleshy leaves, brown markings on margins. Propagates easily from rooted stems or leaves. Mine grows well in bright-diffuse light or full sun, likes to dry slightly between waterings.

Pilea cadierei, P. pubescens liebmannii. Two silver-marked creepers for diffuse light, in standard soil kept lightly moist. *P. cadierei* is from Vietnam, *P. pubescens* from Cuba.

Rechsteineria leucotricha. Although called Brazilian edelweiss for its silvery leaves, this tuberous-rooted gesneriad has red flowers. Grow in filtered light, pot in humus-rich soil, keep on dry side. Propagation from seed, not easy from cuttings. I think this is one of the finest foliage plants available.

Tillandsia usneoides. Hanging silver-gray garlands of this unusual brome-liad will grow where humidity is at least 50 percent. Bright light, mist daily, drape over branches of tall plants or grow on tree-fern pole.

Tradescantia sillamontana. Creeping Mexican silver-leaved species some-times offered as white-velvet or white-gossamer, may be labeled *Cyanotis veldthoutiana.* Well worth growing in a sunny location where the silver fuzz shows best. Tolerates low humidity, grows well in standard soil, slightly dry between waterings, cut back in spring.

Red to Purple

Acalypha wilkesiana 'Ceylon'. Bushy shrub that can be kept under two feet with pruning. Leaves dark maroon with bright-red band. Bright light best brings out the color. Standard soil kept evenly moist.

Aechmea 'Foster's Favorite'. A bromeliad with leaves bright red when grown in strong light. Chapter 8 gives full culture for this genus.

Cordyline terminalis 'Firebrand' and 'Flame'. Two good cultivars chosen for bright color and ability to hold lower leaves. Sprouts from cane sections like willow wands. Standard soil lightly moist, diffuse sun, no cold drafts.

Episcia 'Ruby'. This is only one of several recent hybrids with deep-maroon to red foliage. Episcias need high humidity, warmth, humus-rich soil. Good in terrariums, under fluorescents.

Fittonia verschaffeltii. Creeper with red veins making an overall red effect. Culture as for episcias.

Gynura aurantiaca. A lovely trailer from warm Javanese jungles where it thrives in filtered sun. Pot in humus-rich soil or standard mix, but keep lightly moist, for it wilts easily. Pinching makes it bushy and makes leaves larger. If left untouched, it will trail. My greenhouse plant, in diffuse light, sends out three-foot stems, but a pot plant in a sunny window stays bushy, blooms often. Roots well from stem cuttings in water or propagating mix. Dense purple-velvet hairs on leaves and stem.

Oxalis hedysaroides rubra. Called fire-fern for its delicate cloverlike glow-ing red foliage. My plant thrives in standard soil at a sunny window, gets bushy with pinching. Flowers are small but a nice contrast of sunny yellow. Propagate from tip cuttings. Adult plants should be grown on dry side.

Rhoeo discolor (R. spathacea correctly). Moses-in-the-boat. A low-growing Mexican plant which grows in coral walls around southern Florida. The clusters of foliage show olive-green on top but deep purple beneath and on stems. Easy to propagate from seed, which may not germinate for a month or more. Also if top is cut and kept in a few inches of water, it will sprout new plants. Pot in standard soil, keep evenly moist.

Ruellia makoyana. A Brazilian slender-stemmed creeper with small olive-green leaves suffused with purple. A warm grower for diffuse light and humus-rich soil kept evenly moist. Good in terrariums, and it has pretty rose-red flowers when properly grown.

Setcreasea purpurea. Bright light or dim light, this adaptable trailer from Mexico still grows, but with enough light it bears orchid-colored flowers at the stem tips, and in full sun stems and foliage have best dark-purple color. It endures but does not prefer low humidity. Pot in succulent mix or well-drained soil, and grow on dry side, or put root stems in half-strength Hyponex solution for water culture.

Siderasis fuscata. Low rosette of fuzzy olive-brown foliage tinged purple in good light. Lavender flowers. Pot in standard soil, give bright-diffuse light, let dry slightly between waterings. A slow-growing plant related to *Tradescantia.*

Tradescantia blossfeldiana. Purple-stemmed creeper, olive-green silver-haired leaves purple beneath. Flowers are light lavender. Culture as for *Setcreasea.*

Metallic Blends

Aechmea fasciata 'Silver King'. Rosetted leaves covered with glowing silver scales. See Chapter 8 for culture.

Alocasia chantrieri, A. cupres, A. 'Fantasy', *A.* sedenii'. These two species and two hybrids have shiny coppery or silvery-purple leaves. See culture in "Veined Leaves" section.

Begonia rex cultivars. See Chapter 11.

Calathea species. These jungle-floor plants require humus-rich soil kept evenly moist, humidity above 60 percent, bright-diffuse light, minimum night temperature 65°. Nice in large terrariums. Many leaf patterns and colors available from specialists like Alberts and Merkel Bros.

Maranta species. Close relatives of *Calathea* and need same culture. Most are compact plants four to fifteen inches high. Propagate by divisions of large clumps. Leaves fold up at night.

Peperomia metallica. Compact plant with leaves marked silver, red veins. Culture as outlined for peperomias in "Green Marked White or Gold" section.

Piper ornatum. Warm-preference vine for a humid location, diffuse light, humus-rich soil. Train on a sphagnum-moss pole or tree-fern stick.

Multicolored

Caladium cultivars. See Chapter 14.

Codiaeum cultivars. Crotons. Small richly colored shrubs for bright-diffuse light to full sun, humidity above 60 percent, humus soil kept lightly moist. Fertilize when active. Many leaf forms and color combinations; deepest tones in strong light.

Coleus blumei hybrids, *C. rehneltianus.* The *C. blumei* hybrids come in a wide range of colors and leaf shape, of rich somewhat velvety textures, from green with white to glowing red or almost black. *C. rehneltianus* is a trailing species. Full sun brings out best colors in coleuses, but they tolerate less light. Pot in standard soil, keep evenly moist, avoid cold drafts, pinch to keep bushy. Increased easily from cuttings rooted in water and from seed. Flowers are light to deep blue in short upright spikes.

Ctenanthe oppenheimiana tricolor. A gaily colored cultivar of a maranta relative, having cream splashes over green-and-pink erect lance-shaped leaves. Usually under three feet high. Grow in moist humus soil, filtered light, nights 62° to 68°. The type species has plain or green-and-silver leaves, maroon beneath, and is less showy than the cultivar but more vigorous.

Episcia cultivars. Currently, many-colored hybrids are being introduced. Fine for terrariums or fluorescent-light gardens. See Chapter 11.

Neoregelia carolinae tricolor. Low rosette of shiny foliage, pink, green, silver, even red in bright light. Delightful on a low coffee table. See Chapter 8 for culture.

Zebrina pendula cultivars. Fast-growing trailers with metallic striped leaves, purple stems. Tolerant of low light but color is best in bright-diffuse. Standard soil or peat-lite. Easy to root from cuttings in water. Nice as ground cover around the base of small shrubs or to hide pots in a window box.

Mature *Monstera deliciosa* produces succulent fruit that takes more than a year to ripen but is worth waiting for. The flavor is a combination of pineapple and banana. Bits of black calcium oxalate, found naturally in the fruit, are washed away before segments are eaten.

Agave parrasana

91

Araucaria excelsa,
the Norfolk Island pine
(*Everett Conklin and Company*)

Fatsia japonica
(*Everett Conklin and Company*)

Chamaerops humilis, palm for intermediate temperatures

Dizygotheca elegantissima, a warm-preference shrub from the New Hebrides (*Everett Conklin and Company*)

Dracaena marginata, a Madagascan species (*Everett Conklin and Company*)

Ficus diversifolia, the mistletoe fig of India and Malaysia

Pittosporum tobira from warm areas of China and Japan will thrive in cool to intermediate temperatures. (*Everett Conklin and Company*)

An Indian epiphyte, *Humata tyermannii*, thrives in a hanging tree-fern container with diffuse light and moist conditions.

The low-growing *Begonia* 'Erythrophylla' (center right), *B.
semperflorens* cultivar (top
left), *Chlorophytum elatum vittatum* from South Africa (bottom), coleus hybrids from
Asian species, and *Nephrolepis
exaltata* (center left), a fern
from Old and New World tropics, make an international picture in bright-diffuse light.

'Silver King' is an especially
durable *Aglaonema* with bright
silver-green markings and pale-
green spathes, seen at center.

Many popular green foliage
plants are available as variegated clones, such as this *Ficus
elastica variegata,* the heavy
green foliage marked cream
and yellow.

95

Aphelandra squarrosa, the zebra plant, is grown for striped leaves and waxy yellow inflorescence. If plant gets leggy, it can be topped. Base will resprout; cut top can be rooted.

Tradescantia sillamontana, creeping white-velvet vine, sprouts hairy new growth after being cut back in early spring.

On the jungle floor between Colombia and Brazil, I found this *Calathea medio-picta* growing near a crinkle-leaved *Miconia*.

Metallic colors are found on three compatible Brazilian foliage plants. At left, *Maranta leuconeura kerchoveana*, center, *Calathea makoyana*, and *Peperomia caperata* 'Emerald Ripple'.

Piper ornatum, a black-pepper relative from the Celebes Islands, thrives on a post covered with sphagnum moss held by wire. Stems are flushed red; waxy deep-green foliage is silver-pink.

97

7

Vines and Flowering Shrubs

S OME OF THE MOST UNUSUAL HOUSEPLANTS are flowering shrubs, climbing vines, or colorful trailers. They create an atmosphere of tropical
beauty. They extend the possibilities of plants as decoration from low trays
on up to graceful heights, frame a window in green, or hide greenhouse
posts. Shrubs require space, and vines must have support. Trailers, in baskets
or hanging pots, require less room unless you want to let them grow without
restraint; pinching keeps them shapely. Gentle pruning will train shrubs and
vines to fit your window or greenhouse. For a small window or small light-
cart, there are dwarf shrubs (such as forms of *Carissa* and *Malpighia*),
miniature roses, and diminutive vines like *Thunbergia* or *Manettia*.

Vines

Some flowering vines thrive in bright-diffuse light; most require several
hours of direct sun every day to produce abundant bloom. Only a few, like
the hoyas, will burn if the foliage is subjected to hot winter sun or direct
summer sun. In shady windows you can still have graceful vines, but these
should be foliage plants such as pothos, cissus, piper, and syngonium, which
thrive in spite of reduced light.

To bloom well, vines in active growth are given bright-diffuse light to
some direct sun, even moisture at the roots, balanced fertilizer every few

waterings, and good circulation of fresh air. Species grown for foliage and needing less light will likewise need less fertilizer and water.

Where to Grow Flowering Vines

Vines that are to grow for some distance, around a window, over an indoor trellis, or against a greenhouse wall, need an adequate root run. An indoor planting bed can provide this, as can a large pot or tub of rich soil. My passion vine has a root run of four by ten feet in a perlite-filled bench in the greenhouse. This happened by accident because the ten-inch pot was shoved to the back of the redwood bench, behind pots of orchids. The stems grew up the rafters where I wanted foliage for natural shade over the orchids. By the time I decided to repot my passiflora it had sent an extensive root system through the pots, and the bench was filled with fine roots that utilized all the fertilizer draining from the orchid pots.

With special care, almost akin to bonsai work, you can grow vines on small stakes or a trellis under fluorescent lights, but this is not where vines look best. Give them room to reach their full potential. Picture windows, a sun porch, and greenhouse rafters are suitable places for climbing vines. The trailers, grown in baskets, are easier to place, and you can put hangers anywhere that light is strong enough to encourage sturdy growth. Some of my hoyas are grown in baskets and decorate windows with a southern exposure from late fall through early spring. Then, when the sun gets too strong, I just move the baskets to a protected place.

Control

Vines must be pruned to keep them in bounds and to control overluxuriant growth. In one season a bougainvillea or passiflora can take over a small greenhouse or large picture window. Prune just after major flowering or before the yearly spurt of new growth, generally in spring. Light pruning and training can be done any time you see a need for it.

The vines discussed here require humidity above 40 percent. Check the undersides of leaves often for red spiders. If pests are discovered on a vine that is too extensive for thorough spraying, apply a systemic insecticide, Isotox granular, for example, to the roots. This is absorbed by the roots and moves up into the tissues throughout the vine, where feeding insects are poisoned by it.

Selections

I have listed here some durable and spectacular flowering vines generally available in the better nurseries. Some of the rarer vines are available only as imported seeds.

Allamanda cathartica williamsii. Sunny yellow cup-shaped four-inch flowers against dark-green glossy foliage on a ten- to fifteen-foot vine or, if pruned, a semishrub. Blooms in the spring and summer. Frequently grown outside on fences and walls in tropical countries. Propagate from stem cuttings. Grow in full sun, humus-rich soil kept evenly moist.

Aristolochia elegans. A Brazilian species with three-inch heart-shaped leaves, delicate twining stems, and white flowers veined purple outside and purple-brown within. *A. grandiflora* has foot-long flowers that smell of rotten meat, so in close quarters it is better to grow *A. elegans. Aristolochia* requires humus-rich, evenly moist well-drained soil and bright-diffuse light (not strong direct sun). I have grown both species from seed, which does not produce blooming plants for two years or longer. If you buy a sturdy potted plant grown from cuttings, it will have flowers as soon as it makes four or five feet of growth. The average height of *A. elegans* is twelve to fifteen feet, but it can reach twenty feet if you grow it well and don't prune.

Bougainvillea cultivars. Easy in full sun on a trellis, wire, or stakes or pruned as a short shrub kept eight inches under four forty-watt Gro-Lux Wide Spectrum tubes. Cultivars are available with bracts in several glowing colors: crimson ('Karst' and 'Crimson Jewel'), pink ('Texas Dawn'), white ('Jamaica White'), and yellow ('California Gold'). 'Tahitian Gold' is a deep-gold double. Flowering is heaviest from early spring to summer on growth made the previous year. Buds are set on short days, so give no more than twelve hours of light in late fall if you are growing plants under fluorescents. Night temperatures of 60° to 65°, standard soil kept on the dry side, and full sun are best for bougainvilleas.

Three species, each with a slightly different mode of flowering, have been intercrossed. *B. peruviana* from Colombia, Ecuador, and Peru blooms mostly at the ends of branches; *B. glabra* from Brazil blooms along shorter side branches; *B. spectabilis* blooms best grown as a true vine on wires, stakes, or trellis. Early hybrids of *B. spectabilis* X *B. glabra* created a wide range of colors; later, variations occurred as sports or mutations. Crosses of *B. peruviana* X *B. glabra* produced the *B.* X *buttiana* group, seedlings of which figure in present-day hybrid clones. The USDA is introducing some clones obtained from the Park Department in Nairobi, Kenya, where I saw many lovely varieties trained as ground covers and as small single-stem trees.

Most hybrids have a normal resting period in late fall when they drop much of their foliage. When this occurs, reduce watering, stop fertilizing, and wait for new growth to start in four to six weeks, longer if under cool conditions. Under fluorescent lights at 60° to 70°, these plants may rest only briefly after heavy bloom.

Propagate from cuttings of half-mature wood dusted with Rootone, then set in rooting mix with bottom heat. If your established plants fail to bloom, let them dry out more between waterings, cut down on fertilizing, and provide brighter light.

Clerodendrum species. These vines require culture outlined for bougainvilleas except that they usually flower with bright-diffuse light rather than full direct sun. Bloom occurs from spring into summer, vines rest for six or eight weeks in midwinter, at which time they will accept night temperatures into the 50's. During growth, *Clerodendrum* thrives with intermediate to warm temperatures, evenly moist at the roots. *C. fragrans*, a compact white-flowered fragrant species, can be pruned to make a shrub. The popular glory-bower, *C. thomsonae*, grows ten to fifteen feet tall, is quite adaptable to indoor culture and is available in a variegated-leaf variety.

In summer the hybrid *C.* X *speciosum* (*C. splendens* X *C. thomsonae*), with dark-green leaves, opens clusters of flowers with a pink calyx around crimson corollas.

Dipladenia X *amoena.* A rose-pink flower that may remind you of a morning glory but which remains open for days. The vine is not too rampant and is easily trained on a small wire trellis or wooden stakes in a six- to eight-inch pot of standard soil mix. This hybrid is a cross of *D. amabilis* X *D. splendens* and has decorative leaves with a crinkled surface. Provide humidity at least 50 percent, but keep roots slightly dry between waterings. Bright filtered light; night temperature 65°.

Gloriosa rothschildiana. A twining vine from a long tuberous root. Slender stems carry oval leaves, each with a grasping tendril. Tubers are dormant through the winter. In summer, after flowering, they can sometimes be rested for a few weeks, by withholding water, and then if a new shoot begins, they are started into growth for another crop of bright-red flowers. The blooms resemble those of *Lilium speciosum* except that they are glowing red with a yellow center and edge. *G. superba*, the flame lily, is similar in flower but with perianth segments much crisped. It is not so easy to bloom more than once per season. Give gloriosas full sun and standard soil, and let them get slightly dry between waterings.

Plant tubers in a six- to ten-inch pot, since each will double in size in one growing season. Tubers generally sprout from a single eye until they become established, when they may send up two sprouts. I store the brittle tubers right in their pots to avoid any chance of damage to the dormant growing point or eye. If the eye is damaged, the tuber may stay sound for months but will not sprout. Get dormant tubers in early spring, plant them horizontally with sharp drainage, and fertilize every two weeks until the foliage begins to die down. If your potting soil is heavy, mix it with 50 percent rough sphagnum peat moss.

Hoya species and cultivars. Fragrant-flowered vines that do well in small pots, up to six-inch size, or in larger pots for vines trained around a green-house or large picture window. *Hoya* 'Exotica' has green, cream, and rose-flushed leaves. *H. carnosa variegata* is similar but with broader heavier leaves more distinctly bordered white. The plain species *H. carnosa* has suc-culent dark-green leaves spotted silver. It is easy to grow and bloom.

Another species with smaller leaves and delicate appearance is *H. bella,* but it is less adaptable—often thrives for some time, then dies for no appar-ent reason. *H. australis* is robust, like a larger *H. carnosa.* Pot hoyas in rela-tively small containers with excellent drainage. In their Australian and East Asian habitats they usually grow in humus-filled tree crotches or along moss-covered branches, so they are hypersensitive to overwatering, soggy roots, or lack of good air circulation.

I put a layer of pebbles, then some hardwood charcoal in every hoya pot, and use a fibrous humus-rich soil. Train stems on stakes or a wire grid above a hanging pot or basket, around a window or on a trellis. Grow hoyas in bright-diffuse light, avoid direct sun through glass, which often burns the thick glossy foliage, and keep them on the dry side at the roots when growth slows in winter. Otherwise, they will thrive with even moisture when active. The waxy white flowers marked ruby-red are fragrant at night. They appear from short spurs on the vines year after year, so take care not to injure these growths. Propagate by stem cutting which root readily in water or in a propagating mix.

Jasminum gracile magnificum. This fragrant white-flowered shrubby twin-ing plant may be listed as *J. nitidum* or *J. magnificum.* It thrives in full sun if kept lightly moist at the roots, at intermediate temperatures, to 55° at night. Flowers most heavily in winter and can be trained on various supports or around a window. Prune after flowering to fit your space. *J. officinale grandiflorum* has double white flowers. *J. sambac* 'Grand Duke' is a shrub, also with double flowers.

Lapageria rosea. From Chile. Best when night temperatures fall into the low 50's. Waxy red bellflowers three to four inches long hang gracefully from slender leather leaved stems. Pot in acid humus soil, and grow on the dry side when not active, otherwise lightly moist. Always keep humidity above 50 percent, and give good air circulation. Bright-diffuse light, no hot sun. If foliage looks yellow, try adding Green Garde micronized iron (Encap Products Company) to the water once or twice. Feed with acid-reaction fertilizer as sold for azaleas and gardenias. Young vines may not bloom, but you can puchase mature ones from rare-plant nurseries.

Manettia inflata (bicolor). A delicate little vine from Paraguay, charming around a window or on a trellis. The flowers, borne in March, almost an inch long, are like tiny firecrackers, brilliant scarlet with yellow at the tips. Pot in standard soil, keep evenly moist, provide diffuse light and 60° to 65° night temperature. Easily controlled, it can even be grown under fluorescent light.

Passiflora species. Vigorous, climbing by strong tendrils. Flowers are spectacular, fragrant, some followed by edible fruits. Passion vines thrive in strong direct sun, need heavy feeding, constant moisture, and can be cut back every year and still make abundant new growth and flowers.

My favorite is fragrant *P*. X *alato-caerulea*. A smaller-flowered species, *P. racemosa*, has crimson flowers. Very delicate are the tiny leaves of *P. super-rosa*, a green-flowered species with blue seedpods. Robust *P. quadrangularis*, the edible passion fruit, or granadilla, has abundant fragrant ornate flowers, but they are not so spectacular as those of *P*. X *alato-caerulea*. *P. trifasciata* has three-lobed satin-textured leaves colored bronze, purple, and silver, so lovely that it is worth having for the foliage. The small yellow flowers are fragrant.

Passion flowers are so named for the religious interpretation of the flower parts. An early Spanish friar in South America was inspired to read the story of Christ's passion from the flower structure. This technique was evidently useful in helping to teach Bible stories to Indians he was converting.

The symbolism begins with ten purple and white tepals representing ten of the Apostles, conveniently eliminating Peter and Judas. Center styles form a pale-green cross held above a circle of purple and white rays. Delicate fringed parts of the corona form a crown of thorns. The five anthers are five wounds from nails driven through Christ's flesh into the cross. Under the flower is a calyx of three green sepals to signify the three days Christ spent in the tomb before resurrection. Three-lobed dark-green leaves represent the Holy Trinity, and twisted tendrils which help the vine climb toward the sky are ropes that bound the Lord to his cross.

My plants grow well at 60° to 68° by night and into the high 80's when sun heats up the greenhouse, yet they grow equally well under slightly cooler conditions at a bright window. A mature passiflora, especially *P*. X *alato-caerulea*, will continue to produce large fragrant flowers over many months on new growth. Flowers open in the morning and perfume the air all day. They last well when cut but only for that day. You may preserve them longer in a shallow dish of water in the warmest part of the refrigerator and remove them for a dinner-table display.

Petrea volubilis. I saw this "purple wreath" trained as a shrub in Zanzibar, but it usually grows as a vine. Violet-blue flowers are abundant on plants established for several years. Young plants do not produce many blooms.

An older plant I saw at Logee's Greenhouses was covered with flowers because it had perfect conditions of humid air, bright light, and nights in the low 50's. *Petrea* is easy to train but should be allowed to reach several feet for the best display. Standard soil suits it.

Solandra species. Where there is room for these tropical American vines to grow ten or fifteen feet, they will create a truly striking display of leathery glossy foliage and, in midwinter, five- to seven-inch-wide fragrant golden flowers. *S. grandiflora* with eight-inch yellow-brown flowers and *S. longiflora* with ten-inch-long tubular flowers opening white, turning yellow with age, will thrive with night temperatures in the 60's. *S. maxima* does best with nights into the 50's. Pot solandras with ample root run in a humus-rich soil, and keep them evenly moist when new growth is evident, then on the dry side, even if they lose a few leaves. If you give them full bright sun, they will produce abundant flowers.

Stephanotis jasminoides. Grown for its fragrant waxy white flowers, which appear in clusters from late spring on into summer, the stephanotis is easy to control on a small trellis in an eight-inch pot. Provide humidity above 50 percent or mist on sunny mornings and bright-diffuse light but shade from hot sun, night temperatures between 65° and 68°. Standard soil suits the stephanotis, and you can let it have slightly cooler nights when not growing or flowering. A well-cultivated plant can reach fifteen feet if not pruned.

Thunbergia alata. Twining vine from South Africa, easy from seed or small rooted cutting. Delicate stems bear 2- to 3-inch medium-green leaves which form a pleasant background for glowing yellow black-eyed 1½-inch flowers, all summer into fall. It is excellent for a six-inch hanging basket, for a small trellis, or around a sunny window. Pot in standard soil mix, keep evenly moist, provide bright light to full sun, night temperature 55° to 65°.

Trachelospermum jasminoides. The Confederate jasmine has richly fragrant star-shaped white flowers, mainly in the winter. It will twine slowly around a support or can be clipped into shrub form and thrives with cool nights into the 50's, fresh air, and acid humus-rich soil that gets slightly dry between waterings. Nourish with acid reaction balanced fertilizer, and if foliage gets yellow, apply iron as recommended for lapagerias. This is an excellent vine for the bright but cool sun porch or greenhouse.

Trailers

For baskets, hanging pots, and wall brackets these plants are eminently suitable. Grow them in peat-lite or well-drained standard soil. Give them a warm shower every few months to keep foliage healthy. Prune or pinch the straggling ends.

Asparagus plumosus	Graceful in baskets.
A. sprengeri	
Cissus antarctica	Cissus vines will trail from baskets or twine around
C. discolor	a support. *C. striata* is diminutive with bronze-
C. rhombifolia	green leaves one inch long.
C. striata	
Cyanotis somaliensis	Leaves narrow-triangular, hairy. Flowers blue or purple in clusters.
Davallia bullata	Ferns for baskets; arching fronds.
D. fejeensis plumosa	
Ficus radicans	Trailer or climber if support provided.
Hedera canariensis	Better indoors than *H. helix*. Leaves to six inches wide, entire or shallow-lobed.
Helxine soleirolii	Tiny creeper, humid, moist, part shade.
Humata tyermannii	Bear's-foot fern for baskets.
Nephrolepis exaltata	Boston fern in several forms; baskets.
Pellionia daveauana	For warm, moist conditions.
P. pulchra	
Peperomia angularis	Grow on dry side at roots; foliage is succulent.
P. obtusifolia	Good terrarium or basket trailers in filtered sun.
P. scandens	
Philodendron oxycardium	Trailer, climber with support.
Platycerium species	Epiphytic ferns for tree-fern basket.
Plectranthus australis	Rugged adaptable trailers, spires of white flowers; good in baskets.
P. coleoides 'Marginatus'	See Chapter 6, page 85.
P. oertendahlii	
Polypodium aureum	Long arching yellow-gray fronds.
Sedum morganianum	Succulent soil, full sun; silver-gray.
Setcreasea purpurea	Dark vivid-purple trailer.
Thunbergia alata	See preceding list.
Tradescantia blossfeldiana	Green-purple creeper for basket.
T. sillamontana	Fuzzy silver for full sun.
Zebrina pendula	Adaptable trailers, silver-purple.

Shrubs

A sunny window or bright plant room rivals the greenhouse as a suitable place for shrubs that will grow indoors. Attractive kinds range from dwarf miniature-flowered roses to towering oleanders. Several are best as arching bushes or cascading from baskets. Others are grown for unique or fragrant flowers.

Shrubs for Baskets

Abutilon megapotamicum variegatum. From Brazil. Delicate in appearance but easy to grow. Deep-green leaves to three inches long, spotted yellow; branches gently pendulous. Hanging lantern-shaped yellow and red flowers appear all year long when plants get bright light. Train stems on a slender pole if you want a standard, or grow in a basket so stems can cascade. Pot in standard soil, keep roots evenly moist, provide bright light to full sun, 55° to 65° night temperature. Roots easily from tip cuttings; train by cutting back or pinching every few months.

Fuchsia hybrids. Graceful arching stems, soft-green or maroon-tinged foliage, and hanging bell-shaped flowers with prominent stamens make fuchsia hybrids most effective in baskets or trained as standards. Single or double forms with flowers of royal purple, white, pink, rose, red, and combinations of these hues. Nurseries offer sturdy blooming plants from spring into summer. Fuchsias are lovely on the patio or in an airy bright window until late fall. These are mainly for spring to fall display, although a few, like *F. triphylla* 'Gartenmeister Bohstedt', with narrow tubular orange-rose flowers against purple-toned foliage, may remain active and in bloom through the winter with nights at 50° to 60°.

Pot fuchsias in standard mix with added sphagnum peat moss and a sprinkle of bone meal. Keep evenly moist, fed with a balanced water-soluble fertilizer every two weeks, provide bright light to direct sun, pinch to induce branching, stake and tie main trunk to prevent toppling. Grow fuchsias outdoors in summer and fall; when frost threatens, bring inside to a dim location. Cut back on watering as foliage drops, since most cultivars will go dormant between late fall and early spring. Maintain plants in a 50° to 55° dim basement or dark room with just enough root moisture to prevent complete drying. Resume watering when sprouts appear in March or April, then provide strong light to direct sun, good air circulation, and humidity above 60 percent. Propagate by seed or spring cuttings.

Lantana camara. Vigorous rough-leaved Caribbean shrub blooming twelve months of the year with clusters of yellow, rose, or orange flowers, sometimes several colors on the same plant. Can be trained as a standard or grown in baskets. Pot in standard soil, keep roots on the dry side, but mist foliage to discourage red spiders. Night temperatures 55° to 60° are best. Full sunlight for best growth and flowers. Will reach three to four feet if not restrained by pruning. Root cut branches to propagate. Foliage is fragrant when crushed. *L. montevidensis* is more graceful, with lilac flowers.

Russelia equisetiformis. Grow this coral-red-flowered Mexican arching shrub in standard potting soil, 45° to 55° night temperature, full sun, and somewhat dry between waterings. The four-sided stems curve over to three feet if not pinched. Tubular flowers all year on well-grown plants. Propagate from tip cuttings.

Shrubs for Fragrance

Brunfelsia calycina floribunda. A Brazilian dwarf evergreen with shiny foliage and violet or lavender white-eyed flowers that soon fade to off-white. Blooms heavily from midwinter into summer when provided with direct sun. Pot in standard soil, give room of a six- to eight-inch container, keep evenly moist, grow 55° to 60° at night. Prune as flowers taper off in late spring. *B. latifolia* has slightly smaller fragrant flowers.

Carissa grandiflora. Natal plum. A South African three- to five-foot shrub that can be kept smaller by spring pruning. The best form for indoor growing is variety *nana compacta* ('Boxwood Beauty'), which is dwarf and spineless and has scarlet fruit after white flowers. Thick glossy evergreen foliage on carissas is always lovely if kept clean by frequent warm showers. Pot in well-drained standard soil, keep evenly moist, provide bright-diffuse light to full sun, night temperature of 55° to 60°.

Cestrum nocturnum. Night jessamine. A West Indian shrub with semitwining branches and thick shiny evergreen leaves three to six inches long. Natural mature height is six to ten feet, but pruning keeps indoor plants smaller. Panicles of trumpet-shaped night-fragrant white flowers appear mostly from spring through summer. Standard soil, full sun, 60° to 65° nights, keep evenly moist at roots. Propagate from tip cuttings.

Gardenia. See Chapter 13.

Murraea exotica. Orange jessamine. A lovely evergreen reaching eight to ten feet out of doors in the tropics or in a large tub indoors in the temperate zones. Native to tropical Asia. I have seen it thriving in southern Mexico, its clusters of white flowers filling the air with a strong jasmine scent. My potted *Murraea* grows well in evenly moist standard soil, filtered sun in summer, direct sun in fall through midspring, nights 55° to 65°. I keep it compact by restraining roots in a four- to six-inch pot and by pinching top growth, but the plant doesn't require much fussing, since it grows slowly.

Osmanthus fragrans. The Asian (China and Japan) sweet olive is a compact evergreen closely resembling holly. Diminutive heavily perfumed white flowers appear on and off throughout the year. Variety *heterophyllus* 'Variegatus' has white-margined leaves; it is usually offered as *O. ilicifolius* 'Variegatus'. Both kinds are slow growing, can be kept under two feet tall but will reach five to eight feet if unrestrained by pruning. Plant *Osmanthus* in standard soil with some slight extra-rough sphagnum peat moss. Keep *O. fragrans* evenly moist, *O. heterophyllus* on the dry side between waterings. Provide bright-diffuse light in summer, some direct sun from fall though early spring, night temperature 50° to 60°. Wash the foliage frequently. These fragrant-flowered plants thrive in bright cool greenhouses and sun-rooms.

Roses. Surprisingly, miniature-flowered roses will thrive indoors if given bright light to direct sun, good air circulation, and night temperature 55° to 60°. They produce flowers at various times, usually in early spring or late fall until Christmas. The dwarf shrubs are available in many glowing colors, red and pink being the most popular. I like the orange-rose 'Talisman' colors best. Hybridists continue to create new cultivars to extend the blooming season and increase flower forms and colors. 'Wayside's Garnet' is a good double garnet-red; 'Pink Surprise' is a vigorous Lyon hybrid. Some varieties have a faint fragrance, a few have a strong fragrance.

Pot miniature roses in four- to six-inch containers, using standard soil with sharp drainage. Keep them evenly moist when growth is vigorous, and fertilize with balanced preparations every two weeks from spring into early fall. When growth slows in winter, keep them on the dry side and slightly cooler, with nights into the 50's. In midspring put potted roses outside. In midfall spray with a garden rose-insecticide-fungicide mixture, cut back straggly branches, and bring the plants indoors. Miniatures are not pruned way back as are the outdoor hybrid teas. They do well under wide-spectrum fluorescent tubes.

Shrubs for Flowers and Foliage

Feijoa sellowiana. The evergreen South American pineapple-guava produces camellia-form white flowers filled with prominent long red stamens. Leathery two- to three-inch leaves are woolly white underneath; the branches are covered with light fuzz. Outdoors, feijoas may reach fifteen to eighteen feet, but in a pot of standard soil you can keep it under two feet by pruning. In a tub where the light is strong feijoas grow into attractive small trees. Flowers are followed by edible guavas. Keep the roots slightly dry between waterings, the night temperature 50° to 60°.

Grevillea robusta. The silk-oak tree is an excellent choice for plant room, greenhouse, or big picture window. In the tropics I have seen it used to shade tea plantations, and in its native Queensland, Australia, it may reach more than one hundred feet in height. Indoors you can confine it to a six- to ten-inch pot of standard soil and prune the top to keep it small. Ferny green leaves and silver-fuzzed stems are attractive all year. Orange-yellow flowers are borne in horizontal one-sided racemes. Provide strong light for plants you expect to bloom, keep roots on the dry side, nights 50° to 60°. *G. wilsonii*, the fire-wheel silk oak, is smaller, usually under three feet in pots, has smooth foliage, and red and yellow flowers in open, slightly pendulous, racemes from September to December.

Ixora hybrids. Modern hybrids join several species in this attractive genus of gay-flowered tropical Asian shrubs. As pot plants they will vary from two to four feet high. *I. borbonica* is cultivated for its shiny leathery lance-shaped leaves, olive-green mottled pale green with red veins. Excellent for flowers are 'Angela Busman', brilliant shrimp-pink; 'Colei', pristine white; 'Frances Perry', glowing rich yellow even in diffuse sun; and 'Superking', a compact bush with red flowers throughout the year but most abundant in spring and summer.

Pot ixoras in a rich standard mix, keep evenly moist, provide full sun or strong wide-spectrum fluorescent light, temperature 55° to 65° at night, to 80's in the daytime, with humidity above 50 percent. Pinch at branch tips for bushiness and more abundant bloom. Half-ripe branches are best for propagation. Mist undersides of leaves on bright mornings to discourage red spiders.

Malpighia coccigera. A West Indian dwarf evergreen much like a tiny holly. Flat pink flowers from late winter into summer. Pot in two-thirds standard soil with one-third coarse peat moss, make sure of sharp drainage, and keep on the dry side at roots but never completely dry, since foliage will drop. Provide full sun or at least bright-diffuse light, nights 55° to 60°. *Malpighia* is normally under two feet tall but may be kept smaller by pruning. I grow mine in a five-inch pot at a sunny window in winter, outside during the summer.

Medinilla magnifica. A Philippine tropical shrub that will eventually reach five feet tall but is quite slow growing and therefore often expensive at nurseries. The "flowers" are striking: large pink bracts above pendent panicles of red blooms. Established plants have inflorescences up to a foot long, usually from early spring into summer. Pot in humus-rich mix, using a rather small pot with good drainage, then keep evenly moist in bright diffuse light, provide humidity 65 to 70 percent, nights 60° to 65°. In midwinter, when *Medinilla* slows growth prior to blooming, keep slightly drier and nights to 60°.

Nerium oleander. Slender upright open shrubs with narrow-lanceolate leaves, native to North Africa and extreme southern Europe. Long popular in

Bermuda and on the French Riviera, they used to be plain rose or white but are now seen in various tints and mixtures. I like the double salmon-pink yellow-blushed 'Mrs. Roeding' and the red-flowered *N. oleander variegatum,* which has white-edged leaves. Flowers are produced on new growth, so you can prune oleanders every year without losing flowers; cut in late fall after a summer outdoors or in spring before new growth is under way. Oleanders in large tubs will provide striking small trees covered with clusters of flowers if you give plants direct sun and airy conditions. Pot in standard soil with added coarse peat moss; keep on the dry side during winter and evenly moist during warm months when growth is most active. Oleanders are easy to train as standards or as bushy somewhat willowy shrubs. Flowers, leaves, and stems are extremely poisonous if eaten.

Pentas lanceolata. Compact winter-blooming shrubs from tropical Africa, with rose, lavender, or white flowers. You can purchase seed or small plants, since they grow with vigor. Branches are flexible, covered with downy hairs. Starry flowers are in clusters. Pot in standard soil, keep evenly moist, provide full sun, 55° to 65° night temperature. When shrubs become straggly, replace them from fresh soft-wood cuttings or from seed.

Punica granatum nana. Dwarf pomegranate is a delight for its shiny foliage into late fall and colorful orange or scarlet flowers in early summer, usually followed by edible fruits. Variety *legrellei* has very double flowers. Pot in standard soil, fertilize moderately late spring through summer, and keep evenly moist while growing, then on the dry side for winter rest. *Punica* naturally drops most of its foliage in winter and does best with nights at 45° to 50° until growth resumes in spring, when minimum at night of 65° is suitable. These lovely little trees can be kept under one foot tall by careful pruning and potting in small containers.

Rivina humilis. I have found this quick-growing South American rouge plant easy to raise from seed. It responds to pinching, so it can readily be shaped into a bushy shrub in diffuse to bright light. Smooth green foliage, rose-white flowers, and glowing red berries are most attractive. My plant thrives in standard soil with added rough sphagnum peat moss, nights at 60° to 65°, evenly moist at the roots. *Rivina* matures at two feet in containers, and I like to put several in a six-inch pot if they are grown from seed. Cuttings from large plants can be pinched back to make bushy specimens at home in four- to five-inch containers. Mist underside of leaves on sunny mornings to discourage red spiders, especially when plants are outside for the summer.

Scutellaria mociniana. A Mexican shrub that grows fifteen to twenty-four inches tall in pots, having purple-tinged stems, metallic dark-green quilted leaves, and terminal spikes of glowing red flowers over many weeks. Midwinter into summer is the period of greatest bloom. Supply a standard mix kept on the dry side between waterings, bright-diffuse light, night temperature of 60° to 65°. Propagate from stem cuttings in spring.

Thea sinensis. Closely related to camellias and having essentially similar flowers, this is the source of that caffeine-rich beverage, tea. Glossy foliage and lightly fragrant white flowers are attractive all year. Tea shrubs can take drastic pruning, so they are no trouble in pots. Grow them in a humus-rich mix, provide bright-diffuse light (full sun in winter), keep roots evenly moist, and give 50° to 60° nights. Older plants in tubs or eight- to ten-inch pots are handsome on the sun porch or along a greenhouse aisle.

Tibouchina semidecandra. The Brazilian glory bush is always lovely, thanks to silvery leaves and a graceful branching habit, and is a true glory when the three- to four-inch royal-purple flowers begin to open, usually in midwinter on through spring. Give it standard mix kept evenly moist, bright-diffuse to direct light, high humidity, and nights at 50° to 60°. Prune in late spring. Specimens in large tubs will reach eight to ten feet but can be kept smaller by annual pruning. A two-foot plant in good light should bloom well.

These *Passiflora alato-caerulea* flowers were high on my greenhouse rafters, so I put them in a centerpiece on a Tanzanian bark cloth for intimate viewing.

A beautiful *Aristolochia elegans* flower I found on a vine in a courtyard in Zanzibar

Cissus antarctica, of New South Wales, Australia

Pellionia daveauana, trailer for terrarium or warm humid window with diffuse light

Near the Bundibugyo forest in Uganda, I found these big clumps of *Platycerium angolense*.

Platycerium alcicorne, an Australian epiphytic fern, thrives on a cork-bark slab hung from the ceiling in a bright humid room. *P. bifurcatum* is slightly larger. *Monstera deliciosa* is in the background.

Frond of *Polypodium aureum* shows sori, or spore clusters, sometimes mistaken for scale insects. Spores sown on moist sphagnum moss grow new ferns. Arching fronds are lovely in hanging baskets.

Thunbergia alata, a dainty trailer

Plectranthus coleoides 'Marginatus'

Fuchsia 'Gartenmeister Bohnstedt'

Lantana montevidensis variety in hanging basket

Malpighia coccigera

Tibouchina semidecandra

Hibiscus rosa-sinensis hybrids grow two to four feet, are pruned yearly to keep them compact, and require strong sun and high humidity.

8

The Brilliant Bromeliads

BROMELIADS ARE CHARACTERISTIC of the American tropics, often growing side by side with epiphytic orchids. The most spectacular species
are tree-perching, but a few attractive sorts do grow in humus accumulations
on the jungle floor or in sharply drained sandy places. One species, Spanish
moss, grows in our southeastern states, where the thin gray garlands festoon
whole groves of trees. This is *Tillandsia usneoides*, not a moss but a bromeliad, as is the familiar pineapple.

For decorative material, vase-shaped bromeliads are striking exotic
choices. Those with ornate colored foliage endure low light and brighten
dim corners. Flowers, often sprouting from a tall scape growing out of a
leafy rosette, may be red, yellow, blue, pink, green, white, or of combined
colors. The flower spike of some vriesias looks like a glowing red sword. The
mixture of pink, yellow, and blue in some tillandsia blooms is unlike that in
any other flower.

Papery bracts around inflorescences in many billbergias are bright pink
and last in perfection for months. Some species set seed and later produce
pearl-sized berries, prolonging the plant's decorative appeal. *Aechmea
miniata* has glowing red fruit. Terrestrial *Cryptanthus*, or earth-star, has
banded or metallic-colored leaves. Most aechmeas, billbergias, and
guzmanias have fascinatingly patterned foliage in addition to their dramatic
flowers.

Anyone can succeed with six to ten popular bromeliads. Many more kinds

117

will thrive if given a modest amount of care. But a few very attractive ones challenge even expert horiculturists. As a family they are stunning plants for a wide range of decorative schemes and environmental conditions. In the following descriptions those plants that are especially adaptable are marked with an asterisk (*).

Aechmea angustifolia. Narrow, upright, light-green, purple-spotted, eighteen to twenty-four inches tall. Flowers are small, but pearly berries follow and persist for months. Epiphytic.

*A. fasciata.** The best aechmea to begin with, a one- to two-foot urn-shaped rosette of toothed green foliage striated bright silver. Attractive even when without the pink-bracted flower spike and blue flowers. The bracts last in perfection for three to five months, then mature plants produce offsets, which bloom in less than two years. Pot in epiphyte mix. Keep center cup filled with water. Several selected clones are available; one is all silver, another has purple bands, *variegata* has vertical white stripes.

*A. luddemanniana.** From a rosette of green leaves flushed silver-red beneath, an erect inflorescence sprouts from mature thirty- to forty-inch plants, creating a striking panicle of rose and green flowers. These are followed by blue and white berries. After a month, berries turn bright purple and persist for several more months.

*A. miniata discolor.**   A shiny open rosette of olive-green leaves, maroon on the back, from ten to fifteen inches high. The erect spike of blue flowers is followed by long-lasting red berries. Give bright-diffuse light with a few hours of direct sun in early morning. Keep center filled with fresh water. Berries glow like fire under Gro-Lux tubes.

A. pineliana minuta. A compact green rosette with black spines along the leaf margins, bottlebrush-shaped flower spike with red bracts, yellow flowers. In bright light leaves turn rose-copper under a dusting of silvery scales.

*A. 'Royal Wine'.** A hybrid of *A. miniata discolor*, retains *discolor* foliage with underside of leaves brilliant wine-red, tops shiny olive-green. Spike is semipendent, flowers blue followed by enduring orange berries.

Ananas comosus. The edible pineapple is actually the fruit of a terrestrial bromeliad and follows, in about eight months, the purple flowers produced at the top of an erect stalk and crowned with a tuft of leaves. I saw the lovely variegated form, its leaves striped ivory, green, and rose-red, growing under fluorescent lights at the Oceanographic Museum in Monaco. You can succeed with this same form in a sunny window or under four-watt growth tubes.

A. nanus. A dwarf pineapple under one foot tall, often producing small fruits on stiffly attractive stems. More practical for small windows than the thirty- to forty-inch *A. comosus.*

Give ananas direct sun, pot in a gritty terrestrial mix, water heavily when dry, then let the soil almost dry before watering again. New plants from offsets at side or on top of the fruit.

*Araeococcus flagellifolius.** Thin gracefully arching reddish-green leaves from a bottle-shaped rosette. I raised my plants from jungle-collected seed, and germination was so good that I gave many plantlets away. Mature plants reach to ten inches tall, but curved foliage may be fifteen inches long. Small pink flowers develop into blue berries. The root system is fine, like a tough spider web, and I found this species grows well in three-inch clay pots of semiterrestrial mix. Leaves color best, bronze-green, in bright light.

Billbergias grow well in osmunda or a well-drained semiterrestrial mix. Species and hybrids are grown for both foliage and flowers.

Billbergia 'Fantasia'. Compact hybrid blotched white, suffused with rose over green. Tubular, tight leaf cluster flares open at top, pendent inflorescence has red bracts and blue flowers; a dramatic hybrid.

B. 'Muriel Waterman'.* A tubular twelve- to eighteen-inch vase which, if given a few hours of direct sun each day, blushes burgundy over silver-banded green leaves. The pendent inflorescence, typical in billbergias, has pink bracts, blue flowers.

*B. nutans.** A clustering species, under one foot tall when mature. Inflorescence composed of pink bracts, then blue and green flowers, usually in winter. Thin leaves from an upright rosette which turns red in bright light (although the plants will grow and bloom without direct sun).

B. zebrina. Another species that I have grown from jungle seed and found easy when given bright light, tight potting in a semiterrestrial mix or plain osmunda, and clean water in the twelve- to eighteen-inch upright rosette. Bracts are pink, shoot up and over leaves like a glowing rocket. Yellow flowers are followed by interesting swollen seedpods.

Cryptanthus species and hybrids are two- to twelve-inch terrestrial plants suitable for dish gardens and terrariums or at the base of coffee trees or crotons or around a bromeliad assortment on a driftwood tree. Small white flowers are pretty enough, but the feature of these species and hybrids is their spectacular banded or striped leaves. Pot these plants in semiterrestrial mix or plain osmunda, keep humidity above 50 percent, and sprinkle the foliage on bright mornings. These are good dwarf bromeliads to grow from six to eight inches under fluorescent tubes. In natural light give them bright-diffuse sun.

*Cryptanthus beuckeri.** Dwarf, greenish red mottled with lighter green.

C. bivittatus roseus pictus (*C. bivittatus minor* correctly). Curving wavy green leaves have narrow stripes of creamy pink. Plant matures about three inches tall, may spread to six inches across.

C. bromelioides tricolor. Delightful rosette, ten to twelve inches tall, of wavy foliage striped white, pink, and green, fine in an otherwise predominantly green dish garden or terrarium.

C. fosterianus. Large Brazilian species, more than two feet across with good culture but still of low stature, among the most beautiful bromeliads for its bronze to gray leaves, showing pink to magenta over cross-bars of dark brown, much resembling snakeskin. *C. fosterianus* hybrids* are adaptable, well worth seeking out from specialists.

C. zonatus. Leaves striped brown-green and silvery-gray earn this the popular name of zebra plant. Growth is restrained, to eight inches across. Easy in a gritty terrestrial mix.

Dyckia fosteriana. A cactuslike bromeliad forming a spiny rosette of silver-green leaves that blush purple in sun. A lovely species, easy to grow in strong light and gritty soil on the dry side, with sharp drainage. Flowers are orange, but this plant is grown mainly for form and foliage. Watch out for the spines.

Guzmanias thrive with somewhat more humidity (50 to 70 percent) and shade, need no direct sun except very early in the day or in midwinter. Night temperatures above 65° are best for these rain-forest plants.

Guzmania lingulata. Matures at fifteen to eighteen inches tall, sends up a glowing orange inflorescence, which remains a show for weeks. The cultivar 'Major' is vigorous, shiny green, and has an especially large and colorful flower spike.

G. 'Magnifica'. Green rosette marked with thin red lines. The inflorescence of shiny red bracts in a star shape looks best when viewed from above.

G. vittata. Semitubular upright rosette of green foliage barred a striking dark maroon. In my enthusiasm to collect this species in its Brazilian jungle habitat I forgot about the fire ants and ended up with the guzmania plus a few painful strings; nests of fire ants are common in orchid and bromeliad clumps. Keep this one away from direct sun.

Neoregelia gets my first prize as the most adaptable easy-to-grow bromeliad genus. Some species are epiphytic, some terrestrial, in jungle habitats. I have had success with both types in three- to five-inch clay pots filled with osmunda fiber. They also thrive in sharply drained terrestrial mixtures. Spreading rosettes reach ten to fifteen inches across, about one foot high. Thin glossy leaves provide a circle of foliage around flowers which open deep within the water-filled cup. Put *Neoregelia* plants on a low coffee table to enjoy both the white or blue flowers and the foliage.

Neoregelia ampullacea. One of the smaller species, to eight inches tall, up to twelve inches across, an upright rosette with open flaring top, mahogany bands on both leaf surfaces, blue flowers within the cup.

*N. carolinae.** A spreading glossy rosette which turns striking red at approach of blooming time. Color lasts at least six months, often longer, then main plant makes offset. Variety 'Tricolor' has variegated white stripes over copper-green foliage, which turns red as flowers appear just above water inside the cup. Provide bright light for the best coloration, but once the leaves are stained red, the color endures in dimmer light, too.

N. 'Marmorata hybrid'.* Called fingernail-plant because of maroon tips on yellow-green leaves. Best forms have red tips. Flowers are lavender to white, deep inside the water-filled cup.

*Nidularium innocentii.** A low-spreading rosette similar to *Neoregelia* but will endure less light. Leaves are dark maroon, the center of the rosette changing to red just before the white flowers appear, usually in the summer. Culture as for *Neoregelia.* Variety 'Nana' is smallest; 'Striatum' is striped yellow-white.

Tillandsias are somewhat of a challenge to beginning bromeliad growers, but a few species are easier than most and can be obtained as established plants. This is a genus of epiphytes, and if the particular plant has been grown from seed and has an extensive root system, it should be set tightly in a clay pot of osmunda, tree-fern, or semiterrestrial mix. Some smaller sorts can be grown on twigs or slabs of tree fern, as they are often sold by nurseries. These will thrive if you keep them in bright light and dunk them in warm water on sunny mornings. Pot-grown plants are kept on the dry side at the roots, but the rosette cup is filled with fresh water every few days.

Species that require humidity of 60 to 70 percent for best growth include *T. cyanea* and *T. lindenii*, both warm-growing jungle types. The silver-scaled *T. ionantha* endures lower humidity and bright light. All tillandsias need a good circulation of air and dislike confinement in terrariums or still corners.

Tillandsia cyanea. A green-leaved low rosette cultivated for the wide paddle-shaped pink-bracted inflorescence which has violet flowers.

T. 'Emile'. (T. cyanea X T. lindenii). A hybrid somewhat easier to grow than either parent, same beautiful pink overlapping bracts, blue flowers lasting only a day but appearing for many days, one after the other, through the flat spike of bracts.

*T. fasciculata.** The silver-gray rosette holds a quart or more of water, Branched inflorescence consists of red bracts with blue flowers. Grows on cypress trees of southern Florida, in full sun.

*T. ionantha.** A miniature tuft of spiny silver-gray leaves which turn red in the center during the spring blooming season. Flowers are blue. Grow on a slab of tree-fern fiber.

T. lindenii. A neat rosette of light-green leaves penciled purple. Upright flat pink spike with large blue flowers is spectacular. Grows twelve to fifteen inches high.

T. usneoides. The curious rootless Spanish moss will thrive in a very humid place, doesn't mind cool nights, looks nice draped over tropical shrubs.

Vriesias require the culture outlined for guzmanias. The best-known species are those that have tall sword-shaped inflorescences—the flaming-sword plants—but other species are worth growing for their colorful foliage. Pot these in fine-grade tree-fern or osmunda fiber, using small clay pots. Keep the rosette filled with water, and don't let roots get soggy. Some seed-grown vriesias sold by florists have excellent extensive roots which prosper in sharply drained pots of terrestrial mix. Maintain humidity above 50 percent, provide bright-diffuse light or fluorescent growth lamps. Propagate by offsets which grow up in between older leaves once a mature plant flowers.

Vriesia carinata. Compact pale-green rosette with an upright spike of yellow bracts, red base, and yellow flowers. A hybrid of this Brazilian species, *V.* 'Marie' with longer-lasting bracts, red in the center, yellow sides, above green leaves, is easier than the species.

V. hieroglyphica. Purple markings resemble hieroglyphic writing on light-green rosettes. Yellow flowers appear on a branched spike, usually in late winter to spring, but this large species (to two feet) is grown mainly for its unusual foliage.

V. saundersii. This will take stronger light than other vriesias, and with bright light the silver-gray rosette develops purple spots. Yellow flowers are borne on an upright spike from a neat attractive leaf cluster.

V. splendens. A flaming-sword spike with yellow flowers towers above green leaves banded dark maroon, a favorite gift plant. It grows well in diffuse light, and I have one clump thriving under Gro-Lux tubes. After flowering the spike turns green as seeds develop. Eventually the flowered rosette dies but not before producing several offsets. Hybrids 'Illustrious' and 'Vigeri' are similar.

General Bromeliad Culture

Temperatures for tropical bromeliads are 60° to 68° by night with a 5° to 10° rise during daylight hours. Mine thrive at 65° to 68° at night in a living-room window and in a greenhouse, too. Some few semitropical and high-altitude species, like *Tillandsia fasciculata,* accept night temperatures into the 50's.

Humidity is provided easily for plants that require water in center foliage rosettes. Basic humidity above 40 percent is satisfactory for most, although a few I have mentioned thrive best with slightly moister air. Succulent sorts like *Dyckia* endure less humidity, more sun.

Bright-diffuse light with a few hours of direct early morning sun is excellent. Thin-leaved species, often with patterned leaves, accept less light than the silvery tillandsias and succulent sorts. Pineapples thrive in direct sun.

If your water supply is heavily chlorinated, draw water the day before applying it to the bromeliads, so gas has a chance to escape from the open-top container. Bromeliads do well outdoors for the summer and are even grown in garden beds and trees in southern California and Florida, but where summers are apt to be rainy, some protection from too much moisture at the roots must be provided.

Nutrition

Epiphytic bromeliads are not parasites, although they do dwell on tree branches throughout the American tropics. Their nutrition comes from rotting leaves, dead insects, bird droppings, and dust. Bromeliads absorb food through leaf scales, usually within a water-filled rosette. Those without a water-holding cup have powdery scales, like tillandsias, and these scales absorb night dew to keep the plants alive even under dry conditions.

Bromeliad roots are mostly for support; the foliage rosette of some species holds a water reserve of several quarts. I have discovered aquatic zoos inside jungle bromeliads, especially those that grew near rivers where floods sometimes cover the plants. In these bromeliads you may find a minnow along with frogs, insect larvae, snakes, and seeds of other plants germinating in the moisture. Even if you don't want such organisms growing in your windowsill bromeliads, do keep the rosettes filled with water. I fertilize my plants with a quarter-strength fish-emulsion solution during their summer growing season but avoid any strong chemical fertilizers.

Potting Mediums

Epiphytic species thrive in tightly packed osmunda fiber, tree-fern chunks, or a sharply drained mixture of equal parts builder's sand, rough-chopped sphagnum moss, and medium-grade orchid bark. In small clay pots you can also get good results with commercial mixes like McLellan Wonderbark Mix, formulated for orchids. Always use small pots with very good drainage: crocks, pebbles, hardwood charcoal chunks.

Osmunda and tree-fern fiber have the advantage of packing tightly in the pot; best for unestablished plants that don't already have a good root system, as in recently collected jungle species or offsets. To pot with osmunda fiber, put a two- to three-inch chunk under the plant, the fiber grain pointing vertically to aid drainage, then fold it up around the sides to just cover the plant base. Hold the plant in the pot on top of the crocks and charcoal chunks, and add cut chunks of osmunda from the sides, pressing toward the center, until the plant seems fully centered and potted. Now continue to force in walnut-sized chunks of osmunda from the pot edge, using a potting tool or sturdy wooden spoon. The idea is to make the osmunda tight in the center so that an unestablished plant is held firmly. Remember that even a twenty-four-inch aechmea can be potted in a four- or five-inch pot.

Terrestrial Bromelaids

Species that live in forest-floor leaf mold or on well-drained hillsides can be potted in a porous mixture of sphagnum peat moss, sharp sand or perlite, rotted leaf mold, and humus. Even easier are the prepackaged humus-rich houseplant soils mixed 50-50 with fine fir or redwood bark. The terrestrial orchid mixtures sold by orchid firms are excellent for bromeliads, too.

Container Ideas

I use three-quarter-size clay pots for bromeliads. Some smaller epiphytic species, like *Tillandsia ionantha*, can be affixed to slabs of tree-fern fiber or cork bark. Use plastic-covered wire or nylon fishline to hold the plant base tightly against the slab until new roots are secure, usually after several months. Unmilled sphagnum moss or a small pad of osmunda makes a buffer between plastic wire and plant. Fertilize hanging bromeliads with half-strength solutions misted on the foliage every few weeks during spring through early fall.

Sturdy sections of driftwood (well washed if from the sea; leave outdoors a month or two) can be drilled to make pockets which hold bromeliad roots and thus form a bromeliad tree. A more elaborate tree can be delightful in a bright sun porch or greenhouse. Begin with a driftwood tree, sink the base into a cement mold, let it cure a few days. Put the tree on a wide plastic tray, fill gravel in around the base as camouflage over the cement. Plant terrestrial *Cryptanthus* in a leaf mold and sand mixture in the tray. Put a semiterrestrial *Neoregelia carolinae* or *N*. 'Marmorata' just above the tree base. On the tree, grow miniature *Tillandsia ionantha* and a few small aechmeas; wire these on with a sphagnum or osmunda pad. Hanging Spanish moss completes the display. Place the tree in a bright location where humidity is above 50 percent. Mist the plants on bright mornings. Small orchids (epidendrums, oncidiums) also thrive on a tree like this. Note that this is not a practical method of culture in a small window of a dry home.

Blooming

Bromeliads take from two to five years to bloom from seed, but mature specimens bloom on each new growth. Full-grown bromeliads bloom, then produce offsets before they gradually die. If a mature plant seems stubborn to bloom, put the rosette into a closed plastic bag along with two ripe apples. The ethylene gas given off by the ripe fruit would blast most flower buds, but this same gas prompts bromeliads to initiate an inflorescence. Remove the bag and apples after twenty to thirty days. Another system to force blooming on healthy mature bromeliads is to mix a quarter ounce of calcium carbide (from any drugstore) with one quart of warm water and fill the bromeliad cup (rosette) with this solution. Pour off the solution after twenty-four hours, refill the rosette with plain water, and wait for bloom—in one or two months with most aechmeas, billbergias, and vriesias.

Propagation

Propagate bromeliads by seed or offsets from mature plants. Let the offsets stay with the mature plant for a year or at least until they develop small active root systems; they are much easier to establish that way. Bromeliads raised from seed develop extensive root systems in the sowing mix of sphagnum moss, perlite, and vermiculite recommended in Chapter 5. The species I grew from seed were epiphytic, yet they retained extensive roots when potted in small clay or plastic pots over an inch of pea gravel with a mixture of unmilled sphagnum, coarse perlite, and granulated charcoal. I fertilize bromeliad seedlings three out of four waterings with half-strength water-soluble fertilizer poured into the rosettes.

Ailments and Pests

When properly cultivated, bromeliads are rarely troubled by serious pests or diseases. Of all the species I've grown only a few ever suffered from any insect pest. One plant I received as a gift had a few mealybugs in the new growth, but these I removed by hand and then the whole plant got a wash in mild Malathion solution (the powder is less harsh than the liquid). The next day I washed the whole plant in warm water, and as a standard precaution I kept it isolated for a few weeks.

Scale is one other insect that sometimes troubles bromeliads, especially on new plants imported from jungle collectors. Again, the best cure is hand washing to remove the insects; use an old toothbrush with a soapy solution of warm water. To be extra safe, spray with Malathion. Bromeliads as a group don't accept most insecticides very well. If the insecticide sits in the rosette or heavily saturates plants with scaly foliage, damage often results. The best remedy, as for all your houseplants, is prevention.

Keep new plants isolated for several weeks, even after checking them over for troubles. If you have a clean collection, it takes only a little precaution to keep it that way. Disease, in contrast, can appear as the result of improper culture rather than as an outside introduction. Give bromeliads plenty of air circulation; let foliage dry by nightfall (but not the center rosette); keep roots of epiphytes on the dry side; use small pots with extra drainage to keep roots healthy.

Epiphytic *Aechmea* plants thrive on an oak branch outside Chichen Itza, the famous Mayan temple in Yucatán.

Aechmea fasciata, a Brazilian bromeliad, with faded inflorescence and two sturdy offsets

Small plant of *Ananas comosus variegatus* (top) and the compact *Cryptanthus fosterianus* are terrestrial bromeliads, perfect for dish gardens or set around the base of tall plants.

Nidularium innocentii lineatum, an adaptable Brazilian bromeliad

Tillandsia species vary from the miniature *T. ionantha* (upper right) to sturdy *T. lindenii* (center right), treasured for broad pink spike and large blue flowers. The mosslike *T. usneoides* is draped between larger species in clay pots or on tree-fern slabs. *T. streptophylla* is at lower left center.

On the slopes around Colombia's famous Chivor emerald mine I found this cloud-damp vriesia exposed to direct sun for only a few minutes each day, since the heavy Andean mist seldom lifts. Epidendrum roots growing into the bromeliad foliage rosette can tap water for the orchid.

9

Geraniums for Bloom and Scent

THE GERANIUMS WE GROW INDOORS are impressive for their glowing colors, fragrant and often patterned leaves, and carefree nature. Botanically they are pelargoniums. Somehow "geranium" seems a pleasing name for these verdant friends that we enjoy in the summer garden and winter windows, but the true geraniums are slightly different in flower structure and are mainly temperate zone hardy plants, not suited to indoor culture.

In my southern New York garden *Geranium sanguineum* creates a pink-flowered creeping carpet. The lavender-flowered *G. maculatum* is one of our purest and loveliest native woodland and meadow plants. In our homes we cultivate pelargoniums, species from South Africa, but I admit that I still call my pelargoniums geraniums, as do many people.

Flowers are the primary attraction on *Pelargonium hortorum* hybrids, a group called zonal geraniums, yet a few are grown for their handsome patterned foliage. Dwarf and miniature hybrids are favorites where space is limited; the large standard garden-variety zonals are more generally effective out of doors. If you want to have geraniums in terrace or window boxes for the summer and to bring the same plants indoors in the fall, select some of the compact dwarfs that reach twelve to fifteen inches in the garden, eight to ten inches as potted specimens. The zonals (or *hortorum* hybrids) are the easiest geraniums to grow.

Scented-leaf geraniums include many adaptable species and a few hybrids, often with a bonus of lavender to red flowers. Scented sorts may be raised from seed or purchased as named clones. Older plants of favorite varieties can furnish cuttings for home propagation.

Trailing or ivy-leaved geraniums (*P. peltatum* hybrids) have single or double flowers on graceful cascading stems, best in hanging baskets or raised containers. I like to use them wandering over the side of terrace planters for outdoor summer enjoyment. There are a few clones that will do well inside at a sunny window. The best ivy geraniums I've ever seen were in cool regions of northern Spain where housewives take pride in second-story window boxes and balconies overflowing with masses of flower-covered trailing stems.

Pansy or Martha Washington geraniums, sometimes called the Show or Regal group, offer large flowers in glowing velvety colors with unusual markings in dark contrasting hues. These are *Pelargonium* X *domesticum* hybrids, not easy to grow indoors unless you can provide cool conditions and humidity of 50 to 60 percent, higher than required by other geraniums. In a cool greenhouse or sunny enclosed porch they thrive, and out of doors where summers are not especially hot, they can be rewarding for months, sometimes reaching heights of three to four feet. I have seen plants of *P.* X *domesticum* hybrids growing in rusty tin cans outside Andean farmhouses in Colombia, and with the cool moist mountain conditions they were indeed regal.

Hortorum Types; the Zonals

Geraniums are constantly being improved by hybridizers working for larger and longer-lasting blooms and resistance to heat. Hybrids bred to withstand summer heat will also do better indoors in winter. Iowa State University has introduced a series of geraniums that remain free-flowering in spite of temperatures that cause rank growth and flower color changes in older varieties.

I grow some of these Iowa State hybrids and find them compact delights easy to grow in a sunny window and under fluorescent growth lamps. 'Summertime' is a freely branching plant with large heads of glowing semidouble coral-rose flowers. 'Skylark', introduced in 1970, is a vigorous clone, of which my plants respond wonderfully to pinching by becoming extra bushy. The flowers are dawn-pink, developing rose-pink margins with maturity. 'Toreador' is another, with brilliant deep-red flowers.

These heat-resistant hybrids will approach perfection when you give them night temperature of 65° or even better, of 60°. I note that in my living room, where the night temperature thermostat is set for 68°, the actual temperature close to picture windows in winter is 60°. Throughout the temperate zone you can rely on outdoor weather to keep immediate window areas several degrees lower than the rest of a room. Use this microclimate to keep geraniums cool. Where possible winter nights to 55° are not merely safe but desirable.

Miniatures and Dwarfs

Diminutive zonal hybrids now come in many bright colors, and some have patterned foliage. The miniatures seldom require pots over three inches in size, so quite a few of these four- to eight-inch gems will grow in a sunny window or close under fluorescent lamps. Some excellent miniatures are:

'Frills'. Pink flowers with fringed petals.
'Pigmy'. Small foliage, tiny double red flowers, vigorous.
'Pompeii'. Dark foliage, small double red flowers.
'Red Brooks Barnes'. Orange-scarlet flowers over dark foliage.
'Ruffles'. Light salmon, semidouble.
'Salmon Comet'. Dark-salmon single.
'Sugar Baby'. Miniature ivy-leaf type, double pink flowers.

I grow my miniatures with strong sun, standard soil mix slightly dry between waterings, and balanced fertilizer every third watering when they are most active. They are grown in two- to three-inch plastic pots because I find small clay pots dry out too fast.

Dwarf geraniums are ultra-compact and normally eight to ten inches high when mature, but some sold as dwarfs must certainly be pinched to stay this small. The dwarfs are generally easier to grow than true miniatures. A semidwarf means that the plant will reach twelve inches; even semidwarfs are more suitable for window culture than standard garden-size geraniums. Some nice fancy-leaved dwarfs are available, but the bright-foliaged sorts, especially those with much white or gold, are somewhat weaker than plain-green clones; their root systems are not so vigorous as those of hybrids that have only dark rings as foliage patterns. Some of the more adaptable colored-leaf dwarfs are:

'Alpha' and 'Pink Alpha'. Red rings over gold-green leaf.
'Golden Oriole'. Salmon flowers, gold leaf with red ring.
'Mrs. Parker'. Double pink flowers, white-variegated foliage.

My plants of 'Pink Alpha' bloom constantly when grown in a southeast window where they receive direct morning sun. I find 'Pink Alpha' almost a trailer, with stems gracefully bending over the pot, bright pink flowers set against lovely green-gold foliage, each leaf ringed in red. 'Mrs. Parker' is a semidwarf, so will need some pinching.

Dwarf geraniums are featured in the catalogs of Merry Gardens, Logee's, and Wilson Brothers, but a few will also be found in general nursery catalogs. A few proven dwarf cultivars are:

'Bashful'. One of the Rober series named after the Seven Dwarfs, this one having single light-lavender flowers over dark foliage.
'Goblin'. Double scarlet flower.
'Minx'. Dark-purple double.
'Pixie'. Salmon-pink single.
'Polaris'. White single flower with faint pink edge.
'Robin Hood'. Double cherry-red; plant to fifteen inches tall.
'Sheraton'. Strong growing; double dark-salmon flowers.
'Small Fortune'. Compact free-flowering double white.
'Sneezy'. Rose-red single flowers, white center.
'Sparkle'. Dark foliage, glowing scarlet flowers.
'Vixen'. Salmon-pink single flowers over dark-green leaves.
'Zip'. Orange-red single.

Named dwarfs are propagated by cuttings, but the Read's strain of dwarf geraniums (Geo. W. Park Seed Company) will produce about 50 percent dwarf plants from seed. 'Little Big Shot' is another seed-grown F_1 hybrid that produces five- to six-inch plants which later have three- to four-inch flower heads. Seeds are available of 'Little Big Shot' in separate colors: pink, red, salmon, or scarlet with white center.

Unusual Flower Forms

Among the *P. X hortorum* hybrids are several rare flower types that are as yet not generally available except from geranium specialists. Cactus-flowered hybrids have rolled or twisted narrow petals that present an informal effect. Some nice clones include pure-white 'Noel' and the fire-red 'Tangelo'. Rosebud hybrids are ultra-double flowers with half-open florets resembling tiny tea roses. I especially like 'Apple Blossom Rosebud', delicate white with a deep-rose edge on each petal. Rosebud types come in red and pink, too. Bird's Egg geraniums have flowers with small spots on the petals, and of them I think the single-flowered types the most charming. A good sturdy one is offered as 'Bird's Egg—light pink' (Merry Gardens). There is also a double deep-pink Bird's Egg hybrid listed in a few catalogs.

Fragrant or Unusual Foliage

In a small sunny window you can grow enough scented geraniums to rival all the perfumes of the Spice Isles. These are easy to grow, even under fluorescent lights. Currently available as plants or seed are many "flavors." Some of the best:

Pelargonium capitatum. Rose-scented, ruffled foliage, lavender flowers.

P. crispum. Compact crinkled-leaf, pyramidal growth, strong lemon scent. Cultivars of this species include 'Minor', a citronella scent from small stem-less foliage; 'Prince Rupert', largest crispum leaf, heavy lemon fragrance; and the small-growing crinkled-leaf 'Prince Rupert Variegated' with white-edged foliage, same lemon fragrance.

P. denticulatum 'Filicifolium'. Finely cut pine-scented leaves on tall stems.

P. X fragrans cultivars. Two of the best are 'Nutmeg' and 'Old Spice' (*P. odoratissimum* X *P. X fragrans*). Both have gray-green leaves. 'Old Spice' is compact, upright; 'Nutmeg' rather open, rangy.

P. graveolens. Cultivars of this species smell somewhat like roses (as geraniums go!). The foliage is large, finely cut. Two good compact sorts are 'Lady Plymouth' and 'Little Gem'.

P. grossularioides. A trailer if not pinched, smooth dark-green leaves with coconut scent.

P. X nervosum. Small sharp-toothed foliage with lime fragrance, compact habit.

P. odoratissimum. Rounded fuzzy leaf with apple scent, trailing stems if not trained, small white flowers.

P. papilionaceum. Vigorous South African shrubby species I grew from seed and found easy, trained as a small standard about twenty-four inches high. Foliage is medium green, very fuzzy, citron-scented. Flowers are white with dark-purple markings, suggesting butterflies.

P. quercifolium. Variety 'Staghorn Oak' because it smells like a pine forest to me. 'Pretty Polly' smells like almond to some people, has deeply lobed dark-centered leaves, pink blooms.

P. radens. The lemon-scented cultivar 'Dr. Livingston' has deeply cut leaves, vigorous growth. A leaf crushed in tea is delightful.

Some fanciers cultivate certain types for interesting foliage or curious plant form. Among the better-known ones are: *P. acetosum,* rambling, climbing, with small cupped silver-green leaves, salmon flowers; *P. dasycaule*, thick-stemmed, succulent foliage; *P. echinatum*, gray-green fuzzy leaves, single white flowers splashed red, easy grower; *P. gibbosum*, fleshy knotted stems, night-fragrant green-yellow flowers, grayish leaves. Others are available from specialists. For details consult *The Joy of Geraniums* by Helen Van Pelt Wilson.

Trailing Ivy-Leaved Hybrids

A large window box overflowing with ivy-leaved geraniums in full flower is a memorable sight when these lovely trailers have enjoyed high humidity, bright light, and rather cool temperatures. Under dry, shady, or too warm conditions the *P. peltatum* hybrids are apt to be disappointing. Some cultivars are more adaptable than others for indoor growing, and these are good ones to begin with:

'Charles Turner'. Double dark pink.
'Galilee'. Semidouble pink on bushy plant.
'Gay Baby'. Tiny deep-green leaves, white blooms marked lilac; dwarf plant. 'Sugar Baby' is the double 'Pink Gay Baby'.
'La France'. Easy-to-bloom dark lavender.
'Mexican Beauty'. Old favorite semidouble dark garnet.
'Sybil Holmes'. Double rose-pink, rosebud form.

A hybrid of *P. peltatum* with a *P. X hortorum* cultivar is 'Alpha', mentioned before under the colored-leaf types. I find this a good trailer that is less fussy about temperature than other *peltatum* hybrids.

The true ivy-leaved hybrids thrive with night temperatures around 55° and 10° to 15° higher by day, bright light, humidity 50 to 60 percent, and good air circulation. Let soil dry slightly between waterings to prevent clear warty swellings on foliage, called edema. Spray with Kelthane if the slightest infestation of red spiders occurs (see Chapter 18). Sturdy plants are produced from cuttings taken in spring or summer; older plants can be cut back more than halfway to encourage new growth. Although trailers are grown in baskets or hanging pots, they should still be densely foliaged, not stringy. Pinching and strong light will help make attractive specimens. Fertilizer is fine for active blooming plants but not for resting plants in winter or for any plants when weather is really hot.

Pelargonium X Domesticum

Regal or Martha Washington geraniums have the largest, boldest flowers of all, sometimes individual florets being four inches across. Plants can tower to three and four feet and extend as much across. In England, cool regions of the Pacific Northwest, and other parts of the world where temperatures don't reach extremes of heat or cold, you will find the best *domesticum* specimens.

Flower colors are blends of purple, rose, deep pink, and white, most often blotched with contrasting eyes or splashes; these lead to the popular name pansy-geranium. Florists frequently offer these hybrids in the spring, covered with bloom. To grow them well, you must provide cool temperatures of 45° to 50° at night and not much above 70° by day. Humidity is best above 50 percent, but leaves must be kept free from standing water. Keep the soil evenly moist for active plants, slightly dry between waterings on less active plants, but always for this type of geranium, humidity above 50 percent.

Standard potting soil is suitable but not with much fertilizer. Bright light is required for sturdy growth, maximum bloom. A cool sun porch or place right next to a large window will be best.

Some free-flowering clones are:

'Chorus Girl'. Lavender marked salmon, overall effect glowing salmon.
'Dubonnet'. Deep glowing wine-red, blooms early, repeats later.
'Easter Greeting'. Large rosy-carmine blooms marked deep black. Continuous bloom under favorable conditions.
'Josephine'. Relatively constant production of rose-marked white flowers.
'Mrs. Mary Bard'. Delightful pure white with deep-purple pin stripes.
'Springtime'. White centers, broad rose blotch, thin white edge on petals, large flowers.

General Culture

Species and succulent sorts are grown in small pots with the standard mix cut 25 percent with coarse builder's sand and kept dry for a day or two between waterings. Standard potting mixture for X *hortorum*, X *domesticum,* and fragrant-foliage sorts is:

3 parts standard packaged pasteurized houseplant soil.
1 part leaf mold, humus, or rough sphagnum peat moss.
1 part coarse builder's sand (or coarse perlite).
½ cup powdered dolomite limestone per bushel of mix.

If you like to use a slow-release fertilizer in your potting soils, sprinkle a dusting of low-nitrogen organic fertilizer on the mix, and stir in completely. Good types are the formulas made for bulbs, like Espoma Bulb Tone. Omit this for any slow-growing species and X *domesticum* cultivars.

Geraniums also grow well in soil-free peat-lite mixtures, but they then require weekly fertilizing with a half-strength solution of balanced fertilizer; hence, for the least amount of trouble pot them in a soil mixture, and go easy with fertilizer on slow-growing species like *P. crithmifolium* and *P. dasycaule*. The X *domesticum* cultivars tend to grow too much foliage at the expense of flowers if fertilized often, so try them in the soil mix, without fertilizer, first. Active hybrids of X *hortorum* zonal geraniums potted in soil can utilize a fertilizer solution, higher in potash and phosphorus than nitrogen, every third or fourth week under good growing conditions.

Potting

Pot firmly over good drainage material. I like clay pots best for species and larger sorts; plastic pots for the miniatures.

Watering

Let geraniums get almost dry between waterings to encourage vigorous roots. Fragrant-foliage types can use somewhat more water than others; keep resting species driest of all to prevent rot.

Humidity

Geraniums are less dependent on high humidity than many other tropicals, but maintain it at least 40 percent for optimum growth. See notes under X *domesticum* and ivy-leaved sorts.

Temperature

Sturdy growth is made with night temperatures in the low 60's for standard X *hortorum* cultivars and lower, as mentioned earlier, for X *domesticum* and ivy-leaved hybrids. Daytime temperatures of 70° to 78° are good. Under less than ideal light, the temperatures should be toward the cooler end and watering reduced. Night temperature for optimum growth in X *hortorum*, fragrant-foliage sorts, and many species is 55°.

Light

Grow plants in a south or southwest window. Any less light is likely to produce spindly growth, few blooms. Geraniums will succeed under horticultural fluorescent lamps, and I have grown excellent plants with Gro-Lux Wide Spectrum tubes four to six inches above the foliage. Give fourteen to eighteen hours of light per twenty-four-hour period for rooting cuttings and growing young plants. Geraniums are indeterminate or neutral day-length plants and will normally not require short days to initiate blooming, but some sorts—*P.* X *domesticum* hybrids, for example—bloom best when given two months of short days (ten to twelve hours) once they have produced bushy growth. Follow this with long days of fourteen to sixteen hours, during which time the plants will flower.

Outdoors, give geraniums full sun, keep roots lightly moist.

Ventilation

Free circulation of air helps keep plants healthy. During mild weather open a window where plants grow; in cold weather open a window in an ajoining room to avoid direct cold drafts. In a closed room keep a fan going to circulate air, and open the door at least several hours a day to bring in new air; this is especially important with basement light gardens.

Dormancy

If you are interested only in zonal, ivy-leaved, or fragrant-foliage cultivars, you don't have to be concerned with leaf-losing. However, there are some strangely beautiful deciduous species that are dormant for several months each year. Some such species are *P. apiifolium, P. ardens, P. crithmifolium, P. gibbosum,* and *P. tetragonum.* Tuberous-rooted cactus-type species naturally drop foliage as they begin slowing growth, normally in late spring for these South Africans, adapted to survive long dry periods in their arid habitat. When your captive plants drop leaves, let them have the dry season they are expecting. Withhold water until soil is dry, use no fertilizer at all, and maintain temperatures under 70°. With humidity above 40 percent these succulent sorts may go a month or two without needing water.

Since such pelargoniums are usually dormant during the warm summer months in the Northern Hemisphere, it may not be possible to keep them cool, but do protect them from hot sun at midday and from rain in wet summers. Sprouting foliage signals an end to dormancy. Then increase watering, and begin light fertilizing only when leaves fill out, perhaps not at all if your plants are in soil and growing satisfactorily. Some Southern Hemisphere species may adjust to varying environmental conditions and thus change their period of dormancy, so, as with all tropicals, it is best to watch individual specimens for indications of activity or dormancy.

Training

Miniatures will require little pinching to remain attractive when confined to three-inch pots or smaller. Dwarfs and larger cultivars must be pinched several times each year to keep them bushy. For winter bloom, pinch from late summer on into fall. If you desire summer flowers, keep plants debudded and pinched until midspring. In fall it is easy to find blooming zonal-hortorum hybrids in commercial greenhouses. Such plants are branched, bushy, ready for flowering all winter, and usually don't require pinching that first season. During the summer keep them outside, where after a brief rest they usually continue to grow and flower.

In fall, several weeks before the first frost, cut back the stems about three quarters, dig up roots, and prune back longest roots to fit into six- or seven-inch pots. Put newly potted plants in a bright location, and keep on the dry side until leaves sprout, then increase watering. By late winter flowering should begin. A more suitable procedure, where space is limited or plants are several years old, is to make top cuttings in early summer.

Propagation

Propagate from stem cuttings as outlined in Chapter 5. Let geranium cuttings sit for a day to form a callus. Strains offered by seed firms are now so good that you can grow hybrids of uniform quality and even select the colors you want. The 'Carefree' F_1 hybrid strain, All America Award winners, were picked for sturdy adaptable growth and abundant flowers in five-inch heads: white, rose, and red.

'Carefree' hybrids get to sixteen inches tall and are very vigorous, so be sure you have enough room for them before sowing seed. A double seed-grown strain, 'Double Dip' geraniums, is available in various pink pastel shades (Geo. W. Park Seed Company). The 'Floradale' strain (W. Atlee Burpee Company) produces eighteen-inch mounds with flowers in white, pink, salmon, and scarlet to crimson. For hybrids more in scale with limited indoor growing space I suggest the dwarf strains: Read's to produce 50 percent plants under six inches; 'Nittany Lion' strain of ten- to twelve-inch red-flowered hybrids, developed by Pennsylvania State University; 'Little Big Shot' strain mentioned earlier under X *hortorum* hybrids.

Scented-leaf geraniums can also be easily raised from seed, as can the *P. peltatum* hybrids. Clones with fancy leaves and variegation are propagated from cuttings. Geranium seed has germinated easily for me, but sometimes germination is uneven because of the hard seed coat. Some firms offer seed that has been scarified (scratched), a treatment that fosters uniform germination in less than ten days. The strains developed to be grown from seed will, with correct culture, produce flowers in four to six months.

Health

Geraniums are normally rather trouble-free when given enough fresh air and good cultivation. If they are too wet, they may develop stem rot, in which event you had better quickly take cuttings from sound portions of any plants you wish to save and improve culture for unaffected plants.

Leaf spot may develop from overhead watering, especially under cool, humid, and close conditions. The cure is to improve air circulation and be sure foliage is kept dry. A spray that will help halt the spread of leaf-spot botrytis fungus is made with Fermate powder or the DuPont benomyl fungicide Benlate used according to package directions.

The most serious diseases of geraniums are virus infections. Crinkle disease (*Marmor pelargonii*) is the most common. Sometimes a plant is infected with virus but does not show the typical leaf-curl symptoms or spots surrounded with lighter white rings and distorted new growth that indicate crinkle disease. Commercial growers or friends who give you a plant may thus unwittingly introduce a virus to your healthy plants.

The only way to control virus is to destroy any plants affected. Sucking insects and unclean cutting tools will spread the virus from a sick plant to healthy ones.

Aphids, mealybugs, and white flies that sometimes bother pelargoniums can be controlled with Malathion spray used according to the package directions.

Scented geraniums, front left to right: crinkly lemon-scented 'Prince Rupert Variegated'; *Pelargonium denticulatum* with pine-scented wavy-edged foliage; rear right: soft-fuzzy camphor-scented *P. graveolens*

Zonal hybrid grown mainly for colored foliage, 'Mrs. Henry Cox', an old clone worth growing today for its bright pink, green, and yellow-white leaves

'Little Big Shot', an introduction in F_1 hybrids that comes uniform and true in color from seed, blooms in three to four months. (*Geo. W. Park Seed Company, Inc.*)

Delicate light-lavender bloom
on pungent-scented 'Fair Ellen',
a *P. quercifolium* cultivar

Pelargonium X *domesticum*
'Earliana'

Miniature geraniums thrive in
a model house designed by
Francis C. Hall, a lighting en-
gineer. He grows these hybrids
with fluorescent tubes suspended under the roof and with
several incandescent bulbs between the fluorescents to provide added red-spectrum light.
I find that geraniums thrive
under my conditions without
incandescent bulbs if I use
wide-spectrum fluorescents.

10

Begonias at Home

O NE AFTERNOON WHILE EXPLORING jungle tangles on a misty Andean slope in Colombia, I came upon a rushing stream where the banks were covered with begonias blooming against soft green moss. *Begonia foliosa*, a miniature species long a favorite in hanging baskets, was the most abundant. There, in its tropical habitat, it had diffuse light, humus-rich soil, high humidity, constant moisture around the roots, and good air circulation.

On a spring day in Arusha I admired a mass of cane-type begonias thriving under bright Tanzanian sun where the soil dried out between heavy East African rains. For part of each day hot sun burned down on the thin angel-wing foliage, and leaves on the floriferous plants were yellowish but healthy.

By finding begonias in their various habitats I have discovered what a diverse and interesting group they are—a great many species native to many warm countries around the world. They thrive from high altitudes with diffuse light and cool temperatures down to hot river valleys in bright sun. Each species, of course, does best with its particular requirements met, but within the genus you will find a number of fascinating plants suited to the conditions you can provide.

Types

Horticulturists recognize several groups of begonias, classified by kind of roots and secondarily by leaf form. Most familiar are the wax begonias,

B. semperflorens hybrids, a fine array of shiny-leaved fibrous-rooted ever-blooming plants for winter windows and summer bedding.

Almost as popular are the angel wings, also fibrous-rooted, with wing-shaped leaves, often spotted silver, and clusters of white, pink, orange, to bright-red flowers. Plant habit gives to them the alternate common name of cane-stem begonias. Some, like the Brazilian *B. coccinea* and its hybrid 'Corallina de Lucerna', grow to ten or fifteen feet and are used as hedges in southern California. Others, like 'Pinafore', have a dwarf compact habit suitable for indoor growing without constant pruning.

Rhizomatous species are of varied leaf color and form, but all grow from thick creeping stems. Some grow over rocks in their jungle habitats, but I have noticed that the roots are always found in pockets of rich humus. Because rhizomes store food and moisture, these begonias can endure hardship better than other sorts. Well-known is the beefsteak begonia 'Erythrophylla' with thick shiny leaves, green above, red below. Airy sprays of pink flowers are abundant in the spring. New hybrids from the Mexican *B. boweri* offer a multitude of attractive miniatures with black eyelash hairs along leaf edges.

The glowing foliage of rex begonias emerges directly from the rhizome, although some upright plants, sold as rex, may have fibrous roots without a noticeable rhizome. Since catalogs usually list rex begonias in one section, look under "rex" rather than "Rhizomatous" when you are ordering. The rexes are available with leaves in numerous colors and in metallic blends of silver, sparkling pink, or green spotted bronze, gold, or silver.

The fibrous-rooted begonias are classified according to habit or leaf form as upright, trailing, hairy-leaved, and a catchall group of "odd and rare" types, mainly pure species. Hirsute, or hairy-leaved, plants are favorites for their adaptability. The hairs may be quite evident as in *B. scharffi* (*B. haageana*) with large velvety silvery olive-green foliage, or not so prominent as in *B. metallica*, which has shiny dark-green purple-veined leaves covered with delicate silver hairs.

Begonias suitable for hanging baskets are such practical charming additions to any display that later in this chapter I have a special list of the best kinds. These are begonias that adapt themselves to average conditions.

If you are interested in unusual begonias, you will enjoy the catalogs of begonia specialists listed in Sources of Plants and Supplies. My selection here is of the generally available begonias that are not too difficult to grow, a good way to begin enjoying this fascinating genus. The winter-blooming Christmas begonia (*B. X hiemalis*) hybrids are discussed in Chapter 13 on holiday plants.

Fibrous-Rooted

Semperflorens

For their tolerant constantly blooming habit, the wax begonias win world-wide appreciation. Among the new hybrids are some interesting flower and foliage color combinations, including single, double, and crested flowers. In the crested types, sometimes called 'Cinderella,' the center of the single flower holds a waxy yellow ball of stamens and anthers.

Some varieties grow into mounds a foot tall and wide, but most hybrids are bred for compactness. These smaller plants will mature to bloom under eight inches. All the wax begonias have glossy foliage and juicy stems and will propagate easily from seed or stem cuttings. For best flowering and sturdy growth, night temperature should be 65° to 60° with daytime highs 5° to 10° higher. Bright light is required for maximum flower production.

Clumps I have grown outside for summer color do well when I dig them up in September's first cool days, separate clumps to fit into four- to six-inch pots, then cut back tops halfway. In a sunny window by midwinter the clumps resume blooming.

The original wax begonia hybrids were created from the species *B. semperflorens* and *B. schmidtiana*. Plant breeders have been crossing the resulting hybrids back and forth now for almost a hundred years. One group, the calla-lily variegated-leaf semperflorens hybrids, are slightly temperamental growers.

Calla-Lily Begonias

If you want to grow calla-lily types, keep them under 68° by day; the lower 60's are even better. Let their roots stay confined to relatively small pots, four to five inches. Give water only as the soil begins to dry out, maintain humidity above 50 percent, and provide bright-diffuse sun but not the strong direct sun that common semperflorens require, unless you keep relative humidity above 60 percent and temperatures stay below 70°.

Calla-lily cultivars are slower growing, so they won't need as much fertilizer. If you find a window or sun porch where they do well, leave them there; they don't like to be moved about. Very bright light often causes a rose blush on foliage, a normal and healthy reaction but perhaps out of key with their green-and-frosty-white beauty. Two calla-lily types that are more adaptable than others are 'Charm', a pink-flowered plant with green leaves spotted yellow, not so striking as the white-leaved cultivars but a pleasant variation from the usual wax begonias, and 'Fire 'n' Ice', variegated white foliage, semidouble red flowers on a vigorous plant. 'Calla Queen' is a strong grower, too, with white new leaves but large light-green foliage at the base. Flowers are single deep-rose color.

Other Semperflorens Types and Named Clones

Among popular semperflorens are several strains or cultivars that come very uniform from seed. Many of these are F_1 hybrids, so the seed is produced by crossing the two parents each time seed is required. Because this takes time and special skill, seed tends to be rather expensive, but you can be more sure of getting just what you have in mind than with uncontrolled seed mixtures.

Vegetatively propagated clones are offered by some growers. These individual plants are selected from hundreds for their desirable characteristics. 'Carol', for example, is a compact bronze-leaved plant, easy to grow, with large balls of glowing deep-red flowers. 'Pink Wonder' is bushy, green-leaved, nearly covered with large double pink flowers. 'Ballet' is one of my favorites, with bronze leaves and double white flowers.

Wax begonias offered as seed-grown strains sometimes produce an outstanding clone that is then propagated as a named variety. To grow many plants, you are better off with seed of a select strain. 'Cinderella' strain is dwarf and comes with single rose, white, or pink flowers over green leaves. 'Thimbleberry' plants are bushy, have double thimble-shaped flowers, and are sometimes further separated as secondary named clones. 'Green Leaved Thimbleberry' (Ernest Logee's) is a double red with medium-green leaves.

'Scarletta', a single bright-red flower is an Award of Merit winner; 'Pink Comet' has single blush pink flowers. Both thrive as pot plants. For double flowers from seed look for 'Jewelite' strain with bronze-red foliage and double flowers in delicate rose shades or 'White Christmas', which comes 75 percent true-double from seed, its pure-white flowers set off by shiny green foliage on twelve-inch plants. Largest flowers yet on wax begonias are of the 'Butterfly' strain, a group with three-inch flowers available in red, white, or rose; plants grow ten to twelve inches and have green foliage.

Angel Wings

Angel wings are more tolerant of heavy soil than most begonias, but they must not be kept constantly wet. Pot them in clay containers if you tend to overwater. Low-growing angel wings can look well in hanging baskets after several months' growth, but they are not so graceful as truly rambling or pendulous begonias. Propagate angel wings from seed or stem cuttings. Younger, less woody, plants bloom better indoors than do two- or three-year-old ones.

Five favorite angel-wing cultivars are:

'Corallina de Lucerna'. Easy constant bloomer in bright light, deep-green leaves silver-spotted, clusters of coral flowers. Must be pruned yearly, but it's so easy to grow that you will like it.

'Di-Erna'. Hybrid of B. *dichroa*, easier to grow than that species and taller, but prunes well. Keep in relatively small pot, dry side. Coral-orange flowers.

'Lulu Bower'. Everblooming salmon-pink, good in basket.

'Pinafore'. Low compact hybrid, crimped-edge slate-green foliage, silver-spotted above, deep red beneath. Long season of salmon flowers.

'President Carnot'. Satiny pointed leaves, large clusters of red to pink flowers. Color of foliage and flowers changes with light exposure. Can take almost full sun for deep-colored flowers.

Miscellaneous Fibrous-Rooted Species and Cultivars

These are mostly upright and hairy-leaved but vary considerably in leaf shape, texture, and other details, and possess individual and diverse charms. They will respond to pinching by becoming bushy but are handsome as large specimens if you have room. Be sure to stake the larger growers before they get too tall. Grow all on the dry side at the roots but with humidity at least 40 percent; 50 to 60 percent is desirable. Succulent B. *venosa* requires brighter light than most and will endure low humidity. Hybridizers keep introducing new treasures.

'Alleryi' (B. *metallica* X B. *gigantea*). Easier than straight B. *metallica* but retains that species' shiny dark purple-green foliage. Pink flowers in fall.

'Dresden Gold'. A Kartuz hybrid, semiminiature, foliage glistening with gold above, deep red below. Soft-pink flowers with deeper-pink wings appear all year round for me. I grow it in a semitransparent plastic pot.

'Duscharf'. Broad hairy olive-green foliage and long-lasting white flowers heavily covered with red hairs on the outside; lovely.

B. *hispida cucullifera*. An upright species with foliage that sprouts tiny leaflets along the veins. White flowers.

B. *involucrata*. Erect habit, large green leaves with white hairs, fragrant white flowers. Avoid direct hot sun.

B. lubbersii. Dark-green leaves attached at the center, red below. Good in a raised pot, staked, or in a basket; unique.

B. metallica. The leaves, on upright stems, have a reddish-green shine. Hybrids of this are easier to grow, but you can succeed with the species if you let it dry out slightly between waterings and watch out for attacks of red spiders. Try misting the foliage to raise humidity and keep away the mites.

B. sanguinea. A bushy leathery leaf, striking deep red on the underside. Top of foliage is olive-green covered with silver hairs.

'Templinii' (*B. phyllomaniaca* sport). Delightful sturdy one- to two-foot waxy-leaved green-and-yellow-variegated plant with sprays of delicate pink flowers in late winter. Sometimes tiny plantlets on older leaves. Best propagated from stem-tip cuttings, although a rare leaf-plantlet may grow. Provide rather sandy soil, 60 percent humidity, and nights at 60° to 65° for best leaves.

B. venosa. A true succulent species with fragrant white flowers but grown mainly for foliage, which develops best in strong light. Grow on the dry side at roots.

'Zuensis'. Adaptable hybird with puckered green foliage, red-toned veins, hairy deep-pink flowers.

The pure species listed above can be grown from seed, but hybrids must be propagated by vegetative means outlined in Chapter 5.

Rhizomatous

Rex Cultivars

Rex begonias must have a porous woodsy humus soil and relatively low and wide containers, since the rexes have shallow roots and creeping rhizomes. I use three-quarter-size containers or bulb-pan pots. Plastic pots are fine if they hold plenty of drainage material. Plant the rhizome at soil level, never covered. The fleshy rhizomes hold lots of moisture, so although the relative humidity should be above 50 percent, the soil need not be constantly wet. A slight drying on top between waterings will maintain healthy roots.

Propagate rexes as outlined in Chapter 5 from leaf or rhizome cuttings or seed. Certain fine clones are selected for vigor and constant growth (some rexes rest in winter), so these are propagated by vegetative means. Some clones are a challenge to experts, but those that I have listed below are both lovely and adaptable. With warm temperatures, bright-diffuse light (fluorescents are fine), and high humidity, the rexes will provide months of glorious color.

'Fire Flush'. Fragrant white flowers, velvety red leaves. Mine thrives under fluorescent growth lamps.

'Granny'. Upright miniature, calico foliage design in silver, rose, and red.

'It'. Low growing. Silver-spotted metallic foliage. Takes brighter light than other rex types; produces many clusters of lightly fragrant pink flowers throughout the year.

'King Edward'. Shiny purple-black leaves spotted red. Pink flowers.

'Merry Christmas'. One of my favorites for its brilliant color, low growth, and dark-green leaves marked silver, rose, and red.

'Peace'. Silver with a pink blush that intensifies to rose in bright light or close under fluorescent tubes; six- to twelve-inch leaves.

'Shirt Sleeves'. Ultra-bright silver with pink blush on sturdy bushy plant. Mine thrives under fluorescents.

'Silver Sweet'. Upright habit, metallic silver foliage marked black along the veins.

'Thrush' ('Robin'). Crimson maplelike leaves dotted silver; many pink flowers over long period.

'Wood Nymph'. Charming bushy and low-growing miniature, coffee-brown-green foliage suffused and splashed silver. Good vigor.

Other Rhizomatous Selections

Some of the nicest miniatures are found in this group, mainly hybrids derived from a tiny Mexican species, *B. boweri*. In this same horicultural section are much larger hybrids like *B.* 'Erythrophylla', a profuse spring bloomer with thick leaves and robust rhizomes. Most of the rhizomatous begonias are easy growers. Soil, containers, and potting directions are just as recommended for the rexes. The sorts listed here take much more light than the rexes, so provide them with several hours of direct sun each day for sturdy plants and maximum floral display.

Phalaenopsis hybrid (upper left), white orchid, warm-temperature preference; *Dieffenbachia picta* (lower left), spotted with white; *Amaryllis (Hippeastrum)* hybrid (center), red flowers; *Chamaedorea elegans* 'bella' (Neanthe bella), palm at lower right; *Nephrolepis exaltata,* or the Boston Fern (upper-right background); *Aechmea fasciata,* a bromeliad, foliage seen in background right

'Soleil d'Or' narcissus, an easy-to-bloom indoor bulb for one-time use

Columnea 'Yellow Dancer', an everblooming hybrid, grows best in a basket.

RIGHT: Trailing Brazilian *Begonia solananthera*, with fine fragrance in the flowers

Living-room window garden. The yellow orchid, *Epidendrum tampense* (right),
gives out a honey scent; other orchids fill plastic boxes, the containers concealed by ferns and creeping *Setcreasea*.

The night-fragrant *Angrecum* Orchidglade 'Talisman Cove', hybrid of *A. ses-quipedale* X *A. eburneum giryamae*. The former species was brought from Madagascar to England in 1855 and flowered there in 1857. Charles Darwin saw it and deduced that a night-flying hawk-moth existed with a tongue long enough to extract nectar from the base of the twelve-inch spur of the flower. Some years later, such a moth was discovered on Madagascar.

Miniature African-violets
'Snow In' and 'Tiny Blue',
growing in a coffee measure.

'Frills', one of the many popular miniature geraniums.

Seemannia latifolia, a trailing gesneriad from the mountain rain forests of Bolivia and Peru. Grown under fluorescent lamps, this blooms on and off throughout the year.

Guzmania X *magnifica*, with waxy bracts that last from fall into spring

Mulch around the rhizomes with bark chips or gravel. Some miniatures will do best with chopped sphagnum moss around the rhizomes, but don't let this stay soggy. Humidity between 40 and 50 percent is best for foliage growth. Some few, like *B. goegoensis* and *B. pustulata,* must have 60 to 70 percent humidity to reach their maximum beauty. Provide temperatures between 60° and 65° by night with a daytime range 5° to 10° higher. Again, a few warm-jungle sorts like *B. goegoensis* and *B. masoniana* look better when they are grown a few degrees warmer.

Propagate rhizomatous sorts by division, rhizome cutting, layering, or seed. Some sorts propagate from leaves in water. Small-growing *B. boweri* hybrids root best in the propagating mix discussed in Chapter 5. For plenty of cheerful winter flowers and a year-round display of foliage, rhizomatous begonias are excellent choices. Some of the best medium to large growers are:

'Beatrice Haddrell'. Velvety greenish-black foliage, pink flowers in spring.

'Bunchii'. A ruffled crisp green-leaved sport of 'Erythrophylla', undersides toned deep pink in bright light.

'Erythrophylla' ('Feastii'). Thick glossy green leaves, deep red underneath, many pink flowers in early spring.

'Freddie'. A rapid adaptable grower with large bronze-green leaves, red undersides, many pink flowers.

B. goegoensis. A delightful species from Sumatra. Keep warm and humid, diffuse light, no hot sun.

'Joe Hayden'. Upright with bronze-green satin-finish foliage, red undersides, reddish-pink flowers in winter, adaptable grower.

B. masoniana. Called 'Iron Cross' for the Maltese cross design on each leaf. Provide bright light but no direct hot sun except in winter (when it is usually safe). Keep humidity above 50 percent, grow on the dry side at roots. Does well under fluorescents.

B. pustulata. Dark brownish-green leaves splashed silver on rambling stems. Attractive in a basket if in a warm humid place.

'Ricky Minter'. Robust hybrid with ruffle-edged green leaves tinged bronze, darker in dim light, veins much lighter color, pink flowers in winter.

'Verde Grande'. Name means big green in Spanish. An easy grower, sprays of delicate pink flowers mainly in winter.

Compact dwarf or miniature rhizomatous begonias are excellent in open-top terrariums, dish gardens, and ornamental planters; also under fluorescent lights. Hybrids with *B. boweri* in their background usually retain eyelash markings along leaf edges and are more adaptable than the parent species.

Recommended dwarf to miniature rhizomatous types are:

'Baby Perfection'. Small chartreuse leaves marked black, pink flowers on a very compact plant.

'Black Knight'. Heavily flowered dwarf with deep bronze starry leaves, reddish undersides.

'Black Magic'. Low growing; velvet sheen over blackish-green foliage, lighter center markings.

B. boweri nigramarga. A selected type of the species, tiny light-green leaves. Mulch with unmilled sphagnum, and let rhizomes creep all around shallow container or fern-root pot. Mist with warm water on bright mornings.

'Bow-Joe'. Star-shaped brownish-green leaves with lighter veins, more compact than 'Joe Hayden'.

'Bow-Nigra'. Light veins on star-shaped brown-toned foliage, small plant.

'China Doll'. Hybrid with *B. boweri* twice in its lineage. Tiny pointed light-green leaves with brown veins, eyelash hairs on leaf margins, pink flowers in winter.

'Maphil' ('Cleopatra'). Easy grower. Many pink flowers, red-spotted petioles.

'Nora Bedson'. Very small leaves marked chocolate, edged with lighter eyelashes.

'Robert Shatzer'. Bushy olive-green foliage with brown eyelash markings. A strong-growing *boweri* hybrid introduced at Logee's Greenhouse.

'Zaida'. Compact hybrid of *B. mazae*, the Mexican species with stitch-marked foliage. 'Zaida' has shiny greenish-brown leaves, sprays of pink flowers in winter, easier than species *B. mazae*.

Evergreen Begonias for Baskets

Here are some delightful plants for hanging containers. I like the plastic baskets that have built-in saucers to prevent drip on furniture or rugs. Some newer plastic containers have built-in reservoirs so plants absorb water as required, an excellent device for reducing care.

B. cubensis. A tiny-leaved dark bronze-green Cuban species with many white flowers from fall through winter, then on and off the whole year under optimum conditions.

'Ellen Dee'. Light-green foliage, glowing clusters of orange flowers mainly in winter.

'Florence Carrell'. Everblooming trailer with glossy crimped leaves and coral-red flowers pendent from graceful branches.

B. foliosa. Tiny oval leaves, dark-red stems, and white flowers, tinged rose. A graceful pot plant or charming basket display.

B. limmingheiana. Shiny pointed light-green foliage and pendent clusters of coral flowers from late winter into spring. Parent of several good trailing hybrids. Provide bright light, nights at 65°.

'Lulu Bower'. An angel wing with bronze-green leaves and salmon-pink flowers in large clusters that look lovely when viewed from below. Three bushy plantlets in a seven- to eight-inch basket will make a fine specimen quickly.

B. schmidtiana. I grew this easy species from seed, and the plants did well in baskets and windowsill pots. Small white to pink flowers, leaves green above, red beneath, covered with tiny hairs. Compact.

B. serratipetala. Glossy reddish-green crinkled leaves spotted iridescent pink, trailing stems, pink flowers (the pistillate flowers with red-toothed petals). A fine species from New Guinea. Let it dry out slightly between waterings.

B. solananthera ('Brazilian Heart'). Trailing, with fragrant white flowers, each marked red in the center. Well worth growing for fragrance, foliage, and flowers.

Fern Poles and Tree-Fern Containers

You can also grow some begonias on moist poles of sphagnum moss and tree-fern fiber. Small-size hybrids of *B. boweri* and a few epiphytic species like *B. herbacea* from Brazil do well in containers carved from tree-fern trunks. They create unusual displays when grown in pots with a log or slab of tree-fern fiber to climb on. Begonias will send roots into the moist fiber and thus climb higher than if given only the standard humus-rich potting soil. An alternative to tree-fern material is unmilled sphagnum moss stuffed into plastic or nylon cloth mesh. Such poles are available in garden shops or by mail order.

Tuberous Begonias

Summer-blooming tuberous begonias reach a peak of perfection when grown under cool moist conditions. Hot dry air, direct strong sun, and low humidity are detrimental. Indoors, the tuberous sorts are generally not successful except in damp basement fluorescent-light gardens or cool humid glassed-in porches. Although relative humidity of 50 to 60 percent is best, plants also require good air circulation to avoid fungus attacks, which can quickly ruin buds and foliage. If you wish to experiment, begin by growing multiflora types. They have smaller flowers than the giant tuberhybrida 'Camellia form' sorts but make up for lack of size by producing a profusion of bloom. The overall effect is usually more colorful.

In recent years the larger-flowered tuberhybridas have been crossed with the multifloras. 'Maxima Switzerland' is one fine hybrid that typifies the resulting strain. It incorporates the response to simple culture and multiflowered characteristics of one parent with increased flower size and unusual red color of the second. 'Mrs. Helen Harms', a bright yellow, is another good hybrid of the kind.

A third class of summer-flowering tuberous begonias consists of the pendula or hanging-trailing types. These make a lovely show but are often difficult to protect from wind, too much sun, and low humidity, unless they are grown in a protected area. *Begonia sutherlandi* is an orange-flowered species which goes dormant in the winter like other tuberous begonias. Hybrids for baskets are generally sold by color as *Begonia pendula*: red, white, salmon, yellow, and orange, usually with semidouble flowers.

Plastic baskets lined with sheet moss, redwood baskets, or even the plastic baskets with built-in saucers are satisfactory containers, provided they are shallow. Deep containers are likely to remain wet too long and cause root rot. Also squat pots are harder to tip than standard types. Pot in humus-rich soil with sharp drainage. For slow-release fertilizer, stir in some organic fish meal with the potting soil underneath the tuber, then put plain soil between the enriched mix and the tuber.

Start tubers as suggested for callas in Chapter 14. I like to sprout them in the propagating mix of equal parts perlite, sphagnum peat moss, and vermiculite, or chopped sphagnum moss with perlite. When roots are several inches long, transplant tubers to their pots or baskets. Smaller tubers will do well in four- to five-inch pots. Larger tubers that are several years old require seven- to eight-inch pots. If you mass the plants for display, give the small tubers six to eight inches of space and larger tubers eight to twelve inches.

Feed with a half-strength balanced fertilizer every other watering when leaves begin to open fully. I alternate fish emulsion or seaweed fertilizer with a water-soluble chemical fertilizer not too high in nitrogen. At midsummer, when blooming begins, cut out the high-nitrogen fish emulsion.

Day Length

Tuberous begonias flower on long days, more than twelve hours of light per twenty-four-hour period. Shorter days slow growth and encourage the formation of tubers in preparation for dormancy. The camellia-flowered types need at least twelve to fourteen light hours to bloom, and the smaller multifloras at least eleven hours. After the plants have bloomed under fluorescent lights, on long days you can cut the day length to ten hours or less to force formation of tubers, then dormancy. In natural light give them bright-diffuse light with care to avoid sunburn.

Grooming

For tuberhybridas pinch out all but three or four sturdy stems as they sprout, leaving only the largest to grow. The resulting flowers will be larger. Pinched-out stems can be used to grow additional plants. Follow directions given for secondary gloxinia shoots in Chapter 5. For more flowers just let all stems develop. When stems are about six to eight inches tall, support them with inconspicuous stakes. I use green-plastic-coated wire to gently tie each stem.

Multifloras and the multiflora maxima hybrids won't have to be pinched, but one or two pinchings (take out top inch of each stem) will develop extra-bushy plants. Hanging hybrids can be pinched once when they are about six inches tall. Hanging begonias do not require stakes.

Temperature

Summer temperatures under 75° are best, which is why the finest tuberous begonias grow in areas where the summers tend to be cool and somewhat moist. Actually plants may thrive with higher temperatures, but frequently the buds blast or the opened flowers don't last long. In the fall, as weather gets cooler, you will notice better flowers. Leave plants outside until the first frost. Leaves will begin to die in midfall, but the tuber is still building up energy for next year.

Hold off water as foliage dies away. When all leaves are gone, rest the tubers in a cool (45° to 50°) place in their pots or in plastic bags of un-milled sphagnum moss. Some gardeners clean off the tubers, dusting them lightly with Fermate to prevent rot, and then place them in open plastic trays where air can circulate freely. This will work if the humidity is above 50 percent; otherwise, store the tubers in barely damp sphagnum in bags, or just buy new tubers each year. All but the named hybrids can be had for less than a dollar each.

Begonia Culture Review

Soils

Begonias require a potting medium that is porous, moisture retentive to a degree, well drained, and slightly acid. The humus-rich mixes listed in Chapter 3 are satisfactory. In the wild, begonias live in humus accumulations on the forest floor, in pockets of rotted organic matter among rocks, or in tree crotches where leaf mold builds up.

Fertilizer

The general instructions given in Chapter 3 apply to begonias. I like to alternate chemical and organic products. Every four to six weeks, give plants a deep plain-water drench to carry away accumulated salts. If your water is very hard, it may be necessary to repot plants every year, as mineral salts keep building up in the potting mix.

Containers

Even tall-growing begonias thrive in three-quarter to half-size pots, since they have shallow root systems. I like standard clay or terra-cotta pots for angel wings and other large growers; the weight helps prevent toppling. Plastic containers are suitable for medium to small varieties. Hanging baskets of plastic, with built-in water-catching saucers, are perfect. Stick to the porous humus-rich mediums, since heavy soils in nonbreathing plastic pots quickly lead to root rot.

Begonia herbacea and any other rare epiphytes you may encounter will thrive in tree-fern containers. With high humidity and moisture at the roots, many small rhizomatous cultivars will grow well on sphagnum-moss poles, big chunks of lava rock, or artificial Featherock. To achieve a pleasing composition with plants growing on lava, arrange species in keeping with natural lines of the rock.

Find the best way to position the lava chunk, then hollow out space for each begonia. Use a strong chisel or heavy knife to cut out rock segments. Make the hole somewhat smaller than the pot in which each begonia is growing. Wash away the rock dust, then with an ice pick pierce drainage holes in the bottom of each hollowed-out opening. The lava or Featherock is porous, but it is wise to make these drainage holes in each opening to avoid soggy roots. The planted rock should rest on a tray or dish to prevent damage from draining water.

If you are planting small rhizomatous kinds, you can actually put just a little soil into the holes, then fill in around the roots with unmilled sphagnum moss. Eventually roots will grow down into the rock itself. Fertilize these rock-grown plants as you would a potted begonia, according to their growth. I recommend planting lava rocks with the smaller hybrids like *B. boweri* offspring and some of the more compact rhizomatous hybrids like 'Black Knight'. Keep the lava container in bright-diffuse light or under fluorescent growth lamps.

Temperature

Begonias thrive in a temperature of 60° to 65° at night to 70° or higher by day. Rex begonias like it a few degrees warmer (65° minimum nights), as do species from lowland regions like *B. dichroa* from Brazil, *B. goegoensis* from Sumatra, *B. masoniana*, and *B. pustulata*. Avoid rapid changes in temperature. A natural drop of several degrees in the evening is desirable. Nights should always be cooler than days.

Christmas begonias (a group known as *B. hiemalis*, though hybrids not a species) require cool humid conditions, and I don't recommend them for the house. (See Chapter 13.) Some begonias, the popular 'Erythrophylla' and many angel wings, for example, adjust to a wide range of temperatures. For some people these begonias thrive in a store window that may go to 50° every night; other growers report equal success in a house with 68° minimum night temperature. We are lucky to have such adaptable plants for problem places and beginning window gardeners.

Humidity

Mimimum humidity of 40 percent will keep most begonias healthy, but I have noted certain exceptions in the descriptions of some species. Any lower humidity causes stunted growth, brown leaf edges, and leaf drop. *Begonia leptotricha* 'Woolly Bear', the fuzzy silver *B. venosa*, and its hybrids 'General Jacques' and 'Venepi' all tolerate drier conditions because they have succulent foliage.

Light

Semperflorens and the succulent begonias grow well in full sun, even at a south window if humidity is maintained. Many angel wings bloom best and remain more compact if they, too, receive bright light, yet they tolerate less intensity. Watch foliage; let it take as much light as it can without turning yellow or developing burn spots.

Rex begonias are not very attractive if given too much light from the sun, yet mine thrive under fluorescent intensities that also grow good gloxinias and a few orchids. Fluorescents can give bright light without high heat or low humidity. Constant, unvarying fluorescent light produces symmetrical growth, bright glowing foliage, and maximum-size flowers. I use Gro-Lux and Gro-Lux Wide Spectrum tubes for many begonias. Outdoors in summer be sure to provide dappled shade for all but the succulents and angel wings.

Grooming

Pinch tall growers to keep them within bonds; pinch shorter types to get bushy growth and more pleasing form. Once a begonia makes a good root system you can cut it back one-third to one-half, and it will survive to become a more compact specimen.

Plants that have been outside in summer should be trimmed back before being brought indoors in fall. If an old plant is quite large and woody, you will do better to root half-mature top cuttings than to keep the old plant.

If you want a bushy plant fast, pot three or four cuttings in one container, then give them a pinch or two, and in a month or so they will look like one big plant. For hanging baskets put a cutting in the center, then three or four others around the outside.

Propagation

All named clones must be increased by vegetative means if you want duplicates. Species will come quite true from seed if they have been self-pollinated or crossed with another clone of the same species. Check the catalogs of dealers and also the seed exchange of the Begonia Society for some exciting begonias to grow from seed. See Chapter 5 for sowing details.

Resting

Rex begonias sometimes stop active growth for a month or two, usually in midwinter. More often it is older plants that do this. A rex grown under artificial light with a constant temperature above 65° for winter nights will often keep growing, although it may slow down somewhat. Plants under cooler conditions or with low humidity are more likely to lose their leaves and rest. Eventually the rhizome will begin to send up new leaves, so save a favorite variety.

Keep resting rexes just short of dry at the roots. Give them no fertilizer, and put leafless plants in a dim location with night temperature of 60° to 65°. Plants that retain some foliage should be kept in bright-diffuse light with temperature 65° to 70°. Some leaf drop in rexes is attributable to the change in conditions between a summer outdoors and the inside environment, especially in late fall when central heating normally causes a drop in relative humidity. Minimize such troubles by moving rexes indoors before your heater begins to work constantly.

Some rexes that have a good chance of maintaining foliage all winter (under good growing conditions) are 'Old Faithful', a bright green splashed silver; 'Merry Christmas'; 'Orient' with mainly green leaves; 'Winter Queen' with round-lobed leaf marked silver, reddish-brown in the center and along the edge; and 'It'. Keep an eye on specialists' catalogs for new introductions that are listed as winter vigorous.

Begonias bear male and female reproductive parts on different flowers. Here flowers of 'Man's Favorite', a winter-blooming tuberous hybrid, show pollen in upper (male) flower, sticky stigma in center of lower (female) flower.

Begonia 'President Carnot' grows nicely with *Chlorophytum* around the base.

Rex hybrids, grown from select German-strain seed, show many patterns and colors, equal in beauty to named clones.

Begonia masoniana, or 'Iron Cross', and *B*. 'Bow-Joe' (right), a small growing pink-flowered hybrid

Trailing species *B. pustulata* in a hanging basket

Begonia 'Maphil'

Begonia 'Dresden Gold'

Begonia 'Templinii'

Succulent *Begonia venosa*

11

Gesneriads, the African-Violet Family

Astonishingly varied, the gesneriads have been relatively little known until recent times except for one famous and immensely popular member, the *Saintpaulia*, or African-violet, which is not a true violet but definitely African. Other fairly well known genera are the trailing *Episcia*, exotic *Gloxinia* (now named *Sinningia*), and the exquisite *Streptocarpus*. Virtually all cultivated gesneriads come from tropical or subtropical regions. Saintpaulias are found in Kenya and Tanzania. I've seen episcias covering the jungle floor in Colombia and Brazil. The vermilion-flowered aeschynanthus vines grow in India, Malaysia, Java, and Borneo, the sinningias in Brazil, and the spreading achimenes in Mexico and Guatemala. Truly an international family!

Among the gesneriads are tiny minatures, tall shrubs, and hanging vines. The downy leaves of episcias and *Smithiantha* are treasured for glowing colors and patterns. African-violets may have variegated, crinkly, or veined leaves. Flowers vary from quarter-inch trumpets of *Sinningia pusilla* to four-inch flaring bells of streptocarpuses and gloxinias (*Sinningia speciosa*). Some gesneriads are evergreen. Others go dormant for part of each year.

Temperatures of 60° to 68° by night and into the high 70's by day suit the majority of cultivated gesneriads, which is an important reason for their popularity; they thrive in the same temperatures we prefer in our homes in the cold months. Humidity above 50 percent, to 60 percent if possible, is required for their best health. Species grown mainly for foliage grow satisfactorily in diffuse light; those grown mainly for flowers should have bright-diffuse light. All kinds thrive under fluorescent growth lamps where it is easy to control light intensity, duration, and temperature. And for all, a humus-rich soil with a high proportion of organic matter is correct.

The culture of gesneriads may be considered according to root habit, as fibrous episcias and saintpaulia, tuberous gloxinias and rechsteineria, scaly-rhizomed achimenes and smithiantha.

Fibrous-Rooted Genera

Aeschynanthus

Sometimes called lipstick-plant because of the tubular red flowers of several species, aeschynanthuses are graceful trailers, usually grown in hanging baskets. Gesneriad specialists list about ten species and several hybrids. The more common species may be found on general houseplant lists.

A. lobbianus has yellow-throated red flowers, several together in clusters. My plants bloom all winter, rest awhile in late spring, then set buds again in summer. If well grown, aeschynanthuses will flower on and off throughout the year.

A. speciosus is one of my favorites for its large orange flowers freely produced in terminal clusters, set off by glossy leaves. *A. marmoratus* has olive-green brown-striped flowers against long pointed waxy leaves, mottled green and maroon, most atractive when light shines through the foliage. *A.* 'Black Pagoda' with red flowers and dark-green maroon-marbled leaves combines the features of these two species.

To simulate natural growing conditions of accumulated rotting organic matter in the crotches of jungle trees, I pot aeschynanthuses in a mixture of humus-rich soil with a sprinkling of medium to fine fir or redwood bark. Aeschynanthuses require brighter light than do African-violets, and supplemental fluorescent light, from fixtures hung above vines, will encourage a long blooming season. Less light means fewer flowers.

Some may stop growing for a few weeks in winter if the temperature drops below 65° to 70° at night. If your plant isn't making new growth, reduce watering, don't fertilize, and wait for new foliage to appear before resuming standard culture. Drafts, too much or too little watering, and damaged roots may cause lower leaves to drop. If this looks unsightly, cut back the stem to two inches, and improve culture. After blooming, cut back longest shoots to keep the plant shapely. Propagate by tip cuttings or seed.

Columnea

The South American and Central American columneas grow on moss-covered branches in the jungle, on fallen trees, and on large boulders matted with rotting vegetable debris—all places where their roots are kept moist but never standing in water. Cornell University has introduced some excellent hybrids, several of which bloom on and off all year. Individual hybridizers are further expanding the list of exciting everblooming kinds.

Since hybrids are generally more adaptable than the species from which they are bred, you might begin with a few of these Cornell clones and other hybrids offered in gesneriad catalogs. 'Oneidan', a red-orange Cornell selection, has a winter-through-spring blooming period. 'Joy' is an everblooming clone. Trailing 'Yellow Dancer' also blooms throughout the year. 'Yellow Dragon' has two-toned foliage, red underneath, green above. 'Robin', a Kartuz hybrid, has large red flowers continuously and small leaves on vigorous stems. A contrast to normally trailing columneas is 'Cornellian', an almost upright grower with dark-orange yellow-throated flowers and red-backed leaves.

Recent hybrids and the commonly grown fuzzy-leaved species *C. gloriosa*, *C. hirta*, and *C. tulae* have done well for me with nights at 62° to 68°, but 'Stavanger', a hybrid from northern Europe, needs nights in the 50's to bloom well.

Let the attractive berries develop from pollinated flowers on any established columnea. The fruit is interesting, and seeds within can provide new plants. Columneas are usually propagated by stem cuttings for named clones, and such tip cuttings may bloom while still in a rooting flat.

Episcia

Episcias require more warmth (65° to 70° nights) and humidity (to 70 percent) than do other gesneriads. With careful culture their downy leaves and glowing flowers provide year-round decoration. Smaller kinds—*E. dianthiflora*, *E.* 'Cygnet', and *E. lilacina*, for example—can be nicely grown in covered bowls or terrariums. Larger cultivars must have more room, as in a hanging basket, raised pot, or small strawberry jar.

Although episcias are grown mainly for their colored and beautifully veined foliage, they have attractive one- to two-inch flowers. Pinching out young runners increases leaf size and bloom, but you will want to keep most of the runners in a basket plant. I have grown single-stemmed specimens in four-inch plastic pots, kept all the runners pinched out, and developed very floriferous upright plants with especially large leaves.

'Acajou' and 'Silver Sheen' are red-orange-flowered cultivars with shiny silver leaves edged in marbled brown. For a lovely contrast 'Moss Agate' has glistening red flowers against quilted moss-green foliage, veined in silver. For smaller foliage, downy rather than glossy, and equally striking orange flowers on looser trailing stems, grow 'Colombia Orange'.

Velvet brown-green leaves veined silver-green and red-orange flowers are features of 'Bronze Queen' and 'Shimmer'. Deep-orange flowers and glossier bronze leaves are found on 'Canal Zone', which I find takes stronger sun than do other cultivars. Somewhat more difficult to please, since it requires very even root moisture and constant high humidity, is 'Pink Brocade' with a mélange of green, pink, and white variegations, almost clashing with the orange flowers. Easier but also with much pink in the leaves is 'Ember Lace', pink-flowered.

Even in a greenhouse some episcias begin to look bedraggled by late fall and may not regain full beauty until winter wanes. Don't throw them out just because a few leaves die; simply reduce watering, and stop fertilizing, but maintain high humidity and proper temperatures. After a month or two, new growth will start. I find that fluorescent lights and warm temperatures help most cultivars avoid these midwinter slumps. Propagate episcias by rooting runners or stem cuttings or by seed.

Hypocyrta

Hypocyrta species and hybrids are mostly trailing plants, smaller than the long vines of aeschynanthuses or columneas. Five or six species are generally available from specialists, all offered for their red or orange pouched flowers. *H. selloana* and *H. perianthomega* are upright twiggy growers. Other species do well in raised pots or baskets or staked on a small trellis. Look for *H. nummularia*, a small glossy-leaved trailer with reddish-orange flowers, marked yellow inside, tipped black.

A neat trailer with small closely set waxy green leaves and almost round flowers is *H. radicans*. A free-flowering sort for basket culture is *H. strigulosa*. Two hybrids by William Saylor are 'Rio', upright with green leaves and red flowers, and 'Tropicana' of spreading growth, dark-green leaves marked with dark red, and russet and wine-red flowers.

Propagate *Hypocyrta* by stem cuttings.

Nautilocalyx

Shiny olive-green to black-maroon foliage on upright stems one to two feet tall are the attraction in cultivated *Nautilocalyx* species. My favorite is *N. forgettii* of Peru, a species with yellow tubular flowers in the axils against wavy-margined green leaves patterned with red veins. *N. bullatus* is a robust sort with olive-green hairy crepe-textured foliage and small yellow flowers. *N. lynchii* from Colombia has shiny red-green leaves shaded purple underneath and small light-yellow flowers.

Pot *Nautilocalyx* in humus-rich soil or one of the soil-free mediums designed for gesneriads. Keep evenly moist, pinch stems for bushy growth, cut out older stems at the base as they begin to die; this will result in continuously attractive new foliage. My plants accept bright-diffuse light, and in winter full sun, but require dappled shade in hot summer.

Saintpaulia

Their range of flower shape, color, leaf form, and plant habit have earned for African violets worldwide love and attention. The relative ease of culture and propagation increase their popularity. The best way to decide which of the thousands of available African-violets to grow is by seeing plants in bloom and checking color-illustrated catalogs of dealers. Although every year a hundred or more new clones are introduced, there are some basic types that will be around for a long time, such as the Rhapsodies, developed specifically for their large flowers on robust plants.

For disease resistance, constant bloom, and adaptable nature, the various Rhapsodie clones are a wise choice. For smaller plants choose some minatures. Lyndon Lyon has introduced some delightful miniatures that bloom well on plants in 2½-inch pots, notably 'Tiny Blue' and 'Snow In'. Other miniatures with pink, purple, and maroon flowers are available.

For extra-large flowers grow some of the standard-size hybrids like 'Butterfly White', a huge double white with yellow stamens, 'Floral Fantasy', a double lilac with red-tinged foliage, and 'Triple Threat', a giant double pink. 'Helen Van Zele' is a Tinari hybrid of formal habit, semidouble ivory-white with frosted-pink wavy edges. Such clones require at least a foot square of space when they reach full mature splendor.

TRAILING TYPES

Saintpaulia grotei has been used to develop hybrids with a trailing habit, well suited to basket or strawberry-jar culture. The stems trail much like those of episcias and since the species is blue, most of the hybrids are in blue tones.

Saintpaulia magungensis is a miniature species from the lower warm humid Usambara slopes of Tanzania, where it creeps along a few inches above the shady ground. It is available from a few specialists (Lyndon Lyon; West Coast Gesneriads) and is being used as a parent for still more unusual trailing hybrids. Let the trailers develop multiple crowns and runners for the fullest display.

VARIEGATED FOLIAGE

Some African-violets are grown for their beautiful white- or gold-variegated leaves. One of my favorites, 'Wintergreen', has variegation most intense in the center and double blue and white flowers.

Variegated-leaved plants grow somewhat slower than green-leaved ones, but their culture is the same. If they have too acid a soil, the variegation is likely to be less pronounced. If so, a sprinkle of powdered dolomite limestone scratched into the soil will bring the pH to 6.5–6.8, best for African-violets of all types. Some growers report brighter variegated effects with cooler temperatures (to 65° at night) than plain green plants require but you will have to see how the plants react in your own house. I have found the unusual variegated hybrids just as easy as any other *Saintpaulia*.

Variegated types are at their most colorful when forming new leaves. Center foliage may be nearly white but blends into greener tones as leaves mature. Variegated clones are the result of a mutation or sport, so they are propagated by vegetative means (leaf cuttings, division).

SOIL

African-violets thrive in humus-rich soil such as those commercial mixtures formulated for gesneriads. There are many variations in growing mixtures for *Saintpaulia*, but the basic recipe for humus-rich soil is given in Chapter 3. You come out ahead by getting pasteurized packaged growing mediums and sticking to one that gives good results under your conditions.

POTS FOR SAINTPAULIA

Plastic or glazed pots are preferred over plain clay, since I find that leaf-damaging salts don't accumulate along the pot rim nearly so fast as they do with porous clay. Plain clay pots can be covered with aluminum foil or dipped in hot wax to coat the rims, but plastic pots are a lot easier and lighter to work with. See Chapter 4 for containers, including the wick-fed self-watering pots.

Pot with no more than two inches between plant center and pot rim. Overpotted plants look odd and usually suffer from the medium staying wet too long. Containers ½ to ⅓ the diameter of the plant are adequate. Thus a violet specimen eight inches across would be at home in a 2½- to 3-inch pot. Repot *Saintpaulia* when it is slightly dry; the foliage will be less likely to break.

TEMPERATURE

Once an African-violet is adjusted to its location, there should be no difficulty in having abundant bloom, fall through late spring, perhaps off and on all year with some clones. A temperature range of 65° to 68° at night with a few degrees warmer by day will produce moderate compact growth. A range several degrees warmer will produce somewhat faster growth but of equal health if enough light is available. In my collection blooms are most abundant with nights at 65°, and for young plants and propagations at 68° to 70°. African-violets are one of the few tropicals that thrive without much variation between night and day temperatures, but slightly cooler nights are not detrimental.

LIGHT

Professional growers have found that *Saintpaulia* will still grow well in low light (three hundred to four hundred footcandles) if the light hours are extended sixteen to eighteen hours per twenty-four. Even putting a plant under a table lamp for a few hours every evening is some help, but check Chapter 2 for details on better light arrangements. Cultivars with dark foliage and flowers accept more intense light than those with pastel flowers and lighter leaves.

At a window all thrive with bright-diffuse light in summer and direct sun in winter for abundant bloom. Higher-than-necessary light intensity increases bloom, but plants grown with the proper amount of light are more attractive. A great part of *Saintpaulia* charm is lovely foliage to provide a soft background for delicate flowers. Too strong light will yellow leaves and make foliage unnaturally compact.

Streptocarpus

Large-flowered streptocarpuses, the rexii hybrids, are popular florists' plants but can be easily raised at home with African-violet culture and temperatures several degrees cooler. Lesser known but equally rewarding are the species *S. caulescens* with small white-throated purple flowers on shiny-leaved ten- to twelve-inch plants, and succulent *S. saxorum*, a trailer with silver-haired foliage and abundant lavender flowers. This thick-leaved plant requires less water and more light than other streptocarpus.

Night temperatures of 60° to 65° are suitable for streptocarpuses, and in the winter most will endure nights in the 50's, but growth is retarded. Soil must dry slightly on top between waterings, for these plants are easily rotted by soggy roots; don't let the pots sit in water. Older plants may grow leaves that are difficult to keep off the plant tray or ground, so a hanging basket or inverted pot under them is the answer. In extreme cases you can cut back by one-third any foliage that is too long.

S. 'Constant Nymph' does well for me under fluorescent lights or in a south-east window. Larger flowers and plants are seen in the Weismoor and rexii hybrids which will bloom in six to eight months from seed. Some growers treat these as annuals, but they do propagate from divisions and leaf cuttings. *S. saxorum* will bloom in six months with diligent culture. Other species may mature more slowly, from fifteen to eighteen months. Many die after

producing flowers and must therefore be reproduced from seed or by frequently taken leaf cuttings.

The strange *S. dunnii* grows a single leaf one to three feet long and after
sixteen months produces a six- to eight-foot scape of rose to brick-red
flowers. Check the seed lists of gesneriad societies for rare species.

Tuberous Genera

Gloxinia

These handsome and best known of the tuberous gesneriads have been
favorite florists' and windowsill plants since the early 1900's, when hybrids
were developed by European nurserymen from the Brazilian *Sinningia speciosa*. A well-grown gloxinia is a spectacular plant indeed, with green hairy
leaves to form a perfect twelve- to fifteen-inch circle around brightly colored
three- to four-inch flowers. Some cultivars have spotted throats; others contrasting colors bordering the petals; and there are varieties with pure white,
red, and velvety deep-purple flowers.

Until a few years ago we had to be content with large-growing European
hybrids, but recently American hybridizers, like Ted Bona and Albert Buell,
have introduced a wide variety of new colors and growth habits. Now you
can grow double-flowered gloxinias, miniature hybrids that bloom in a three-
inch pot, and of course cultivars in new color combinations.

One of my favorite gloxinias is the slipper type. It has gracefully drooping
cornucopia-shaped flowers on plants normally smaller than standard hybrids.
S. regina has deep-purple slipper flowers on six- to nine-inch plants with
silver-veined foliage, red underneath. Another charming compact species is,
white-flowered glossy-leaved *S. eumorpha*, which thrives in my living-room
window where it puts on a six-week show although only in a three-inch pot.

S. eumorpha is used as a parent for some unusual X Gloxineras, hybrids
between *Sinningia* (*Gloxinia* in horticulture) and *Rechsteineria*. It usually
imparts compact growth and charming slipper-flower form to its hybrids.

GLOXINIA CULTURE

Gloxinias grow from a fleshy tuber, each of which will sprout several stems,
but in order to have a symmetrical plant, only one stem is usually allowed
to grow. Removed secondary shoots are excellent for propagation. Gloxinia
tubers are sold during their dormant period and are offered by mail-order
nurseries or in garden shops, where they may be seen packed in peat moss
or in plastic bags. Get your tubers from a reliable dealer to be sure that they
are fresh, clean, and undamaged by improper storage or shipping.

I start gloxinia tubers in flats filled with the propagating mix detailed in Chapter 5. With care in watering you can also plant dormant tubers directly in humus-rich soil, placing the top one half to one inch under the soil surface. Water once, put in a warm (68° to 75°) place with bottom heat, and don't apply any more water until roots and leaves are active. I pot standard-size hybrids in five- to six-inch azalea pots (three-quarter-size pots), usually plastic. Dwarf and minature growers are planted in two- to three-inch plastic pots.

LIGHT

Give gloxinias brighter light than for African-violets. They will accept direct sun in early morning even in the summer, and in fact, if you want compact plants, they should receive all the light possible short of turning foliage yellow. With too little light intensity the plants may well grow and bloom but will be quite tall, and flowering will be reduced. Under fluorescent tubes keep the foliage four to six inches away until buds begin, then lower the plants or lift the light fixture to give flowers room. My best plants are grown under fixtures with two forty-watt tubes, but even sturdier plants, and more of them, will result under fixtures of three or four bulbs.

SECONDARY BLOOM

If the top part of the stem is cut off, most gloxinias will produce a second crop of flowers before they go dormant. Cut off the topmost stem section with one set of leaves and the faded flowers. A new set of leaves and subsequent flowers should develop within two months. The freshly cut top section can be rooted whole, or each of its healthy leaves used for propagation, as outlined in Chapter 5.

DORMANCY

Gradually withhold water as tubers lose foliage. Pull off dried leaves, dust any cuts with Fermate or Rootone, and store the tuber in its pot in a dim place at 60° to 65°, as in a cellar or cool closet. Keep soil just moist enough to prevent tubers from shrinking; too much water will cause a dormant tuber to rot. Most cultivars stay dormant at least a month, some up to ten weeks.

When new growth begins (leaves look like kitten ears), begin gradual resumption of watering, and provide bright light. Don't fertilize until the shoot is at least an inch tall and foliage has opened fully. I let my gloxinias grow in the same soil for two years, but they can just as well be repotted each season as they are coming out of dormancy.

PROPAGATION

Propagate gloxinias from leaf cuttings, secondary shoots, or seed. With good culture they will have flowers five to six months after seed is sown.

Sinningia

Some of the charming *Sinningia* are miniatures, and one of them, *S. pusilla,* is the smallest gesneriad—a plant one inch high that often blooms constantly if grown well. 'White Sprite' is a pure-white cultivar of *S. pusilla.* Hybrids include 'Bright Eyes', with one-inch lavender flowers, and 'Dollbaby', a delicate blue-lavender that often stays in flower for months. Lavender-pink 'Cupid's Doll', a semiminiature that thrives in a 2½- to 3-inch pot, is actually a Gloxinera, from 'Dollbaby' crossed with a *Rechsteineria.* For all these tiny treasures give African-violet culture but higher humidity, to 70 percent (so they are excellent in terrariums). See Chapter 16 for more information on miniatures.

GLOXINERA (SINNINGIA X RECHSTEINERIA)

The first X Gloxinera I grew was old 'Rosebells'. It grew rangy, even with bright light, and I had to stake the stem, but when it reached two feet tall, delicate slippers of rosy pink opened at the top leaf junctions, and I forgot how tall it was. The newer hybrids do not grow so large but do have very showy flowers and lovely foliage.

Look for 'Alfred K', a compact, dark-leaved hybrid with tubular salmon-pink flowers, and 'Laurie', a white flower with yellow throat on a dark-green plant. Mine thrive in four-inch pots, as does 'Melinda', another compact grower. 'Clarice T' has salmon-red flowers over shiny dark-green foliage. Culture for X Gloxineras is the same as for gloxinias except that these will often stay in bloom longer by sending up one stem after the other, a trait inherited from *Rechsteineria.*

Rechsteineria

My favorite foliage plant is silver-leaved *R. leucotricha,* the only plant I have that everyone wants to pet. *R. cardinalis* is famous for fuzzy red flowers against wide medium-green foliage. Treat *Rechsteineria* plants like gloxinias except that the former may stay in growth longer due to their habit of sending up new stems soon after one finishes blooming. Eventually they will rest for a few weeks. Light for *R. leucotricha* need not be so bright as for species grown for flowers, but on the other hand it will accept very bright light if you have it to offer. The growth is more compact with strong light.

I find these plants easy to propagate from seed, and they flower within a year if grown under fluorescent growth lamps. Most species do well for me from stem cuttings, too, but *R. leucotricha* is reluctant to root under my conditions. It is so quick from seed that I still have enough plants.

R. cardinalis usually flowers around Christmastime, when its bright-red fuzzy flowers are an appropriate note against velvety green foliage. You can get this usually as a dormant tuber which is started into growth as for gloxinias. *R. cardinalis* has been playing an important part as a parent for unusual hybrids with *Sinningia*. Look for some of the miniatures created by Dr. Carl D. Clayberg, of the Connecticut Agricultural Experiment Station. X Gloxinera 'Pink Imp' grows two to three inches across as a flat rosette of downy foliage; tiny flowers, usually three or four, are lavender-pink with a red blush. 'Little Imp' is somewhat smaller and has a magenta blotch on each flower.

Rhizomatous Gesneriads

Achimenes

Achimenes, long popular in hanging baskets, are probably the best-known rhizomatous gesneriads. They grow from underground scaly rhizomes, as do *Kohleria, Seemannia*, and *Smithiantha*. When achimenes complete their summer blooming period, the foliage gradually dies back, but the rhizomes remain alive, waiting to sprout after several months' rest.

More than forty types of achimenes are available from gesneriad specialists. Some of the more adaptable cultivars are 'Ambroise Verschaffelt', white and purple; 'Jewel Pink', compact and glowing; 'Margarita', pure white; 'Purple King'; and 'Wetterlow's Triumph', a lovely flat flower, pink with yellow throat.

Grow achimenes with even moisture at the roots; if they get dry once growth has begun, they often go dormant again. Humus-rich soil, as for gloxinias or *Saintpaulia*, is fine. I put three rhizomes per six-inch pot, but with some of the smaller species like *A. andrieuxi* and *A. fimbriata* you can put as many as six rhizomes per pot for a full effect. Place the rhizomes in a horizontal position, cover with one inch of growing medium. Flowering is best in bright-diffuse light, even full sun if the medium stays moist and humidity 40 to 50 percent. The number of rhizomes per pot doubles each year, and they store best right in the pots (especially plastic pots); or they can be given a dormant rest while packed in vermiculite within a plastic bag. If rhizomes are slow to begin new growth, give them soil heat so that they are 5° to 10° warmer than the air. A soil-heating cable is effective. Achimenes are mainly summer-flowering plants, so they are not to be counted on for winter color.

Kohleria

Underground rhizomes of *Kohleria* may reach ten inches in length and can be broken into several sections to get a number of plants. *Kohleria* is erect, often requiring thin stakes, which I put in the soil after the rhizomes are planted so I don't injure any latent roots or rhizomes. A good plant to grow is *K. amabilis* with ornamental green foliage, heavily marked with purple, and rose-white spotted flowers. It will droop over the pot or basket if not staked. *K. lindeniana* is another possible hanging basket candidate; white flowers are spotted with violet. My favorite is 'Longwood' with large glowing velvety red flowers spotted white. Clusters of flowers are produced against fuzzy dark-green leaves which are blushed red below.

Grow *Kohleria* from rhizomes, from stem-tip cuttings, or from seed. As *Kohleria* finishes flowering you can cut back the older stalks to stimulate immediate new growth and thus keep a plant blooming on and off all year. After two or three flushes of flowers you can let the plant die down for a month or two of rest.

When you want to start it again, knock rhizomes out of the pot, break them into four- to five-inch sections, dust lightly with Rootone, and plant one section per four-inch pot. Water sparingly until new stems are well under way. Provide *Kohleria* with bright light for maximum growth; a window with three or four hours of sun each day or fluorescent lamps with growth tubes is satisfactory.

Seemannia

Seemannia latifolia, a rhizome-rooted Andean rain-forest gesneriad, will grow nicely under fluorescent lights or in a window with bright-diffuse light, somewhat less than required by *Kohleria*. A temperature range of 60° to 80° is correct. Glowing yellow and red flowers are produced throughout the year, and I find that the plant looks best in a hanging basket without staked stems. Since the stems don't get much over eight inches tall, unless staked, you can fit this under light fixtures, too. A four- to six-inch pot is large enough. Provide humus-rich soil to which you add one-third fine redwood or fir bark. Propagate as for *Kohleria*.

Smithiantha

The temple-bell, or *Smithiantha* grows from a sturdy one- to four-inch rhizome into a velvet-leaved plant six to fifteen inches tall, depending on the cultivar. Many kinds have attractive foliage in addition to clusters of bell-shaped flowers. Plant the rhizomes as for achimenes. It is difficult to ship plants without damaging the foliage, so dealers ship the rhizomes during each plant's dormant period.

I like 'Little Wonder', a dwarf *Smithiantha* with rose-yellow flowers and bronze-green leaves covered with red hairs. A sister, 'Little Tudor', has red-orange flowers and maroon-marked leaves. Both bloom well in four-inch pots. Cornell series hybrids grow to fifteen inches high. Names of green-leaved Cornell hybrids recall church bells, as in 'Abbey', peach; 'Cathedral', yellow-orange; and 'Vespers', orange-red. Cornell clones with red-marked plush foliage, worth growing even without the lovely blooms, are named for California missions: 'Capistrana', red-orange with spots; 'Carmel', cherry-red; 'San Gabriel', orange; and 'Santa Barbara', buff-orange.

Grow *Smithiantha* with humidity 50 to 60 percent to prevent bud blasting and foliage curl. My plants succeed under fluorescent lights or in a warm window where sun is direct in morning, diffuse or reflected later. Keep roots evenly moist but never soggy; rhizomes can store moisture and rot if too wet.

Culture Review

Soil

My favorite potting soils for gesneriads are commercial packaged formulas made especially for African-violets. I have had excellent results mixing a commercial soil-free medium like Black Magic with equal parts of Baccto Peat potting soil or Laviga mix. Some mixes require more fertilizer than others, so follow package directions. A slightly acid soil (pH 6.5 to 6.8) is best, and the commercial mixes are prepared with this in mind. Any mix for gesneriads must be porous and loose; and don't pot tightly—as you might do correctly with geraniums.

Fertilizer

Gesneriads are fertilized according to recommendations in Chapter 3. Plants grown under fluorescent lights require more water and fertilizer than the same plants under variable daylight conditions. Every three or four waterings, even for plants in wick pots, flush out the soil with plain water until water runs out of the drainage hole.

Water

Cold water will cause foliage spots on gesneriads. Water them with luke-warm or room-temperature water. Clean foliage with a gentle shower of warm water every few months, then let the leaves dry off in a temperate, shady, but airy place. For healthy foliage on active plants I mist with a quarter-strength fish-emulsion and chemical-fertilizer solution. This nutrient mist is not for resting plants.

Grooming

Remove faded flowers, and cut off dead foliage and damaged stems. *Saintpaulia* will often send up a second flowering stem from the leaf-crown junction if you cut rather than pull off the first faded flower stalk. Use pipe cleaners or a soft camel's-hair brush to clean leaves, but be sure not to spread insect pests. It's a good idea to wash brushes every few days or use throwaway Q-Tips. Small cuticle scissors are handy for trimming faded blooms, snipping out unwanted offshoots on African-violets, cleaning up dead leaves, and general pruning of miniature plants. Dip tools in alcohol or flame between plants to prevent spreading disease.

Propagation

Gesneriads propagate easily from seed, as outlined in Chapter 5. African-violets need six to nine months to ripen a seedpod, gloxinias usually two to three months, and other gesneriads somewhat less. For best germination sow seed as soon as it is ripe. For details on hybridizing see a specialized book such as Helen Van Pelt Wilson's *African-Violet Book*.

Gesneriads root readily as stem cuttings, and most will propagate from leaves. Large tubers sometimes form secondary tubers; scaly rhizomes are broken into sections for more plants (both outlined in Chapter 5). *Saintpaulia* and *Streptocarpus* can sometimes be divided after they form clumps.

Clinic for Gesneriads

Healthy gesneriads are the best testimony to your cultural techniques, but even well-grown plants are susceptible to attacks of insects. Mealybugs can enter your collection from infested gift plants or from garden plants in warm weather. Sometimes potting soil (unpasteurized) contains mealybugs or mealybug eggs and microscopic nematodes. If you discover mealybugs (see Chapter 18), treat plant with Cygon 2E, one-half teaspoon per gallon of warm water. Use this solution as a drench on the roots. It kills mealybugs in the soil.

Remove any mealybugs you can see. A cotton-tipped Q-Tip soaked in rubbing alcohol is a good tool. You may have to use a nail file to pick out mealybugs wedged in the leaf joints. Spray the plant with a solution of Cygon 2E, mixed two teaspoons per gallon of warm water. This will kill mealybugs that you miss getting by hand. An alternative to the spray is an application of V-C 13 systemic insecticide as directed on the container. This is absorbed by the plant and kills any sucking insects.

In two weeks, if you see any more mealybugs, repeat the spray treatment and of course keep infested plants isolated from other plants. Systemic insecticides in the soil will also help to control thrips, white flies, nematodes, and the tiny soil-dwelling symphilids. With African-violets it is important to use insecticides that have been proven safe for delicate indoor plants; otherwise, you could burn foliage and perhaps kill the plant. In my collection I have found Cygon, Kelthane, Malathion, V-C 13, and Dr. "V" soil insecticide to be safe on gesneriads when used as suggested on the containers.

Mites

Twisted foliage, excessive hairiness, stunted growth, distorted flowers, and blasted buds are symptoms of the tiny cyclamen mite. Gesneriads are susceptible to this almost microscopic pest. Female mites lay an average of six eggs per day over a period of several weeks. In under two weeks the eggs hatch. Young mites eat tender growth for a week, rest, and change into adults, which in turn live three more weeks, sucking juices from the plants' tender center foliage.

To destroy an infestation quickly, spray with Kelthane as directed on the container. If any damage results to the plant from recommended concentrations, you can cut the dose to one teaspoon per gallon water, but beware of such weak concentrations unless required to protect tender plants; weak insecticides just help pests develop resistance. The spray will kill mites but not their eggs, so every spray must be repeated again in a week. The best "treatment" for a serious pest like cyclamen mite is to throw away an infested plant before it can supply pests to the rest of your collection.

Since mites concentrate on tender center foliage at the crown, you can pick larger mature leaves off infested plants, wash the leaves in very warm water, mist with Kelthane, and root them in a covered plastic greenhouse or pot covered with a plastic bag (Chapter 5). Throw away the infested plant. When plantlets show from rooting leaves, mist again with Kelthane.

Crown Rot

A fungus disease that usually begins in tissue that has been injured can cause the whole plant to rot. Overwatering, water in the crown, and extreme alternation between dry conditions at the roots and soaking soil all make a plant more susceptible to rot troubles. The cure is to cut away all infected parts down and into sound tissue. If the plant is badly infected and most of it is brown or wilted, then save only a few healthy leaves. Throw away the rotted plant and root leaves as outlined in Chapter 5.

Keep any partially infected plant on the dry side; water only at the soil, not overhead. Provide good circulation of warm air but no cold drafts. By keeping your gesneriads in the best health through correct culture and environment you will be likely to avoid serious rot problems.

African-violets prosper if they are kept evenly moist. Don't let them go from a wilted dry state to an overwatered one. If you tend to overwater, work in some coarse perlite (Sponge-Rok) with your planting mix. This helps water to drain away but retains enough moisture in the soil to stop roots from drying. Let lower leaves wilt slightly until you learn to water just before that point is reached. Tuberous gesneriads can go quite some time without water, and at the extreme they just go dormant.

Culture Problems

Under less-than-ideal environmental conditions gloxinias and some other gesneriads suffer bud blast and leaf curl. To avoid such problems, keep humidity above 50 percent (see Chapter 3), and be sure that air circulation is good. Gesneriads need fresh air but never any direct drafts or rapid changes in temperature. If you are growing plants near a bottled-gas fixture, a stove, or heater, look into the possibility that bud blast may be caused by minute amounts of escaping manufactured gas. Natural gas is much less harmful, but enough of it leaking might cause blasting with gesneriads as it does with certain orchids.

In gloxinias and their hybrids overfertilization will frequently cause foliage to curl sharply under at the edges. The remedy is to water heavily several times in succession to wash away accumulated salts. Use only fertilizers formulated for tropical houseplants or recommended as safe (Peters, Hyponex, etc.). Some other formulas, made from outdoor crops, may be toxic to gesneriads. Leaf curl from overfertilization is much more common than cyclamen-mite leaf damage, which most growers first suspect.

Too much or too little water on roots of a plant in bud will also cause bud blast. If you are in doubt about when to water, grow two plants side by side. Water one when you think it needs it, but leave the second for three more days. See which does best. I notice that some gloxinias, even under ideal conditions, will open buds perfectly, but then the corolla will drop free of the connecting stem or calyx.

Such a dropped flower has many more days of life and can be floated in a shallow dish or saucer. If the flower is about a half inch in water, at the bottom end, it should last a week. Such fallen flowers are one of my favorite decorations for low candle-holders or for a centerpiece on the dining table.

Episcia 'Cameo', well displayed in a strawberry jar

Episcia 'Acajou' has bright-red flowers against silver foliage.

Episcia 'Cygnet' combines spots of *E. punctata* with fleshy green foliage and fringed flowers of dwarf *E. dianthiflora*.

Chain-hung twenty-watt fluorescent fixtures can be used under a shelf, in the basement, over plant stands. *Saintpaulia* thrives in lightweight Styrofoam pots under fluorescent tubes, here supplemented with low-wattage incandescent bulbs. It is best to keep pots on trays filled with moist gravel or coarse perlite, except for display as shown here. (*House Plant Corner*)

Gloxinera 'Laurie' produces compact stems and shiny foliage like its parent, *Sinningia eumorpha*. Flowers are soft white with a narrow yellow stripe in the throat.

Achimenes show wide variation in flower color and size. Good displays are created by a mixture of colors or by a contrast, as of a deep purple with a glowing yellow. (*Geo. W. Park Seed Company, Inc.*)

Kohleria 'Longwood', a vigorous hybrid for a bright window
or under lights

Smithiantha 'Little Tudor', a
red-leaved dwarf

12

Orchids for the House

SINCE THE EARLY YEARS OF THE EIGHTEENTH CENTURY, plant explorers have risked and sometimes lost their lives in search of rare orchids. From Sumatran jungles to high Andean gorges these men have collected thousands of species for the conservatories of wealthy amateur orchid fanciers and the greenhouses of commercial growers. Recent advances in techniques of hybridizing and propagating have made collecting wild plants less necessary and less profitable, and fortunately the increasing emphasis on conservation in many nations has spread some measure of protection over what species still enjoy their natural homes.

Now, with modern growing methods, you are offered extraordinary orchids at reasonable prices. Even a rare award-winning clone that may have brought over one thousand dollars per division twenty years ago can be yours for fifteen dollars, because of the extraordinary advances in tissue-culture propagations. Better understanding of how to grow orchids away from their habitats and the increased adaptability of hybrids make it possible for you to succeed with many orchids in your window, sun-room, or under lights anywhere.

These exotic plants are so diverse in manner of growth, leaves, flower structure and size, and even fragrance that you could make a lifetime hobby of growing and studying them. The flowers generally last for many weeks, several are pleasantly fragrant, and they occur in all imaginable colors—pure, delicate, muted, brilliant, bold, somber, murky, and fiery. The stems may reach fifteen feet or mature at half an inch, hidden by blooms larger than the plant itself. Some flowers must be examined under a magnifying glass; others extend to ten or more inches across. Certain odontoglossums thrive with chilly 40° to 50° nights, and other orchids from lower elevations will prosper with 65° to 68° nights, the same range we prefer.

Most orchids grow from creeping rhizomes producing upright stems (as in *Epidendrum ibaguense*) or swollen pseudobulbs (as in cattleyas) each growing season. Such orchids are called *sympodial* for their successive upright stems. Sympodial orchids can be divided every few years because each new stem is complete with a growing point and one or two dormant buds on the rhizome below every stem. Several stems or pseudobulbs constitute a sturdy division.

A few orchids have a monopodial plant habit, or single growing point that elongates steadily without branching. *Angraecum, Ascocentrum, Phalanopsis*, and *Vanda* are some showy monopodial orchid genera. Their growth style prevents frequent division, but they do produce offsets and plantlets on old flower spikes.

How to Begin

Hybrid orchids are generally easier to grow than species, but some of the more rugged species are relatively easy to bring to bloom and have such beauty that it would be a pity to restrict your orchid collection to hybrids. For both types, begin by growing flowering-size plants. Leave the seedlings and more demanding small divisions and back-bulb propagations until you have had success with sturdy mature specimens.

Commercial growers offer attractive collections of flowering-size orchids at fair prices; they are always upgrading their stock with new hybrids and will often sell multilead cattleya hybrids in six- to eight-inch pots for less than six dollars, much more if you want them in flower of course. Some dealers offer collections that include a plant to flower every month of the year; others will send every month a plant that is ready to flower.

Mature specimens of the popular genera seldom cost more than ten dollars per plant unless you get them when they have flowers. Select clones propagated by tissue culture (meristems) are gradually making outstanding named orchids available as flowering-size plants for thirty dollars or less. Similar-size divisions of select clones used to cost hundreds of dollars a few years ago. You don't have to be rich to grow fine orchids.

Kinds to Grow

With over 24,000 species and many more man-made hybrids to choose from I have had drastically to restrict my listing in this broad-spectrum book to those types that are most adaptable and generally available. Plants of the genera listed have grown well for me without special fussing but not without love.

In addition to the hybrid genera which were made by crossing two natural genera, there exist numerous others, each containing several combinations of genera. *Potinara*, for example, combines *Brassavola, Cattleya, Laelia*, and *Sophronitis*. You will find other created genera in catalogs of orchid specialists. By understanding the genera and species in each man-made combination you will be able to predict something about the probable character of the offspring.

Here are some select species and hybrids with which to begin:

Angraecum. Epiphytic, white-flowered, night-fragrant, mainly from Madagascar and nearby islands. Best for window and small greenhouses are *A. comorense, A. sesquipedale*, and the hybrids Ol Tukai (*A. comorense* X *A. sesquipedale*), Orchidglade (*A. sesquipedale* X *A. giryamae*), and the oldest hybrid, Veitchii (*A. sesquipedale* X *A. eburneum*). Check catalogs for new dwarf and miniature hybrids which are still rare. Epiphytic mix kept evenly moist, bright light, intermediate to warm temperature.

Ansellia africana. An African species with one- to three-foot canes in a neat compact clump, sprays of yellow flowers spotted dark brown, long lasting. Grow in clay pot with epiphytic mix, keep moist when growing, with fertilizer every other watering, then drier when growth is completed. Usually blooms in winter. Bright light, intermediate to warm temperatures. May be listed as *Ansellia gigantea* or *A. nilotica*.

Ascocentrum. Dwarf six- to ten-inch Thailand monopodial epiphytes with sprays of upright bright-rose flowers in *A. ampullaceum*, orange-red in *A. curvifolium*, yellow-orange in *A. miniatum*. Delightful hybrids with vandas are Ascocendas, compact adaptable bright-flowered dwarfs, better indoors than pure vandas or ascocentrums. Grow these (species or hybrids) in bright light, in relatively small pots with tree-fern or bark mix; keep lightly moist, intermediate to warm.

Aspasia principissa. Epiphytic thin-leaved plant under one foot tall, waxy yellow-green blooms marked brown, white lip turning yellow with age. Easy in bright location. Keep lightly moist until new growth is complete, then dry between waterings. New hybrids with *Brassia* make adaptable Brapasia.

Brassavola. Epiphytes from tropical America. White to yellow flowers, fragrant, long lasting, compact growth, eight to twelve inches tall. *Brassavola (Rhyncholaelia) digbyana* passes its six-inch fringed lip on to numerous hybrids, is worth growing for glaucous foliage, giant night-fragrant, white to creamy-green flowers. Thrives in sharply drained epiphytic mix or on a thick slab of tree fern, needs strong light. *B. glauca,* under eight inches, has four-inch waxy white fragrant flowers, contributes compact growth and wide lip to hybrids. Easiest to grow and most floriferous is *B. nodosa,* lady-of-the-night orchid, bearing sprays of night-fragrant white flowers as new growths are completed, often several times a year. Culture as for *B. digbyana* but keep watering if it wants to continue growing (in contrast to *B. digbyana* that will rest a month or more). A rare, recently remade hybrid is starlike B. David Sander (*B. digbyana* X *B. cucullata*) with dark-green terete foliage tinged maroon, six-inch fringe-lipped white flowers. *Brassavola* plants are intermediate to warm growers, bloom best with bright light.

Brassia. Evergreen epiphytes of tropical America, sprays of spidery white to yellow, brown-spotted flowers on compact thin-leaved plants ten to fifteen inches high. Good species are *B. gireoudiana* with eight- to twelve-inch sprays of fragrant yellow-brown-blotched flowers; *B. maculata,* greenish-yellow with white lip spotted purple; *B. verrucosa* with four- to six-inch fragrant greenish-white purple-spotted flowers. Hybrids between *Brassia* species are especially adaptable and beautiful. New creations of *Brassia* crossed with related *Aspasia* (Brapasia) and *Oncidium* (Brassidium) produce compact gems with unusual flowers. Pot in epiphytic mix, provide bright-diffuse light, intermediate to warm.

Broughtonia sanquinea. Dwarf, pink-to-red-flowered Jamaican for culture on bark or tree-fern slab in full sun. Hybrids with cattleyas and epidendrums are also dwarf, best grown on slabs or in small clay pots. Intermediate temperature.

Bulbophyllum. This is the largest genus of orchids, comprising more than one thousand species from the Old and New World tropics. Two excellent fall-to-winter blooming dwarf species are *B. medusae* and *B. guttulatum* (*umbellatum*). These two thrive in diffuse light, intermediate to warm temperature, and in small containers with the epiphyte mix or grown on a slab with sphagnum moss at roots.

Catasetum. Epiphytic Latin American species with stiff sprays of intricate two- to five-inch flowers, usually male or female but sometimes bisexual. *C. integerrimum* has erect racemes of yellow-green purple-spotted flowers. *C. pileatum* has a wide-lipped yellow-to-white fragrant flower from six- to eight-inch pseudobulbs. *C. warscewiczii* is dwarf with pendent flower spikes. *C. viridiflavum* has a green-to-yellow goblinlike flower. Grow in small pots of epiphyte mix kept lightly moist, then dry as plants rest; many will lose all leaves.

Provide bright light, intermediate to warm temperature, and keep water out of new growth.

Cattleya. Cattleyas are epiphytes four to more than one hundred inches tall, with pseudobulbs and large usually fragrant flowers. Hybrids are improvement over species for vigor, shape, color variations, and growth habit. By crossing cattleyas with related genera (*Brassavola, Epidendrum, Laelia,* and *Sophronitis,* for example) hybridists create orchids with large flowers on small plants, new colors, and extended blooming seasons. Some nice species, backbones of modern hybrids, include *C. aurantiaca,* glowing orange-to-red cluster-flowered bifoliate species for early spring bloom; *C. intermedia* with lavender or white heavy-substanced flowers popular in hybridizing; *C. labiata,* a fall-blooming lavender with two to five flowers per stem; and *C. trianaei,* the national flower of Colombia, winter-blooming and cultivated in many varieties. Cattleya should be soaked well when growing, then permitted to dry out at the roots before being soaked again; bright light for best bloom, intermediate temperature.

Chysis. Epiphytes with pendulous ten- to twelve-inch pseudobulbs and flower spikes. Leaves usually drop when growth is complete, a signal to cut down on watering until new eyes sprout. *C. bractescens* has fragrant white three-inch flowers; the hybrid Chelsonii (*C. bractescens* X *C. laevis*) is adaptable yellow-to-orange flowered. Culture as for *Catasetum* except that *Chysis* is especially good in baskets. Flowers appear from half-completed new growth.

Comparettia macroplectrum. Light-lavender flowers on a graceful spray from a four- to six-inch-high plant. Easy on slabs of tree fern or in small pots of bark mix, intermediate to warm range, lightly moist, good air circulation, bright-diffuse light.

Cycnoches ventricosum warscewiczii (*C. chlorochilon*). The swan orchid is easy with intermediate to warm conditions and culture as for *Catasetum.* This fragrant species has four- to six-inch yellow flowers with a prominent white lip from October to December.

Cymbidium. The intermediate- to warm-growing miniature-flowered hybrids are dwarfer than standard hybrids and will flower without cool fall rests. Good ones are rose-cream Flirtation; yellow, fragrant Peter Pan; and Tiger Tail, yellow with red-spotted white lip. There are many more. Pot in semiterrestrial mix, give strong light to direct sun, fertilize every other watering until growths are completed in fall, and keep evenly moist.

Dendrobium. A genus mainly from New Guinea and Australia, containing almost as many species as *Bulbophyllum.* Range from creeping *D. cucumeri-*

num to the large *D. taurinum* with three-foot pseudobulbs, sometimes grown as garden plants in the tropics. In between are the *D. nobile* hybrids and *D. phalaenopsis* types with one- to two-foot stems. Grow yellow-flowered *D. aggregatum* and *D. cucumerinum* on tree-fern slabs or bark sections, and give dry rest when new pseudobulbs have formed. The *nobile* hybrids require small pots of bark or fern-root mix kept evenly moist when plants are active, then a cool dry rest until buds are seen along the canes. Some leaves may drop. Too high night temperatures (above 55°) will decrease blooms and cause many plantlets to form instead. *D. phalaenopsis*, in shades of white to deep red-purple, are grown the same way except that they don't require a cool rest; leaves are more evergreen. All dendrobiums need bright light for abundant blooming.

Doritis pulcherrima. A genus of only one variable species. Resembles a small stiff upright *Phalaenopsis* orchid. Flower spike is upright, too, with small pink-to-dark-purple flowers. This has been crossed with *Phalaenopsis* to create Doritaenopsis, mostly pink-flowered hybrids with excellent long-lasting flowers on upright to gently arching stalks. Culture as for *Phalaenopsis* except that these hybrids will accept more light and require somewhat less watering.

Epidendrum. A large American genus of spray-flowered orchids, some with pseudobulbs, like fragrant *E. aromaticum* (brown-yellow) and *E. atropurpureum* (rose and white), others with reed stems as in fire-red *E. ibaguense* *(E. radicans)*. All require bright light and intermediate temperature. Many are small enough to be excellent choices for fluorescent-light gardens. Mount smaller species on tree-fern or cork-bark slabs; pot larger growers in baskets or containers with bark or tree-fern mixes. Good species to begin with, besides those already mentioned, are *E. cochleatum*, almost perpetually produced flowers, yellow-green with cockleshell deep-purple lip; *E. secundum*, reed-stemmed with orange to red flowers; and *E. tampense*, honey-scented brownish-gold flowers from southern Florida and the Caribbean. Hybrids of *Epidendrum* with *Cattleya* and *Laelia* make compact adaptable orchids with numerous flowers. A good dwarf reed stem is Epiphronitis Veitchii (*E. radicans* X *Sophronitis grandiflora*), which I find thrives under fluorescent wide-spectrum lamps.

Laelia. A genus of dwarf to two-foot epiphytes with blooms that rival cattleyas in color, size, and abundance. *L. anceps* is under one foot high, but the four-inch lavender flowers are produced at the end of a two- to three-foot stalk. *L. flava*, a cheerful yellow, has cylindrical pseudobulbs, a characteristic it transmits to hybrids. *L. purpurata* resembles a cattleya plant but is somewhat slimmer, about two feet tall, has six- to nine-inch open-form freely borne flowers with deep-colored lips. It is used in hybridizing to contribute these rich velvety purple lips. *L. tenebrosa* as a parent contributes copper-yellow color and purple lip. One of its best primary hybrids is Lc. Martinetii (*Cattleya mossiae* X *L. tenebrosa*), a spring-flowering plant with six-inch bronze-lavender fragrant flowers. A dwarf species that thrives on a tree-fern slab or in a small clay pot is *L. rubescens,* which in spring has up to eight lavender-to-white two-inch flowers on a ten-inch stalk.

Leptotes bicolor. A miniature Brazilian with one- to two-inch fragrant flowers, white with rose lip. Grown on fern-root slab in bright-diffuse light, warm to intermediate range.

Lowara. A man-made genus from *Brassavola, Laelia,* and *Sophronitis.* Mainly dwarf fringe-lipped flowers in yellow, orange, or red tones. Grow with cattleyas; thrives under bright fluorescent light.

Maxillaria. A large genus with many rank growers, usually tiny flowers on large plants but *M. tenuifolia* is restrained, worth growing for its white- or yellow-striped one- to two-inch red flowers which are heavily fragrant of coconut. Small creeping rhizomes are best mounted on tree-fern slab or pole. *M. sanderiana* from Andean peaks, is a cooler grower, has striking white five-inch flowers marked red. Give these bright-diffuse light, no hot sun; keep evenly moist when growing, dry between waterings when inactive.

Meiracyllium. Miniature creeping epiphytes doing best in bright light, intermediate temperatures. Mount the tiny plants on a tree-fern slab. *M. wendlandii* has one-inch lavender-purple flowers long lasting. *M. trinasutum* is similar, not quite so robust.

Miltonia. An American genus of epiphytes; some from high altitudes as cool-preference *M. phalaenopsis, M. roezlii,* and *M. vexillaria*; some from lower regions, as *M. flavescens, M. regnelli,* and *M. spectabilis.* The warmer-growing hybrids, like Miltonia William Kirch, are best indoors or under fluorescent light and intermediate temperature with nights around 65°. Most warm growers have lasting flowers in shades of yellow marked with purple or brown. Cool growers have flowers that are striking on the plant but don't last when cut. Grow miltonias in medium-grade bark or fern-root mixtures, keep evenly moist but perfectly drained, and provide bright-diffuse light. Hybrids with *Brassia* (Miltassia) and *Oncidium* (Miltondium) create lovely new forms and color combinations, usually many flowers in arching sprays. *M. warscewiczii* is a favorite intermediate-growing plant to produce offspring with curly-edged, long-lasting flowers.

Mormodes colossus. A caramel-colored flower produced on stiff scapes from twelve- to fifteen-inch-high plants. Grow as for *Catasetum.*

Neofinetia falcata (Angraecum falcata). Dwarf monopodial orchid with sprays of white vanilla-scented flowers. It thrives in a pot of fern or bark mix, bright-diffuse light, and intermediate temperature. Mine flowers on and off throughout the year, chiefly in winter. Hybrids with *Ascocentrum*, like Ascofinetia Peaches (*Neofinetia falcata* X *Ascocentrum curvifolium*), produce dwarf offspring with great bunches of pastel flowers. Ascofinetia Peaches in my collection has upright fist-sized clusters of pink flowers that almost hide the eight-inch plant.

Odontoglossum. Epiphytes, mainly cool growers from the Andes, but a few will succeed under intermediate conditions. Try *O. bictoniense*, a fragrant yellow-and-white, brown-marked flower with wide white lip, upright stalk, plant about twelve inches high; *O. grande* with four-inch yellow, brown-barred flowers from a squat plant under eight inches high; *O. pendulum* with pendent ten-inch scapes of fragrant white flowers, sometimes flushed pink, compact six- to eight-inch growth. Hybrids of *Odontoglossum* with *Oncidium, Miltonia, Brassia*, and the red-flowered *Cochlioda* create numerous forms and colors, many suitable for growing under intermediate conditions in the greenhouse, under fluorescents, or in a bright window. Flower stalks may reach three feet long, but growth is normally compact. Pot in small containers of bark or tree-fern mix, and keep evenly moist, slightly drier when growth is complete. *O. crispum* hybrids are cool growers (50° to 55° nights).

Oncidium. More than 750 species are included in this American genus of spray-flowered epiphytes. Dwarf fan-shaped succulent-leaved species grow best in very bright light, attached to slabs of tree fern or on driftwood branches, coffee trees, or *Codiaeum*. Good ones are hybrids of equitant species and *O. intermedium*, yellow, *O. pulchellum*, pink, and *O. variegatum*, white, marked brown. Similar is *O. henekenii*. Thin-leaved species thrive in pots of bark or fern-root mix kept evenly moist to slightly dry between waterings. *O. varicosum* and its hybrids are glowing-yellow thin-leaved sorts.

The mule-ear types, like *O. carthaginense*, the fragrant-flowered *O. lanceanum*, waxy *O. luridium*, and *O. splendidum* need sharp drainage, bright light, rather small pots (clay is usually best), and must be dry for more than a month once growth is complete. With high humidity they succeed on sturdy tree-fern slabs. Most produce long-lasting flowers in red-brown and yellow tones marked magenta. *O. splendidum* has chrome-yellow lip, brown-barred tepals. An excellent hybrid is O. Kalihi. Some good species are dwarf yellow-flowered *O. ampliatum*, under 6 inches tall but with a three-foot spray of 1½-inch flowers; dwarf, purple-flowered *O. ornithorhynchum*; and floriferous *O. sphacelatum* with small yellow flowers in three- to four-foot arching sprays, the plant to 15 inches, not for small spaces.

Numerous hybrids between *Oncidium* and other genera have created new colors, forms, and variations, of which Colmanara Sir Jeremiah, combining *Odontoglossum, Oncidium*, and *Miltonia* is a fine example.

Thin-leaved oncidiums require bright-diffuse light; the thick-leaved types, direct sun. Complex hybrids such as Colmanara generally thrive with intermediate temperature.

Ornithocephalus bicornis. A dwarf epiphyte, fan-shaped cluster of flat gray-green foliage, sprays of tiny fuzzy white flowers. A blooming plant will fit into a 1½-inch pot or on a small tree-fern chunk. Bright-diffuse light, intermediate temperature, lightly moist.

Paphiopedilum. This Asian genus was formally listed as *Cypripedium* but differs in technical details; and cypripedia are entirely in the North Temperate zone. Both, however, have the same "lady-slipper" flower shape. *P. bellatulum* is dwarf, has mottled leaves and white two- to three-inch flowers spotted purple; *P. niveum* is similar; both are intermediate to warm growers for diffuse light or good under fluorescents. The hybrid Maudiae has marbled foliage, blooms several times a year, and also thrives under intermediate conditions. The award-winning clone 'Magnificum' is robust.

Since these require less light than cattleya-type orchids, they are excellent choices for windowsill collections or for growing under artificial light. Pot *Paphiopedilum* plants in semiterrestrial mix, and keep moist. Give fertilizer (like 10-30-20) monthly when new growths are being made; don't let roots dry out; keep water out of leaf centers and flower pouch. Hybrids without mottled foliage are usually cooler growers, to 55° at night.

Phaius tancarvilliae. The terrestrial nun orchid produces a one- to two-foot upright inflorescence of three- to four-inch white flowers in the spring and summer. Each bloom is white on the outside, reddish-brown within. The lip is veined with purple, and the tepals form an arching hood. Pot in terrestrial or semiterrestrial orchid mix, keep lightly moist, and give frequent fertilizer when active, bright-diffuse light, and intermediate to warm temperature.

Phalaenopsis. A delightful genus known as moth orchids. Fine choices for a window with diffuse light or under fluorescents, since these are warm growers and don't need bright sun to grow and flower—in fact, they should be protected from direct sun in spring and summer. *Phalaenopsis* orchids are tropical Asian epiphytes with sprays of flowers from less than an inch across up to six or eight inches in some modern hybrids. Flowers are long lasting, sometimes fragrant, as in *P. violacea* and *P. lueddemanniana*, both plants under eight inches with two-inch waxy flowers in lavender to yellow tones, darker magenta markings. *P. equestris* has one- to two-foot sprays of one-inch pink, dark-lipped flowers. I have some *Phalaenopsis* flowers that last more than forty days in perfection. When flowers fade, cut back the inflorescence only three quarters of the way, leaving several nodes. A secondary spike will usually sprout from the topmost joint of the cut-back inflorescence. Pot these species in bark or fern-root mixes, keep evenly moist, and provide diffuse light, some early-morning sun, and warm temperatures.

Most mature *Phalaenopsis* plants, although warm growers, will set buds or initiate flower spikes best with a few weeks of cooler than usual nights, down to 55°, but they can be grown and flowered without this step when they are seedlings. My *Phalaenopsis* thrives with nights 65° to 68° except for slightly cooler nights in late fall into winter. *Phalaenopsis* crossed with *Renanthera* produces Renanthopsis hybrids with yellow to orange flowers. Plants are dwarf, under one foot tall, and require more light than straight *Phalaenopsis*.

Pleurothallis. Tropical American epiphytes, mainly compact species from medium to high altitudes, with stalks of tiny flowers in green, yellow, and maroon. Grown in small pots, diffuse light, no hot sun, lightly moist at the roots, intermediate to cool conditions. Satisfactory under fluorescent lights. Flowers best appreciated under magnifying glass.

Potinara. A man-made genus combining *Brassavola, Cattleya, Laelia*, and *Sophronitis* to produce hybrids in dark-lavender to red tones and recently in orange and yellow. The plants are smaller than the standard cattleya type. My *Potinara* plants thrive under fluorescent lamps, appreciate somewhat more moisture than most of the cattleya alliance, and do well with intermediate temperature.

Renanthera. Monopodial epiphytes with long sprays of small red or red-spotted yellow flowers; need bright light. *R. imschootiana* (to three feet) and *R. monachica* (to two feet) are practical indoors; the brilliant red color of the former is rather rare in orchids. There are hybrids of dwarf stature. Species have been crossed with *Phalaenopsis* to create dwarf-growing Renanthopsis in yellow or orange shades. Plant in sharply drained pots, keep evenly moist, intermediate to warm temperature.

Schomburgkia. Closely related to the laelias, these American tropicals require more light and room for their two- to four-foot inflorescence. Pseudobulbs are hollow; in the jungle usually filled with ants. Hybrids with *Cattleya* and *Laelia* make adaptable orchids with curly flowers. *S. thompsoniana* is the most compact species, about eight to twelve inches high, with its hybrids producing bronze-toned flowers on fifteen- to twenty-four-inch spikes.

Sophronitis. Dwarf Brazilian epiphytes with one-inch orange flowers in *S. cernua*, bright scarlet in *S. coccinea (grandiflora).* The species are cool growing, need high humidity, more moisture at the roots than cattleyas or laelias, but *Sophronitis* crossed with related genera produces adaptable hybrids for intermediate conditions. Primary hybrids are the smallest in plant and flower; later generations become larger as influence of dwarf *Sophronitis* dwindles; Sophrolaelia Psyche (*S. coccinea* X *L. cinnabarina*) is an excellent hybrid, under eight inches tall, with two- to three-inch fiery-orange flowers several times a year.

Stanhopea. Warm-growing Latin American epiphytes with fragrant flowers on sharply pendulous inflorescence. Most species have five to eight three- to six-inch flowers. I like creamy-white *S. oculata*, which smells like chocolate. *S. wardii* has spectacular yellow flowers dotted purple. Grow in open-bottom baskets of osmunda, give diffuse light, keep well fertilized and lightly moist when growing, then somewhat drier as growths are completed. Clumps of four to six pseudobulbs bloom better than larger plants.

Stelis. Dwarf two- to six-inch epiphytic or rock-dwelling tropical American species related to *Pleurothallis.* The tiny triangle-shaped flowers on two- to four-inch scapes are fascinating under a magnifying glass. A nice species for intermediate conditions is maroon-flowered *S. ciliaris.* Pot in bark mix or mount on tree-fern slab, and keep lightly moist in diffuse light.

Trichocentrum. South American epiphytes resembling a dwarf *Oncidium lanceanum* with fleshy leaves, small pseudobulbs, but large (two-inch) waxy fragrant bronze-yellow flowers. The lip is purple below and rose above, or white and rose in the rather similar species *T. albo-coccineum.* Slightly larger, with tepals heavily spotted brown, is *T. tigrinum.* Grow in small clay pots of bark or fern mix or slabs of tree fern or cork bark. Provide bright-diffuse light so that foliage blushes gently rose, give good air circulation but humidity above 60 percent, lightly moist at the roots but never soggy.

Trichopilia. Compact fragrant-flowered epiphytes from Central and South America for intermediate to warm culture. Seldom more than six inches tall. Good species are *T. suavis*, stalk of several four-inch creamy-white fragrant flowers spotted rose; and *T. tortilis* with a pendulous stalk of one or two waxy fragrant white-lipped flowers, greenish-yellow tepals. Grow in small pots of fern or bark mix kept evenly moist in diffuse light. Keep clump of pseudobulbs raised slightly in pot so pendulous stalks can expand freely.

Vanda. An Asian genus of monopodial epiphytes made famous by conspicuous utilization in Hawaiian leis. The narrow terete-leaved types (*V.* Miss

Joaquim, *V. teres*) need so much strong sun that they are suitable only for greenhouse culture or outdoor garden beds in the tropics. Strap-leaved hybrids like blue-toned *V.* Rothchildiana (*V. sanderiana* X *V. caerulea*) and pink-flowered *V.* Manila (*V. luzonica* X *V. sanderiana*) succeed in locations that get five to six hours of direct sun daily; less light means fewer or no flowers. Grow vandas in well-drained pots with large-grade fir bark or tree-fern chunks, slightly dry between waterings to encourage healthy roots. I use chunks of charcoal and gravel for sharp drainage and let the aerial roots hang free or provide a tree-fern pole for them to cling to. For growing under lights or in limited space get the Ascocenda hybrids, delightful crosses of *Asco-centrum* with *Vanda*, which grow six to ten inches high and have stalks of one- to three-inch flowers in shades from pink through orange to mulberry. Grow the strap-leaved vandas and their hybrids intermediate to warm; fertilize well when in growth.

Zygopetalum. Semiterrestrial South American intermediate growers with upright stalks of fragrant 3-inch flowers. Adaptable species are *Z. crinitum*, with inflorescence more horizontal, 12 to 18 inches long, three to ten waxy green flowers marked reddish brown, white frilly lip; *Z. intermedium*, tightly clustered pseudobulbs, erect inflorescence 20 to 28 inches high, yellow-green flowers, usually three to five, barred down, white lips with purple lines; *Z. mackayi*, like *Z. intermedium* but with larger flowers, to 3¼ inches on a three-foot stalk. Pot *Zygopetalum* plants in a semiterrestrial mix, keep lightly moist, avoid water settling in new growth, fertilize every other watering as new growths are made, and give bright-diffuse light and good air circulation. Flowers usually last more than a month.

Mediums and Cultures

Epiphytes

With roots adapted to exposure in freely circulating air the epiphytes require open porous mediums. Their roots are primarily for clinging and quick absorption of moisture, even light dews, and are not like the fine fibrous roots of begonias or geraniums. In regions of Central America I noticed that orchids survive through normal dry seasons of up to six months by absorbing night dew.

One Salvadorian epidendrum I examined had a root system several feet long, running over the tree branch on which the plant grew, down the tree trunk, and penetrating a few inches into gravelly soil. I saw similar adaptations on dry Caribbean islands where epiphytic orchids growing on cacti sent roots into the sandy soil but always where drainage was sharp and most of the roots were exposed to light and air.

Suitable basic materials for potting epiphytes are:

Fir bark and redwood bark (fine, medium, and coarse grinds).
Osmunda fiber (from the osmunda swamp fern).
Tree-fern fiber (fine, medium, coarse; also poles and carved pots).
Sphagnum moss (unmilled coarse natural strands).

Additives to blend with these include coarse builder's sand, rough-ground sphagnum peat moss, perlite, pea gravel, chicken grit, and charcoal. In some tropical areas coconut fiber and lava ash are used. Fir bark, fiberized redwood bark called bark wool, and large-grind perlite (Sponge-Rok) make a good mixture. The commercial mediums prepared by orchid firms for epiphytic orchids are excellent and convenient to have on hand. I recommend these: Dimmick redwood bark products (usually to be mixed with other materials; I use coarse perlite), Lager & Hurrell Mix, McLellan Wonderbark Mix, Fred A. Stewart Mix for cattleyas, and Weyerhaeuser Silvabark Mix.

Prepared potting mixtures are used as they come, unless your own cultural practice indicates modifications. I find that in plastic pots these mixtures, especially those with bark fiber or "wool," may stay wet too long for orchids that should dry out rapidly, so I use clay pots in these cases or dilute the mix with coarse perlite, charcoal chunks, or gravel.

Three parts tree-fern fiber and one part coarse perlite are a combination in which many of my orchids thrive. Since bark and tree-fern mixes do not contain enough nutrients for orchids, fertilizer is required on active plants. Usually a 30-10-10 for bark mixtures and a balanced 18-18-18 for tree-fern mixes. Some steamed bone meal, blood meal, superphosphate, and similar products can be combined with the potting mixture, but it is safer to control fertilizing by using water-soluble products made for orchids grown in the home. With orchids under lights or outdoors for the summer and in terrestrial mixes the solid organic materials mentioned are suitable. I often sprinkle some steamed bone meal around orchids that are outdoors for the summer.

Plain osmunda fiber is a useful material for potting anthuriums, bromeliads, and some orchids, but it must be cut into walnut-sized chunks, and practice is required to pot with it correctly. Get only well-washed fiber, preferably fumigated. If mold develops, spray lightly with Fermate. Osmunda contains enough nutrients to support epiphytes, so feeding isn't essential. However, under good growing conditions, plants respond well to monthly applications of half-strength balanced-fertilizer solutions.

I don't recommend osmunda if modern composts are available to you. Commercial growers developed easy-to-use mixes after years of research. Since they give good results when properly used, they are preferable to osmunda alone.

Mediums for Terrestrials and Semiterrestrials

Some orchids—*Cymbidium, Paphiopedilum*, and *Zygopetalum*, for example
—thrive as semiterrestrials, with more moisture than is required for epiphytes.
Others, like *Phaius*, are completely terrestrial, but even so they must have
a sharply drained humus-rich soil. Pot semiterrestrial orchids in fine- to
medium-grade fir-bark mixes (not plain bark) or in a mix designed especially for semiterrestrials. Some good ones are McLellan's Super Orchid Mix
and Stewart's Cymbidium and Paphiopedilum formulas. You can modify
a mix designed for epiphytes by adding a good-quality pasteurized soil or
one of the soil free-mediums like New Era #5 or Black Magic. This makes
a mixture suited to semiterrestrial orchids.

Some species of warm-growing Asian *Paphiopedilum* like *P. bellatulum,
P. concolor*, and *P. niveum* thrive with a slightly sweet potting mix, so stir
a half cup of pulverized dolomite limestone into each cubic foot of your mix,
or pot in a commercial mix that is definitely balanced for these species. In-
quire about species preference from the nursery that supplies the plant.

Watering

The relationship between water, temperature, humidity, light, and plant
activity is covered in Chapter 2. With orchids these same principles apply.
Orchids with pseudobulbs, terrestrial or epiphytic, are adapted to go days
without water. When they are almost dry, it is time to soak them; then let
the compost nearly dry again before the next watering. This is usually six to
ten days in the winter, three to five days during warmer months. No damage
will be done if pseudobulbs shrink slightly so long as humidity is above 50
percent.

Orchids without pseudobulbs are maintained evenly moist, never soggy
but never completely dry. This is why sharp drainage is so important. *Paphiopedilum, Phalaenopsis*, and *Vanda* are some genera without water-storing
pseudobulbs. They can go a day or so barely moist at the roots if they are
not in a hot dry place, but never let the foliage get droopy. With the recommended potting mediums you can keep these plants evenly moist without
rotting the roots. As humidity increases the plants can go longer between
waterings.

Paphiopedilum plants can actually remain constantly moist if they have a
proper air compost and good air circulation. With all genera, if in doubt about
watering, wait another day. Apply lukewarm water. Chilly or cold water
may spot foliage, shock warm growers.

Just after orchids are potted they must be kept slightly dry at the roots,
since too much moisture rots old roots and discourages new ones. Mist the
foliage and top of the compost every morning until new roots (with green

tips) are seen at least two inches long, then give a good soaking. Potting mixes are used in a slightly moist condition. If you pot with them dry, soak each plant right after potting, then let the compost dry out to encourage new roots.

Orchids on slabs of bark or tree fern can be soaked where they hang, watered with a spray bottle that has a long-throw adjustment, or taken down and dipped in a bucket of water (or weak fertilizer solution every few weeks). If you use the same bucket of water for several orchids, be sure each plant is free of pests.

Temperature

Most of the orchids I recommend will grow well with intermediate temperatures at night (55° to 65°). Mature cattleya hybrids completing growths and those species that normally thrive best with cool nights (*Odontoglossum crispum* hybrids, etc.) thrive with 50° to 55° nights. Seedlings and warm-preference orchids such as *Phalaenopsis* grow best when nights are 65° to 70°. In traditional orchid culture, plants are grouped into cool (50° to 55°), intermediate (55° to 65°), and warm (65° to 70°) growers. Daytime temperatures are at least 5° higher, 10° to 15° higher being better.

Catalogs often list orchids under these three temperature headings, but in my mixed collection I maintain a minimum night temperature of 65°. Plants that like it cooler are hung close to the greenhouse outer wall or kept near cool windows; warmer-growing plants (and all seedlings) are placed where night temperature stays above 65°. Orchids that require low temperatures (under 55° when growth is complete) in order to bloom well are usually so designated by dealers. These include standard *Cymbidium* hybrids (not dwarfs and miniatures) and *Dendrobium nobile* hybrids.

Especially good for culture in the home, because they thrive with nights at 65° to 70°, are *Angraecum, Ascocentrum,* spotted-leaf *Paphiopedilum,* and *Phalaenopsis.* Intermediate growers include the great bulk of cattleya hybrids, epidendrums, oncidiums, and hybrids of *Brassia, Miltonia,* and *Aspasia* crossed with one another. Good selections for cool sun porches include odontoglossums, Mexican epidendrums, laelias, and some mature hybrids of *Cattleya* and *Laelia.* Mature cattleya hybrids generally bloom best when given 55° to 60° nights as growths are completed. Blooms on all genera last longer when the plant is kept slightly cooler than required for growth.

Light

Light for orchids may be from the sun, artificial illumination, or a combination of the two. Bright light (two thousand to three thousand footcandles) is required for normal growth and abundant bloom on many orchids. Some, like *Paphiopedilum, Phalaenopsis*, and many tiny miniatures, thrive with diffuse light (six hundred to one thousand footcandles), the same intensity used for healthy *Saintpaulia*.

Gradually accustom orchids to their maximum light tolerance if you have bright light available. High light, in keeping with the requirements of each genus, helps make sturdy compact growth, abundant flowers of top quality. Only a few green-toned cattleyas and cymbidiums should be shaded during blooming to get the best green color. Other orchids will require bright light whenever they are growing or blooming. Once ripe, one to three days after opening, orchid flowers will last on the plant even though they may be in the shade, so put your flowering orchids where they are most appreciated.

With horticultural wide-spectrum fluorescent tubes (see Chapter 2) you can grow most orchids anywhere that adequate humidity and temperature can be maintained. I also recommend fluorescent fixtures to supplement daylight in any area that receives less than six hours of bright light each day. For orchids, use forty-watt fixtures with at least two, but better four, tubes (wide-spectrum). If you are creating a basement light garden, it would be wise to install high-output fixtures with several ninety-watt tubes each (Sylvania Company).

Light Hours

For some orchids, initiation of flower buds is determined by day length. Most species that you will grow bloom normally under fourteen hours of light per twenty-four-hour period. Seedlings grow faster with sixteen to eighteen hours. Mature *Phalaenopsis* plants, especially those with *P. schilleriana* in their parentage, and *Dendrobium phalaenopsis* will often make vegetative shoots rather than abundant flowers if days are over fourteen hours.

In my own collection, which includes many hybrids and species, fluorescents supplement sunlight and extend the day for fourteen to sixteen hours, depending on the season. Most of the orchids grow and flower normally. But I have noticed a few mature cattleya hybrids and several *Phalaenopsis* plants not blooming even though the growths were sturdy. I have been able to get flowers by giving them short days of less than twelve hours and night temperatures 62° to 65° in the fall. The day length in late fall and winter is naturally short, so you must be sure not to extend it with artificial light if you encounter such problem plants. Effects of day length and temperature on the growth and flowering of orchids are not yet completely understood. It is worthwhile trying a short day (twelve hours or fewer) on any mature healthy orchid that does not bloom normally. At the same time keep night temperatures under 65° for warm growers and to 55° for intermediate growers such as the cattleya hybrids.

Humidity

Orchids grow best with humidity above 50 percent. Chapter 2 has details on how to maintain adequate humidity for tropicals indoors. Outside, during the summer, you may have to mist the orchids and wet the ground under them if midafternoon humidity drops too low.

Air Circulation

A constantly blowing fan, directed away from the orchids, up, down, or against a wall, is good in a greenhouse or basement light garden. I use a twelve-inch fan in an eight-by-ten-foot greenhouse, but fan size depends upon the size of your collection. Moving air helps to prevent fungus troubles and keeps plants supplied with carbon dioxide. Orchids grown in the living-room window or anywhere else that air keeps moving usually don't need a fan.

Warm-Weather Care

When late spring night temperatures stabilize at 60° or above, put most of your mature orchids outdoors under high shade. I leave *Phalaenopsis* inside because the leaves are easily damaged by sun, but all the other mature plants go outside on benches or racks until night temperatures fall below 60°. Cool-growing species like *Dendrobium nobile* and cymbidiums can be left out until nights get into the low 50's, whereas the warm-growing *Angraecum* would be the first to come in. Fresh air and sunlight outside help encourage sturdy growths and somewhat make up for less than ideal growing conditions during the colder months. In mild parts of the subtropical world where there is seldom a frost some orchids will thrive outside all year. Mexican and high-altitude species or their hybrids can be planted on trees or kept in pots on benches or under lath in the garden. Cymbidiums and reed-stem epidendrums thrive in raised beds and produce abundant flowers in full sun.

Propagation

Orchid seedlings offered by commercial firms are produced from seed sown on nutrient agar in glass flasks where the tiny plants grow under sterile conditions. Each orchid seedpod contains upward of a million dustlike seeds, most of which will grow when correctly sown on agar under antiseptic conditions, but in the wild many seeds fail to find a suitable place for germination. Even among those seeds that do sprout, few reach maturity.

Home propagation is best done by gross division—separation of large mature clumps into two or more smaller clumps, each with at least one growing lead. This is easily accomplished when sympodial orchids are repotted. *Vanda*, *Phalaenopsis*, and similar monopodial or single-growing-point orchids can't be divided, but they sometimes grow offshoots.

The photographs at the end of this chapter illustrate how a cattleya hybrid is divided and repotted. This technique works for any type of orchid that has multiple growing points (sympodial growth). Orchids are best divided or repotted only when they are active. I wait until they just begin sprouting new roots but do the potting before roots are so long that they might get broken. If roots start before the last growth flowers, I use the plastic-bag technique.

Back Bulbs

Excess healthy pseudobulbs, sometimes leafless, are removed from front lead division, dusted with Rootone, and set in a warm place with diffuse light, where they usually sprout dormant eyes and in two or three years grow to flowering size. Pot back bulbs when roots are a few inches long. I root the back bulbs in sphagnum moss or perlite kept lightly moist.

Before a plant is ready to be divided and repotted you can cut halfway through a rhizome, behind the first three or four front pseudobulbs, and dust the cut with Rootone; in a few months the back bulbs should have sprouted. By the time you repot the plant there will be a little division already growing. You can also use this technique to develop multilead specimen plants.

Awarded Clones

Among thousands of individual orchids grown from a single hybrid cross are usually several clones outstanding for color, shape, or other feature. These individuals reveal their superiority when they bloom, normally four to eight years after seed is sown. Orchid judges at shows in many countries award prizes to the best clones. Once a clone has been awarded, it carries a fancy clone name along with the initials of its highest award and usually the initials of the society that made the award. For example, "Slc. Anzac 'Orchidhurst', FCC/RHS" means that the red-lavender Sophrolaeliocattleya Anzac (Slc. Marathon X Lc. Dominiana) was awarded a first-class certificate by the Royal Horticultural Society.

Divisions of selected clones are highly prized by orchid growers, and until recently prices for a single-lead vegetative propagation might run to several hundred dollars, sometimes over a thousand. Even when growers wanted to speed up propagation of a select clone, they could divide only so much, since they were dependent on normal growth patterns, slower in orchids than in most ornamental plants. Recently a laboratory process for growing any number of divisions from a single growing bud or meristem was perfected in France.

Now it is possible to remove the growing center (eye) of a good clone and culture the tissue on nutrient agar, where it is encouraged to sprout many clumps of cells which then form tissue clumps of protocorms, later growing into tiny plants. From then on the propagations are handled like seedlings; and they are genetically identical. Even *Phalaenopsis* is now propagated by meristem and culture of dormant inflorescence buds.

You can purchase vegetative propagations of select orchids for the same price as an unbloomed seedling of comparable size. Although most orchid firms still stress their ongoing breeding program and offer hundreds of un-bloomed new crosses, they are starting to sell meristem propagations of their most select clones. The advantage to a hobby gardener is that you will know in advance what you are getting (not sure in a seedling) and thus can pick those orchids you admire most—glowing reds or yellows, for example, which were formerly very rare.

Growing seedlings still has a supreme fascination because you may flower a clone that is a great improvement over older hybrids, and of course the seedling will be unique, being but one of a kind. However, meristem propagation is a boon to growers who desire the beauty of selected clones at a reasonable price. Most of the orchid firms in the Sources of Plants and Supplies list offer meristems of excellent proven orchids.

Cut Flowers

Now that you have grown a windowful of beauty you may like to give some of it away or to put the flowers elsewhere in the house. Pick flowers only after they are fully open, or they will not last long. Orchid blooms require two to three days to open and become ripe. In the case of those with multi-flowered inflorescences, the lowest bud, nearest the plant, will be the first to open. The topmost bud may not open until several days later in cattleyas, to a full month later in *Phalaenopsis*.

Those species that are fragrant signal their ripeness by a sweet odor, usually the third day after the bud opens, or perhaps the third night in those with evening fragrance. Others are best left on the plant for three days after the bud begins to open. Cut flowers close to the stem, using a sharp razor or knife which can be sterilized in flame before being used on another plant.

Place cut flowers in fresh water. Keep them away from excessive heat, but don't put them in a very cold place. If you are picking the orchids for room decoration, there is no reason for putting them in the refrigerator every night. Even orchids picked for corsages will last well at normal room temperature if their stems are one or two inches in fresh water. For extended preservation keep the flower in the warmest section of the refrigerator, about 45° to 50°.

Cut orchids don't fold when they are in a bright spot, in contrast to many other cut flowers, but they will last a few days longer if kept out of direct sunlight. An orchid for a corsage should have around the stem base a small piece of damp cotton, which is then covered with foil and pinched at the top. Tubes and tiny vials with pins for orchid flowers are carried by some orchid firms.

Three blooming styles and bloom variations but all orchids. Left, upright inflorescence of white-and-brown Odontocidium Chiriqui (*Oncidium stenotis* X *Odontoglossum carniferum*); center, Potinara Dorothy Adair with large fringed lip inherited from *Brassavola digbyana*; right, an arching spray of yellow Colmanara Sir Jeremiah, a hybrid involving *Odontoglossum, Miltonia,* and *Oncidium*

The Rift Valley habitat of *Ansellia africana* in Tanzania

One bloom from the 2½-foot spray of a gold-and-brown *Ansellia africana*

Clump of *Ansellia* in accumulated leaf mold of tree crotch near Lake Manyara, Tanzania

Angraecum Ol Tukai 'Talisman Cove' (*Angcm. comorense* X *Angcm. sesquipedale*)

Primary hybrid Brassocattleya Nodata 'Talisman Cove' (*B. nodosa* X *C. guttata*)

Second-generation hybrids of *Brassavola nodosa* still retain the flower form and thin growth habit of that species. At left is the species *B. nodosa*; right, Brassolaeliocattleya Dorothy Friedel; at top, Blc. Lisa Carmichael. The common parent of both hybrids, Blc. Freckles, is *B. nodosa* X Lc. Purcad.

Brassia Edvah Loo, a spider orchid

Brapassia Serene 'Talisman Cove' (*Aspasia principissa* X *Brassia gireoudiana*), a heavy-substanced creamy-yellow hybrid

Brassolaeliocattleya Pride of Salem with splashed petals bred in from *Cattleya intermedia aquinii*. This is sometimes called a three-lip flower.

Chysis Chelsonii, seedling from self-crossing of a hybrid originally made in 1874, has caramel-yellow flowers.

Comparettia macroplectron

Pendent spray of golden blooms on *Dendrobium aggregatum*

203

Dendrobium nobile originates in mountains of South China, Nepal, Thailand, and parts of Vietnam, where it grows at high altitudes with night temperatures in low 50's; sometimes it even endures light frost. In captivity it grows well at intermediate temperatures but will bloom freely only if given a cool rather dry rest after its growing season.

Epidendrum ionophlebium, similar in form, size, and fragrance to *E. fragrans* and *E. radiatum*, photographed in its native El Salvador

Cool- to intermediate-growing *Miltonia* Merriman, a bright-yellow-flowered highly bred hybrid of Andean species

Miltassia Charles M. Fitch combines *Brassia verrucosa* with *Miltonia spectabilis* to create an adaptable multiflowered modern hybrid. Depending upon which variety of *M. spectabilis* is used, offspring will be cream-colored, as this one, or purple.

Odontoglossum California combines Mexican species *Odm. johnsonorum*, an intermediate grower, with Odm. Olinda, a large cool-growing hybrid of *Odm. crispum* lineage. Blooms are white with chocolate markings, last two weeks or more.

Oncidium carthaginense of Central America, a succulent mule-ear species that requires a long dry rest after completion of each growth. Plants are fifteen to twenty-four inches tall but need only four- to six-inch pots; inflorescence has many pink to brown blooms marked white.

Butterflylike *Oncidium* Kalihi produces gold-and-brown flowers from the tip of an inflorescence that will continue to have blooms for several years if the spike is not cut. Plants are a compact six to nine inches and thrive in bright-diffuse light with intermediate to warm temperatures.

Phalaenopsis Baguio has pendent inflorescences typical of its *Phal. lindenii* parent. Light-pink peppermint-striped flowers open over several weeks.

Oncidium Kenny Ku has long sprays of bright-yellow flowers marked red-brown, typical of many oncidiums.

The strictly pendulous inflorescences of a *Stanhopea* tried to develop flowers in this standard clay pot but could not expand properly. Stanhopeas bloom in pots with bottoms knocked out or even better in open-slat baskets.

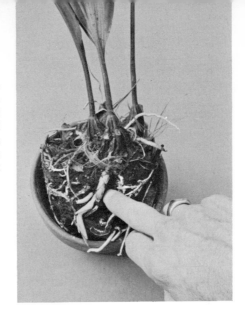

Mediums for epiphytes, top left to right, cork-bark slab, tree-fern slab on which a *Broughtonia* is growing, and a chunk of osmunda. In cups, left to right, tree-fern shreds, fir bark, Wonderbark Mix of fir bark, perlite, redwood bark and fiber, and peat moss. Far right, homemade mix of tree fern with perlite. On foreground cork-bark slab are hardwood charcoal bits, useful as drainage and in potting *Phalaenopsis* and vandas.

My Salvadorian friend shows *Catasetum integerrimum*, one of many orchids that initiate new growth as rains follow normal dry season of several months. Species from habitats with dry seasons are given a comparable rest in captivity.

Orchid seedpods, like this one from a *Catasetum*, contain millions of dustlike seeds.

Some offsets are produced from buds on an inflorescence like this one on *Phalaenopsis* Arcadia. Now that it has a good root system, it is ready to be cut off and potted alone.

Doritaenopsis Purple Gem, mother plant in background. Two offsets, or keikis, have developed on the old inflorescence. One, at right, I potted while it was still attached to spike from the mother plant, a safe way to get small keikis established before removing them from larger plant. At left is keiki with sturdy roots, ready to be potted.

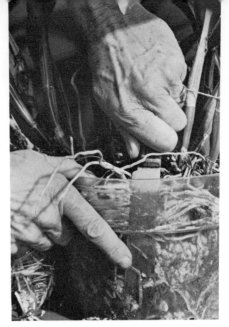

1. *Cattleya* ready for repotting, overgrowing present container. To avoid disturbing the roots before the orchid blooms, I put a plastic bag filled with rough sphagnum moss and perlite under the front lead or rhizome that sends roots outside of the pot. New roots, seen here as white, thrive in loose sphagnum. When repotting is done, the new root system is easy to handle, better than roots grabbing on to other pots or the bench.

2. A dull knife is used to separate roots from pot wall.

4. A knife or large clippers cut through the rhizome and root ball of multilead plants to make divisions of three to five pseudobulbs, each with a live growing lead or eye. Unflowered seedlings are not divided.

3. Remove root ball, and pull out all the old compost from between live white or green roots. Any dead roots, usually soggy and brown, are cut away.

13

Holiday Plants

THE BEAUTIFUL PLANTS WE GIVE and receive at holiday times are raised under optimum greenhouse conditions by skilled plantsmen. When such plants arrive, they are in their prime, ready to provide many days of cheerful color if you understand how to care for them. Some of them may even thrive so well that you will have them for several years. Apart from a few small evergreens, most of these plants come originally from the tropics or sub-tropics and will respond to intelligent treatment based upon their needs in nature. (See Chapter 15 for Christmas cactus.)

Ardisia

Long thick glossy foliage and clusters of coral-red berries make this Malaysian shrub a welcome gift. I find ardisias do best in a cool place, so keep it in a bright but airy location where nights drop into the 50's.

Ardisia crispa (*crenulata*) is the species most often grown in greenhouses. It matures at about one foot tall, but the final height may be three or four feet. Another species, *A. japonica*, is sometimes available. It has white flowers and red berries on a plant twelve to twenty inches high. Both are suited to culture in tubs when large, and the smaller specimens are charming in dish gardens or as compact pot plants in the window. They are frequently propagated from cuttings by nurserymen and so will have berries even though the shrub may be under eight inches tall.

Keep the soil lightly moist but not soggy. If you wish to keep the plant, prune it in spring, and repot in standard soil mix when roots fill the old container. In late spring ardisias have clusters of tiny white flowers which later develop into the berries that make it such a striking long-lasting holiday gift.

Azalea

A flowering azalea often comes with a giant gaudy ribbon, which you will want to remove at once. Next, strip off any foil that might be blocking the pot drainage hole. If the plant is in a nondrained glazed container, you will have to be especially careful in watering. Florists offer four azalea types as gift plants. Tender Indica hybrids are large, double-flowered, and evergreen, originally developed in Belgium especially as flowering pot plants. They are descended from *Azalea indica* of Japan. Except in the mildest parts of the Southeast, these sorts are not truly hardy in the United States.

Two popular Indica hybrids are 'Albert Elisabeth', a dwarf white-flowered clone, each flower heavily bordered in strawberry-pink, and compact 'Hexe de Saffelaere', crimson-flowered.

Reasonably hardy Kurume hybrids (from another Japanese evergreen species, *A. obtusa*), like 'Coral Bells' and crimson 'Hinodegiri', are favorite Easter plants. Through the years I have planted out a number of 'Coral Bells' and 'Salmon Beauty' gifts. Here in southern New York they survive the winter, the leaves turning a deep glossy greenish maroon in late fall, to bloom faithfully each spring. The only damage has been from ice snapping the branches. However, even the hardiest varieties of the Kurume azaleas do not survive in New England or, except near the coast, in many places north of Philadelphia.

A third popular group is the Rutherfordiana hybrids, derived from four or five species. These are vigorous evergreen plants of compact growth. 'Alaska', a sparkling white, and 'Early Wonder', a large semidouble rosy red, are usually offered during the winter holidays. I have had no luck with these outside in the garden, but they can be grown outside in warm weather, then brought indoors before frost, kept in a bright cool spot (50° at night), and should bloom from midwinter on into early spring.

The fourth type of holiday azalea is the Pericat group. These were created by crossing Belgian Indica hybrids with Kurume azaleas, and I find them partially hardy in Zone 6 if planted against a warm wall, though every winter a number of branch tips and some buds are killed.

Your gift azalea won't be labeled Indica, Kurume, Rutherfordiana, or Pericat, but the same kind of care should be given to all types while flowering. In a normally warm room the plant will require about one cup of water per day to keep the roots evenly moist, which is important.

For all the buds to open perfectly the azalea must have bright light to direct sun. Early morning or late afternoon sun is fine. Provide night temperatures down to 60° to obtain the longest period of bloom. No fertilizer will be necessary during the flowering period.

If you want to keep the plant for another year of flowering indoors, continue to give it bright light, cool nights, and even moisture at the roots. Put it outside when nights stabilize above 50°. Fertilize every three weeks with water-soluble acid-reaction plant food (Stern's Miracid, for example), or alternate chemical and organic nutrients. In late summer stop feeding nitrogen, and apply a dose or two of high potassium-phosphorus fertilizer (Peters' 5-50-17 is fine).

Bring the azalea into a cool sunny room when nights begin to reach the low 40's. Keep roots evenly moist and expect bloom in the hybrid's normal season, winter into early spring. If the plant requires repotting, use a humus-rich soil mixed with 50 percent rough sphagnum peat moss, and pot in a three-quarter size azalea pot.

Winter-Flowering Tuberous Begonias

An abundance of long-lasting flowers over round green foilage characterizes winter-flowering tuberous begonias. Two kinds are offered: the original Christmas begonias made from a cross of *B. socotrana* and *B. dregei*, now listed as *B. X cheimantha* hybrids; and the *B. hiemalis* hybrids developed from *B. socotrana* crossed on high-altitude species.

Of these two groups, the *B. hiemalis* hybrids are the larger growing and produce the larger flowers. They come in delicate shades of rose, apricot, pink, and salmon, some with flowers that resemble rosebuds. Both *cheimantha* and *hiemalis* hybrids require high humidity and diffuse light. Night temperatures below 60° tend to make long-lasting flowers. With higher temperatures flowers may be fleeting, and leaves may look sad. Soil should remain evenly moist but not sodden. As flowers fade, cut them off along with any damaged leaves. If the plant is under very moist conditions, a greenhouse, for example, guard against mildew. These begonias are quite susceptible to fungus troubles when air is still and moist. A spray of Fermate or even better, Benlate (DuPont) will keep fungus under control.

When the plant has finished its first show, trim it back if branches are straggly. New growth will normally begin right away. Keep the plant in a cool bright location, always with high humidity, good air circulation, and even moisture at the roots. Fertilize with a balanced chemical formula like Hyponex. With some vigorous hybrids, like *cheimantha* 'Lady Mac' or *hiemalis* 'Apricot Beauty', you often receive a second flush of flowers for your trouble.

By late spring the tuber will go dormant and should be stored in a cool place with only enough soil moisture to keep it plump. In a few weeks new stems will start and you can gently repot the tuber in fresh humus-rich soil. Grow it through the summer with care to avoid sunburn of the foliage. The plant may not grow well if the summer is very hot. Water on the soil; keep foliage dry.

If the tuber grows, the plant will be ready to bloom by late November. The *hiemalis* hybrids look tougher than small-flowered *cheimantha* hybrids, but actually they are somewhat more difficult to grow because they require even cooler temperatures. The tuberous species in *hiemalis* hybrids come from high Andean forests where night temperatures drop into the 40's. Their other parent, *B. socotrana*, is from tropical Socotra Island in the Indian Ocean, so the hybrids we grow will do fine with a night temperature up to 60°, but higher than this prevents good growth and flowering. Daytime highs for *hiemalis* hybrids should be 60° to 65°.

As *hiemalis* hybrids die down, tiny tubers form along the stem, just under the soil. Keep these cool during the dormant period (a month or two), then plant them in fresh humus-rich soil, and begin the growth cycle again. Pinch several times during the summer for bushy plants. Stop pinching by mid-August. Well-grown plants flower for several months.

Citrus

When well cared for, citrus trees indoors have a special appeal, perhaps partly because they are not commonly seen, but also because of their clean-cut leaves, fragrant flowers, and gleaming fruits. Give these plants a cool airy place with nights under 60°, or 50° to 55° if possible. Humidity should be at least 50 percent; the light should be strong direct sun in morning and late afternoon.

With dim light, trees will remain attractive for the holiday season, but when new growth begins, they must have bright light for future flowers and fruit. Keep the soil evenly moist. Use standard soil mix, with additional 50 percent sphagnum peat moss if repotting is required for pot-bound specimens. You can prune citrus trees as required to keep them tidy. Wash foliage with warm water to keep it clean and free; watch for red spiders. Fertilize every other watering when new growth is being made. Some excellent indoor citruses for cool bright places are:

Citrus aurantifolia. This is the Key lime, taller than most dwarf citruses. Pruning will keep it in bounds.

C. limonia 'Meyeri'. Semidwarf lemon, adaptable, green fruit flushed orange, good for juice.

C. limonia 'Ponderosa'. I grew a tree for several years in a six-inch glazed pot. It produced many fragrant flowers and several huge lemons.

C. mitis (Calamondin Orange). Can be pruned as a small bush and grown in a six- to eight-inch pot. Has inch-wide orange fruits. Let soil dry out slightly between waterings.

Fortunella Margarita. A Chinese kumquat, closely related to citrus, best in a terrace tub or big pot on the sun porch. Flowers from spring into summer, then has orange one-inch fruits. Intermediate temperatures, lightly moist, and as with citruses, full sun.

Cyclamen

The florist's cyclamen hybrids are derived from *C. persicum*, native to Greece and Syria. Temperatures in persicum's Mediterranean habitat drop sharply at night but not to the extent that its hybrids would be hardy in northern climates. Required temperatures are the low 50's at night and several degrees warmer by day. Many people get a four- or five-month bloom period from a mature cyclamen when they provide this cool temperature range, keep the plant evenly moist at the roots but not soggy, and give it diffuse light— just enough sun for the buds to develop and open well but no hot sun to burn the leaves.

When flowering ceases and foliage begins to die, put the pot on its side in a cool dry place until early September, when the tuber can be brought into growth again. It is very likely to rot if just put outside for the summer. If the tuber lives and begins growth in the fall, provide bright-diffuse light, cool temperatures, even moisture.

Less fussy than the *C. persicum* hybrids is *C. neapolitanum*, a winter-hardy species from southern Europe. You can pot this small tuber in a three- or four-inch container, let it root outside until mid-November, then bring it indoors for the flowers that come in the fall. Put it outside with a leaf mulch after the pink flowers fade. I am presently trying a hybrid between hardy *C. europaeum* and *C. persicum* (*C.* 'Puck'—Geo. W. Park Seed Company), which should have showy flowers but a less temperamental nature than the familiar *C. persicum* hybrids.

Gardenia

The most fragrant gift plant remains the gardenia. Large-flowered popular types are 'Belmont' and related winter-flowering forms of *G. jasminoides*, all with glossy dark-green leaves and bushy habit. These shrubs are sensitive to cold drafts, overheating, and low humidity. With temperatures under 70°, fresh air, and humidity at least 50 percent, a gardenia will remain attractive for many weeks.

Keep the roots evenly moist, and provide several hours of early morning sun and bright-diffuse light for the rest of the day. When nights outdoors are above 60°, put the gardenia outside in a shady moist place; I sink the pot in peat-lite. Fertilize it every few weeks with an acid-reaction fertilizer, and mist the foliage to keep leaves clean. Bring it indoors when nights start going into the 50's.

If the plant becomes pot-bound, repot it into humus-rich soil or standard soil mixed 50-50 with rough sphagnum peat moss. Prune after flowering to keep tidy, and mist the plant on sunny mornings to keep foliage fresh and humidity high. If foliage looks yellow, apply iron chelate like Sequestrene (Geigy Chemical).

Kalanchoe

During winter holidays multiflowered *Kalanchoe blossfeldiana* is a cheerful and charming sight. Succulent green leaves on compact bushy plants are a lovely background for clusters of starry yellow or red flowers. While the plant is in flower, enjoy it anywhere in the house. After flowers fade, cut off bloom stalks, and put the plant in a sunny window where it can make sturdy growth. I once thought a friend's kalanchoe was a peperomia; she had given it so little light that it made a trailing long-stemmed growth, not at all typical of its healthy normal foliage. Keep roots on the dry side; water after the first top inch of soil dries out. In early spring begin applications of a balanced fertilizer every three weeks. In midsummer add a teaspoon of bone meal, scratched into the topsoil. By early fall stop all fertilizer, but continue to give bright light, no more than twelve hours per day (ten is better); let the kalanchoe have normally short fall days without artificial light after dark.

Flowers should appear by late December. Temperatures of 55° to 60° at night and into the 70's by day are proper. Slightly higher night temperatures are acceptable if the plant is given strong light with good air circulation. You can propagate kalanchoe with stem cuttings or seed sown in early spring for flowering plants the following winter. *K. blossfeldiana* will thrive under sixteen-hour fluorescent-lamp days until it has five or six pairs of leaves, then reduce day length to ten or eleven hours for the initiation of blooming.

To get rid of mealybug, use nicotine sulfate (Black Leaf-40) because the normally recommended Malathion will badly damage or kill kalanchoes.

Some attractive hybrids are 'Brilliant Star', plants to ten inches, large heads of glowing red flowers about three times larger than other hybrids; 'Scarlet

Gnome', a seven-inch plant of rounded compact growth and deep-scarlet flowers; 'Tom Thumb', dwarf with scarlet flowers, available in yellow-flowered strain, too.

Poinsettia

This most famous Christmas flower, *Euphorbia pulcherrima*, was introduced from Mexico by Dr. Joel R. Poinsett about 1830. It now grows outdoors to six feet or more in many warm countries. Indoors we enjoy improved dwarf hybrid forms which hold their scarlet bracts (which we call flowers) for several months. There are varieties with white or with pink bracts.

The poinsettia needs bright light, daytime temperatures in the 70's, nights at 55° to 65°. Avoid rapid fluctuations in temperature. Keep soil lightly moist but not soggy; too wet soil causes lower leaves to drop. No fertilizer is required during the winter.

If you want to keep the plant for another season, let the soil stay on the dry side after flowers fade. In the spring when outdoor nights are above 50° put the poinsettia outside in bright light, sink the pot in moist peat-lite, and keep roots evenly moist. Cut back about one half of the top growth. During the summer pinch new green stems to get bushy growth, but stop pinching by the end of August. New hybrids are quite bushy, so perhaps only one or two pinches will be required. During summer growth apply balanced fertilizer, like Hyponex or Miracle-Gro at half strength, alternated with an organic fish emulsion and seaweed mixture. Or scratch some dry organic fertilizer into the topsoil (Wayside Gardens 4-10-6 or Espoma organic).

Plants that require repotting are planted in a blend of three parts standard houseplant soil, one part coarse sand, and one part rough sphagnum peat moss, plus a tablespoon of dry organic fertilizer per pot. Any stems cut back at repotting or pinched to get a bushy plant can be rooted for additional plants. Poinsettias initiate flowering only with short days—less than twelve hours of light.

From late September through November protect the plant from any light after sunset. It must have no light at all during the night of twelve or more hours, and night temperatures should be 60° to 65°, no higher. With this care your plant should form flowers by the end of December. Once buds are seen, usually by the end of November, you don't have to worry about the day length, but the largest bracts will be produced if you continue to provide long nights until full color develops. Some people put the plant in a closet every evening so it won't be disturbed by house lights. I'd prefer to get a new specimen from the florist every Christmas.

'Red Baron', new cardinal-red poinsettia developed by United States Department of Agriculture in a breeding program to create hybrids of compact growth, bright lasting colors, and extra-large bracts (*USDA*)

Gift poinsettias are available in modern white or pink hybrids to complement the traditional red varieties.

Kalanchoe blossfeldiana hybrid with yellow flowers. Other varieties are available with bright-red or scarlet flowers. (*Pan-American Seed Company*)

Cyclamen persicum hybrid

14

Bulbs to Grow Indoors

Planting a sturdy bulb almost guarantees flowers because bulbs have formed buds the year before. Tropical bulbs will provide spectacular flowers the first year and with optimum culture, for many more seasons. Some few indoor bulbs, not strictly tropical, like paper-white narcissus and fragrant hyacinths, are best started from new bulbs each year.

Amaryllis

Amaryllis are the most spectacular truly tropical bulbs for easy indoor culture. Botanically they belong to the genus *Hippeastrum* but are popularly known as *Amaryllis*, which is a genus that formerly included hippeastrums and other plants. The only remaining true amaryllis is *A. belladonna*, a fall-blooming "lily" of South Africa, not hardy north of Philadelphia. About seventy species are now in *Hippeastrum*, and the ones we call *Amaryllis* are mainly hybrids developed from several species over a period of 150 years.

I always get a feeling of warm excitement when planting an amaryllis because I can imagine the sparkling flowers as I pot each plump bulb. Healthy bulbs offered by professional nurseries always bloom if given good basic starting care, but whether or not your amaryllis will bloom again the second year depends on the care you give it after the flowers fade.

Purchasing

Choose large, sound bulbs from a reliable local dealer, or order before freezing weather from one of the mail-order firms on the Source of Plants and Supplies list. You can get named clones to flower in white, orange, red, deep black-red, pink, pink lined with white, white spotted red or edged red, and some delightful candy-stripe types. Current internationally available favorites include:

ORANGE TONES

'Fire Flame'. New clone from Dutch hybridizer Van Meeuwen.
'Glorious Victory'. Golden-orange, free flowering.
'Halley'. Burnt-orange, easy grower.
'Traffic Stop'. Spectacular tall giant, orange-red.

PINK TO ROSE

'Daintiness'. Light pink.
'Dawning'. Round pink flowers.
'Pink Perfection'. Rose-opal.
'Pygmalion'. Easy-to-grow, soft pink and white.
'Rose Marie'. Sturdy and large, pink, lighter center.

REDS

'Belinda'. Dark red, round shape.
'Fire Dance'. Vermilion.
'Ludwig's Goliath'. Giant, easy-to-grow, scarlet.
'Tristan'. Dark wine-red.
'Wyndham Hayward'. Giant, glistening oriental red.

WHITES

'Early White'. Easy-to-bloom, pure white.
'Ludwig's Dazzler'. Popular vigorous clone.
'White Christmas'. Large perfect white.

STRIPES

'Candy Cane'. Red and white, bold effect.
'Picotee'. Delicate red penciling on white.
'United Nations'. White petals, wide vermilion stripes.

Top-size bulbs of named clones cost from four to eight dollars each, small divisions less. If names are not important, buy bulbs labeled only for color, often equal in quality to named clones if purchased from amaryllis specialists. These are normally under three dollars each, top sized.

Amaryllis that have been rested for early flowering during Christmas holidays sometimes cost a few cents more, but for quick bloom the extra cost is nothing. Some firms sell preplanted bulbs, usually Dutch hybrids in plastic pots filled with a peat-lite or similar mix. This type of mixture holds a lot of moisture, so take care not to overwater. Cultural directions are furnished by dealers who sell preplanted amaryllis.

Potting and Culture

Pot bare-root bulbs immediately. Remove only broken or dead roots; treat remaining live white roots gently to prevent damage.

1. Select heavy clay pot or another container with drainage holes and enough weight to prevent tipping. Amaryllis may split thin plastic pots but grow well in plastic foam pots (Styrofoam, Tufflite). For small- to medium-size bulbs I like azalea or bulb pots, only one-half to three-quarters the size of standard pots.

2. Allow a maximum space between bulb and side of pot of two inches. Roots should fill container as bulb prepares to bloom.

3. Proceed with potting as explained in Chapter 4. Standard mix with a half tablespoon of steamed bone meal and a tablespoon of granulated charcoal per six-inch pot is satisfactory. Stir in a tablespoon of dolomite limestone per six-inch pot if more than one third of your soil mix is peat moss.

4. Fill in potting medium to cover only half of the bulb.

5. Mulch with coarse sand, pea gravel, or stone chips to depth of one-half to one inch.

6. Settle in with lukewarm water poured on from the top.

7. Put pot in a dim place where temperature will be close to 70°. Warmer temperature may cause excessive leaf growth; lower temperature will slow down blooming.

8. Keep lightly moist as roots develop.

9. Bring plant into bright light as lance-shaped scape shows at top.

10. Increase watering on soil as bloom develops, but don't let bulb sit in water.

11. Turn pot every few days to maintain symmetrical growth.

12. When all buds are open, you can place the plant where it is best appreciated or cut the scape for display elsewhere.

Variations

Bulbs prepared for early blooming, usually imported from Holland for flowering around Christmas, should be given gentle bottom heat from a soil-heating cable or by being kept above a radiator on a tray of moist gravel. This will take the place of Step 7 above. Bottom heat speeds rooting and can actually be used with any bulbs if air temperature is not over 70°. Higher temperatures with bottom heat combine to force weak rapid growth, blooms of poor substance. With temperatures 65° and 70° flowers last longer, up to five or seven days. Be careful not to knock fluffy pollen onto the sticky stigma; pollinated flowers don't last long.

After Blooming

When flowers have faded, pinch them off. After a few days cut the scape; some sap will run out but will soon stop, and the cut will heal. Keep the bulb growing in bright light with night temperature 65° to 70°. Stake foliage to prevent it breaking or drooping over nearby plants. Fertilize with liquid balanced preparations every two weeks. I alternate liquid organics with water-soluble chemicals on my plants all through the summer.

Put bulbs outside when temperatures stay above 65°. Move them into almost full sun, but do it gradually. Keep roots lightly moist by sinking pots into peat-lite with an inch of gravel spread under each pot. Sinking pots up to the rims in soil, as some people do, increases chance for slug damage and earthworm troubles (they get in pots and keep soil too loose).

Keep bulbs growing all summer long; the more good leaves they grow and mature, the better flower production will be. Toward the end of August apply only low-nitrogen fertilizer. About September or October most bulbs will begin to lose foliage as you gradually withhold water to bring them into dormancy, a natural part of their life cycle.

I like to turn pots on their sides so that rain won't soak the roots, then I bring bulbs indoors before the first frost. Give resting bulbs only enough water to keep the soil lightly moist and prevent shrinking. Leafless bulbs can go into a dark closet, under a greenhouse bench, or in the basement until they show leaf tips or flower scapes, usually two or three months.

Where bulb flies are a problem, I give the soil a soaking of Cygon solution, one teaspoon per gallon of water, before the pots are brought inside. If any pests are seen, like red spiders or mealybugs, you can also spray with Malathion. Pick off the old foliage and any loose outside bulb covering.

New Soil

Just before established bulbs begin new growth is a good time to scrape away most of the soil and fill in with fresh. Use care not to break live roots. I let my amaryllis stay in the same soil for two years, then fill in fresh soil or repot completely if bulbs are much bigger. Offsets that have roots are removed if desired for propagation (details in Chapter 5).

Seasonal Variations

Amaryllis are generally spring flowers. Normal variations between cultivars do occur, so some bloom in early winter to late January, whereas others won't flower until April. In my collection 'Rose Marie' is early; 'Rembrandt' much later. In order to flower amaryllis earlier than their spring season, the bulbs must be dried off somewhat earlier in the fall. Once they have been dormant for two months at 60° to 65° they will respond to increased warmth, moisture, and light by earlier flowering.

One excellent new small-flowered hybrid is 'Christmas Joy', a glowing red that is easy to bloom in December. A low-growing group of hybrids called 'Gracilis' includes 'Fire Fly', a medium-size red on a ten-inch scape, quite a contrast to the twenty-four- or thirty-inch scapes of standard hybrids.

You can grow amaryllis from seed and create your own hybrids to flower in two to four years.

Caladium

Plant caladiums for a multicolored foliage display from spring into midwinter. These tropical tubers are available in numerous colors and different leaf shapes. Charming miniature *C. humboldtii* grows less than six inches tall, standard hybrids may reach twelve inches, and newer lance-leaved cultivars somewhat less. The most popular caladiums are large-leaved hybrids of *C. bicolor*, but the growing list of lance-leaved types (forms of hybrids of *C. picturatum*) are well worth having for their compact habit and unusual leaf form. I have white and green 'Caloosahatchee', 'Pink Gem' with foliage pink marked white with bronze border, and 'Rosalie', a brilliant red over green.

Plant caladium tubers one or two per five-inch pot of humus-rich soil or standard mix combined 50-50 with rough sphagnum peat moss. Cover tubers with one-inch of the medium, keep warm, 75° to 80°, just barely moist, until good roots begin, then increase watering and keep them evenly moist. You can also start tubers into growth in flats.

Keep caladiums in a bright warm location—65° minimum nights, 75° to 80° optimum as growth begins. Once several leaves have opened, begin fertilizing with half-strength fish emulsion alternated with balanced chemical fertilizer. Bright light increases foliage brilliance, but guard against direct sun through glass in late spring and summer.

Caladiums will provide excellent color for six to eight months, then they rest. Store dormant tubers in the pots of soil or if more convenient, in plastic bags of peat-lite. Miniature *C. humboldtii* will rest for a month, then come into growth again if given temperatures above 70° and moist conditions. Larger cultivars normally remain dormant for two to four months. Keep temperatures above 55° for resting tubers.

Clivia

Established *Clivia* grows well with minimum nights of 50° so it is a good choice for a cool room or sun porch. Plant the heavy roots in the mixture recommended for amaryllises or in one of the soil-free mediums with a table-spoon of steamed bone meal added to each seven- or eight-inch pot. *Clivia* forms very tough roots, which should be confined in their container, pot-bound, for optimum bloom. Provide bright-diffuse light, no hot sun, keep slightly dry between waterings when resting, otherwise evenly moist. *Clivia* plants are evergreen but slow their growth in midwinter. The orange flowers are pleasantly fragrant and long lasting. Hybrids vary in intensity of orange and the amount of yellow in the throat.

Eucharis grandiflora

Amazon lily, or *E. grandiflora* (*amazonica*), produces fragrant white flow-ers several times during the year and has attractive evergreen foliage and compact growth under a foot tall. Plant dormant bulbs in standard soil mixed 50-50 with sphagnum peat moss or leaf mold, one bulb per five-inch pot. Start into growth as suggested for caladiums. Once *Eucharis* is growing it will stay green unless drastically dried off at the roots.

By alternating lightly moist conditions with drier periods every five to six months, the bulb will flower several times a year. Fertilize the growing plant as for caladiums; I use half-strength solutions every two or three weeks. This is a truly tropical bulb and thrives in warm temperatures and diffuse light. Put it outside when the weather is mild; bring it inside before nights get below 50°. Flowers look somewhat like daffodils but are pure white and deliciously fragrant.

Eucomis

The pineapple lily isn't a pineapple, but it is at least in the family Liliaceae. The several species are adaptable summer-blooming bulbs with rosettes of glossy strap-shaped foliage from which sprouts a stalk and then many white, yellow, or green one- to two-inch flowers, mostly spotted light purple. The flowers cluster around the stalk with a rosette of small leaves on top, much in the manner of a pineapple.

Eucomis bicolor alba is hardy in my southern New York garden when I plant it at the base of a warm south foundation wall. It will thrive indoors if you keep night temperature below 65°. Culture is the same as recommended for amaryllises, except that *Eucomis* is planted two inches under the soil, not exposed. Give the plant full sun, although it will tolerate less light.

Among several South African species available from bulb specialists are *E. autumnalis* (*undulata*), under fifteen inches with a six-inch spike of green flowers; *E. bicolor*, about one foot tall with white to pale-green flowers lightly marked purple; and *E. comosa*, up to two feet tall with a one-foot spike of yellow-green scented flowers sometimes marked purple.

Haemanthus

This genus of spectacular orange- to scarlet-flowered bulbs is easy to grow indoors. Flower heads are spheres or half-spheres containing many one-inch glowing flowers. The common name is blood lily. I recall seeing hundreds of them growing where the wide strap leaves were moist with mist from Victoria Falls in Rhodesia.

Culture for these African plants is similar to that for amaryllises. Bulbs are planted with the tops even with the soil level. Under indoor cultivation *Haemanthus* tends to remain green for more than one growing season. The species *H. katharinae* especially tends to hold its foliage up until just a few weeks before new growth sprouts. In any event you can judge from the plant's behavior when it no longer needs water.

Once foliage begins to die back, cut down watering, rest the bulb in its pot at 55° to 60°. After six weeks you can resume watering to encourage sprouting. Don't keep the bulb moist unless growth begins. *H. coccineus* may rest for three months. Once active, *Haemanthus* responds well to fertilizer solutions every two weeks. Six weeks after flowering, fertilize once or twice with a low-nitrogen, high-potash-phosphorus preparation to get sturdy bulb formation. Night temperatures of 55° to 65° are satisfactory. Keep bulbs outdoors for the summer.

Dormant bulbs are available in the fall from specialists, except that *H. katharinae* may not be available until its midwinter dormant period.

Species to look for are *H. coccineus*, with up to two-foot-long leaves and an alliumlike umbel of red flowers on a twenty-four-inch stalk, usually before foliage expands; *H. katharinae*, somewhat more compact, with nine- to twelve-inch-long leaves and orange-red flowers on a ten-inch spotted stalk; *H. multiflorus*, having spotted stems and umbels of up to one hundred small blood-red flowers. A nice hybrid, *H. multiflorus* X *H. katharinae,* is worth growing but hard to come by.

Haemanthus plants are slow growers; they will be at home in five- to six-inch pots for several years, then can be moved to more spacious containers and stay there, since established bulbs produce the largest flowers. Soil can be scraped away on top and replaced every two years without disturbing the roots. Bulbs increase by offsets.

Lachenalia

For spikes of coral or red flowers from December into midspring grow a few pots of lachenalias, African bulbs with overhanging green foliage, spotted all over with purple. These are not common plants, and you may have to search through a few catalogs to find them. I grew some from seed, but it took three years to flower them.

L. aloides var. aurea is a golden-yellow form which has twenty to twenty-five flowers on each stem. My favorite species is *L. pendula superba*, a coral-red flower marked green and yellow. One year I grew a pot of these under two forty-watt fluorescent growth tubes which hung against a cool outside greenhouse wall, and the plants were nicer than the same species in a sunny window because, I think, the artificial light was more constant and the temperature cooler than in the living-room window. Similar results can be achieved in a cool basement or sun porch. These are not bulbs for warm dry places.

Optimum night temperatures are 45° to 50°, but light must be either bright-diffuse or the fluorescent tubes I mentioned. I like to pot five to eight bulbs in a seven- to eight-inch bulb pan or squat pot. Standard soil over crocks with a few charcoal bits is satisfactory. Let growth begin in a cool location with barely moist soil.

Foliage is succulent and easily damaged if crushed or bent. A hanging container will keep it safe. Or put the lachenalia pot on an inverted clay pot to keep leaves off the ground. Waxy tubular flowers are produced on semipendulous to upright stems about ten inches tall. Under proper cool conditions they remain in perfection at least a month, often two months. When foliage dies down, give the bulbs a two- or four-month rest in their pots. When bulbs are overcrowded, repot them in early fall, just before growth begins.

Narcissus

Most narcissus are hardy bulbs for outdoor planting, but the golden 'Soleil d'Or' and paper-white Mediterranean narcissus are excellent forcers that thrive indoors, always fragrant and cheerful. Both are forms of *N. tazzeta*. Start bulbs in early October for flowers around Thanksgiving. By planting a dish of bulbs each week you can create a succession of bloom until after Christmas.

Obtain top-quality bulbs anytime after October in local garden stores or through mail order; buy only the largest bulbs. The Riviera brand of paper-whites has given me good results for several years. White marble chips are an attractive planting medium for paper-whites and 'Soleil d'Or'. Pick a low glazed container, copper bowl, or bulb pan. If you use marble chips, the bulbs are grown in water, but if you prefer pots, they can be planted in peat-lite. I prefer the water and gravel method as easy and satisfactory. Plant five or six bulbs together, their sides touching, and one half of each bulb above the gravel or peat-lite.

Pour in warm water over the gravel just to a level one-half to one-quarter inch below the bulbs' bases. Roots will reach into the water. If bulbs are covered with water, even halfway, they often rot. Put newly planted bulbs in a dark cool place 60° to 65° for two to three weeks. When roots are several inches long, down into the water, bring the bulbs into bright light, but keep temperatures under 70°. Higher temperatures force tall foliage which hides flowers; extreme heat may blast buds.

'Soleil d'Or' starts more slowly than the paper-whites but will eventually make just as lovely a show. Both these species are discarded after being forced indoors; they are not hardy in northern temperate latitudes.

More challenging varieties, like garden-hardy 'King Alfred' (a large trumpet type) and the delightful fragrant 'Cheerfulness' (double-flowering type), can be forced, too, but you need a cold frame or dark unheated room with temperatures 45° to 50° for their long rooting period, then a very bright but cool airy place, if you hope to produce a satisfactory show. These bulbs can be planted out in the garden after forcing and will live for many years, but they are so much more difficult than the fragrant no-fuss paper-whites and 'Soleil d'Or' that I don't recommend them for indoor growing.

Scilla

Two species in this generally hardy genus are suitable for indoor growing. *Scilla peruviana*, a Mediterranean bulb, produces scapes ten to twelve inches high with a head of purple to blue flowers. Pot bulbs in fall as suggested for *Haemanthus*: top of the bulb at soil surface. A four- to five-inch pot is suitable. Provide bright light but cool (40° to 50°) night temperatures; keep lightly moist when growing and dry when dormant. Normal flowering season is late winter to spring.

S. violacea, a succulent South African bulb with two- to four-inch variegated leaves, is an evergreen dwarf. The foliage is its main attraction: shiny strap-shaped, blotched silver, stained purple underneath. Spires of tiny green and blue flowers appear in spring. Pot in a small container, use succulent mix, give filtered sun, intermediate temperatures, and keep almost dry between waterings.

Sprekelia

The Mexican fire lily or Jacobean lily (*S. formosissima*) is a glowing red-flowered relative of *Amaryllis* and succeeds with the same soil and potting methods as for that bulb. Once a pot of *Sprekelia* is established, the bulbs will often bloom more than once each year if you alternate moist and dry conditions every few months as suggested for *Eucharis*. I plant three or four bulbs in a five- to six-inch pot for the best flower display. Normal blooming season is summer, but some bulbs I planted in January flowered in April. If all the foliage dies down, let *Sprekelia* rest a month, then encourage new growth with bottom heat and light moisture at the roots.

Vallota speciosa (purpurea)

This is another bulb that thrives under the conditions right for amaryllises. It tends to remain evergreen, flowering on and off throughout the year and producing the best flowers after it fills the pot with roots and offsets. It may be set back by division or disturbance. Provide full sun or, at the least, bright-diffuse light; keep lightly moist, then let it almost dry out every six to eight weeks. Umbels of three-inch flowers on a two-foot scape are brilliant red.

Veltheimia

Veltheimias are South African bulbs with broad green shiny leaves in a neat rosette about one foot across, with flowers in terminal racemes on twelve- to eighteen-inch stalks, somewhat resembling the garden tritoma. Flowers are a soft red to yellow-green and last for several weeks.

Veltheimias grow well with the culture outlined for *Haemanthus*, but they accept cooler temperatures, down to 45° at night, though mine does well at 60° to 65°. I have success with this bulb under fluorescent lights in the basement. *V. glauca* (*capensis*), which blooms in early spring, has tubular white flowers lightly spotted rose. *V. viridifolia* normally blooms in our winter and takes about a month to open all the florets on the eighteen-inch stalk. The shiny, intensely green, and undulated foliage is always attractive.

Zantedeschia (Calla Lilly)

This is one plant that will actually grow well with wet feet once the roots are active. Treat the tubers as recommended for caladiums (to which it is related), and keep moist in a bright location with nights at 60° to 68°. A good variety that stays under twenty-four inches tall is fragrant *Z. aethiopica minor,* also called 'Compacta' or 'Little Gem'. The white flowers, about five-inch spathes, come from late fall to early summer. Then tubers go dormant for several months. My favorite is *Z. elliottiana,* which grows and blooms easily in spring through summer. My plants have three- to four-inch spathes on eighteen-inch stems softly barred bronze-brown, the leaves with translucent spots that look silver. This species needs bright-diffuse light, in contrast to *Z. aethiopicta,* which accepts full sun. *Z.* 'Helen O'Connor' has white-spotted leaves on an eighteen-inch stalk and an apricot-shaded flower with purple throat (Wayside Gardens).

Also with apricot-colored spathes is a new strain of callas, the 'Sunrise' hybrids. *Z. rehmannii* is a delicate-pink-flowered species fifteen to eighteen inches tall, flowering around Easter if you plant it in midwinter. Because callas grow new roots from the top of each tuber, they do not require very deep pots. I grow them in four- to six-inch plastic pots or three-quarter azalea pots. All hybrids and species respond well to fertilizer during their growing period. Stop feeding as foliage begins to die in late summer to fall, then rest tubers for two or three months with just enough moisture to prevent them from shrinking. Tubers purchased from nurseries in midwinter have already been rested and are ready to be started into growth at once.

Bulb Clinic

The common pests that attack bulbs are discussed in Chapter 10. Some troublesome creatures, like bulb flies, are especially attracted to bulbs and can be controlled with twice-yearly applications of Cygon 2E mixed at one teaspoon per gallon of water. I handle fungus problems and the bulb flies with a spring and fall soil drench that contains Dexon 35 percent wettable powder (one teaspoon per gallon of warm water) mixed with the Cygon 2E. The same solution can be used as a spray to control both fungus rots and bulb flies. Amaryllis, particularly, are most troubled by the flies and fungus, so I treat them as a matter of course, but this treatment is effective for other bulbs as well.

Most amaryllis have blooms five to nine inches across. This is one of the author's own hybrids, flowered from seed in three years.

Amaryllis are potted with limited root room.

Roots will fill the container, usually before the flowers open.

There is normal variation between clones in the amount of foliage produced with flower scapes. These bulbs are potted in three-quarter-size pots; the one at left in a clay-colored Styrofoam pot; behind is bulb in a white Tufflite pot; at right in clay.

Caladiums growing with "Shower of Gold" *Codiaeum punctatum aureum*, the thin-leaved croton, in Izmal, Mexico

Eucomis bicolor alba

Haemanthus katharinae from Natal

Fragrant Dutch hyacinth, hardy outdoor bulb, may be forced indoors in peat-lite or hyacinth glass with water. Keep dark, at 45° to 50°, for six to eight weeks. When buds and foliage show, give bright light, 60° to 70°.

Summer-blooming *Sprekelia formosissima* from Mexico

Veltheimia viridifolia

15

Succulents—Cacti and Their Companions

CACTI ARE THE BEST-KNOWN SUCCULENTS, although plants with water-storing growth are found in more than twenty plant families, many rivaling the cactus in beauty. Bold agaves with sturdy symmetrical spine-tipped leaves, soft-orange-flowered aloes, euphorbias in miniature to tree-sized species, metallic-tinted sedums, and giant-flowered stapelias have much to offer. As a group the succulent herbs stand out from all others for their markedly three-dimensional structure, textures as exquisite as the skin of fruits or as tough as hide, subtle and extraordinary kinds of coloring, and frequently a magnificent armor of thorns.

A true succulent has water-storing tissues in fleshy leaves or thick green stems to help it survive long periods of drought. Cacti, like the euphorbias, vary greatly in size, habit of growth, branching, spines, and flowers. Desert cacti and many other succulents require a minimum of six hours direct sun each day to reach their potential development with abundant bloom. Other succulents—epiphytic jungle cacti, echeverias, creeping stapelias—will grow and bloom in bright-diffuse light; and strong sun coming through a window in late spring or summer can actually scorch these fleshy plants. Even without the daily six hours of direct sun you can grow a number of unusual succulents.

Haworthias, hoyas, and stapelias thrive three to eight inches under wide-spectrum horticultural fluorescent lamps. Best growth is with four forty-watt tubes. Echeverias will grow well, too, if you keep them three inches under the lights, lower when flowers appear.

Succulents are relatively carefree. They require less of your attention than do other tropicals because they thrive with lower humidity and less water, and they don't need frequent repotting. Their generally slow growth, especially in winter, eliminates the need for frequent turning of pots to maintain symmetrical stems. Many succulents, mainly cacti, thrive in a sunny window where daytime temperatures are in the 80's but drop into the 50's at night.

Decorative accents—rocks, driftwood, ceramics—blend well with succulents; and the bold sharp lines of agaves, aloes, some euphorbias, and gasterias combine perfectly with clay, stone, or earthenware containers. Rooms with cool clean architectural lines are good settings for tall agaves, an *Aloe arborescens*, or a spiny *Euphorbia lactea*; and at night, with lighting from below, such plants throw striking shadows on light walls.

For horticultural reasons I divide cacti into two large groups. The first includes familiar desert cacti—*Echinocactus, Mammillaria, Opuntia,* and many lesser-known genera, adapted to live in direct sun under quite dry conditions, usually with a long cool winter rest. Second are jungle cacti, many of them epiphytes—the orchid cactus or hybrids of *Epiphyllum*, Christmas cactus (*Schlumbergera, Zygocactus*), and tiny-flowered *Rhipsalis*, or mistletoe cactus. Jungle cacti need diffuse light, somewhat more water, and a humus-rich potting medium, not sandy as for desert cacti.

Unless you have plenty of room, choose cacti that don't get huge at maturity. If you want flowers, select those sorts that will bloom under conditions you can provide. My list includes the best kinds for decoration and colorful flowers, but some, like *Echinopsis* and *Lobivia*, require 45° to 50° winter nights for abundant flowers, and all the desert cacti reach their full beauty only in bright sun.

Desert Cacti

Astrophytum capricorne. Slow growing, globose-cylindrical, many long curving spines, satiny lemon-yellow blooms marked red in throat in summer.

A. myriostigma. Spineless, gray-green, three to five inches across, shaped like a bishop's cap—a flattened sphere divided into five lobes (in variety *tetragona*, four lobes). Large light-yellow silky flowers.

A. ornatum. Yellow flowers in late summer. Eight-lobed spiny plant body beautifully streaked with white.

Cephalocereus senilis. Old-man cactus. Easy to grow in bright light; covered with long white hairs.

X *Chamaelopsis.* Hybrids of *Chamaecereus* X *Lobivia.* 'Blush' has rose-pink flowers on a one-inch plant. 'Fire Chief', two-inch-wide red flowers in spring.

Cleistocactus straussii. Silver torch cactus. Attractive columnar plant covered with soft silvery spines. In strong light, cool conditions, also may have red flowers.

Echinocactus grusonii. Golden-spined barrel-shaped Mexican species growing to fifteen inches tall (to four feet in the wild). Small plants remain attractive with slow growth, yellow flowers.

Echinocereus. Four- to ten-inch spiny plants which bloom easily after a cool winter rest. *E. delaetii* has clusters of white-haired stems, pink flowers. *E. fitchii,* cylindrical small plant sometimes branching, yellow spines, many rose-pink flowers, deeper color in center.

Echinopsis. Sea urchin or hedgehog cactus. Large flowers on globose to upright cylinder-shaped plants. Remove offsets for best flowering, give full sun, 45° to 50° winter rest. Crossed with *Lobivia* and *Chamaecereus* to make easily flowered Paramount hybrids with flowers orange, pink, red, and pastel blended colors (Johnson Cactus Gardens).

Espostoa lanata. Covered with a dense fabric of finest white hairs. From Ecuador and Peru. Matures at two to three feet but is slow growing.

Gymnocalycium. Neat spherical 3- to 4-inch spiny South American cactus. *G. damsii* has 1½-inch pink and white flowers; *G. friedrichii* (select forms) rose-pink flowers in summer. A mutant cultivar of this is available as a graft, grown for its glowing red body color. *G. quehlianum* has white flowers marked red in center.

Lobivia. Neat-growing Andean plants with flowers among the most brilliant and varied in color of all cacti. Medium-size, flowering freely, needing a cool winter rest. *L. aurea* is yellow. 'Tricolor', a hybrid, has flowers of blended white, red, and yellow. 'White Knight', a hybrid with *Echinopsis,* has many five-inch flowers.

Mamillopsis senilis. Round ball to five inches high, covered with white hair-like spines, red flowers. Cool winter rest, very gravelly soil.

Mammillaria. Pincushion cactus. Mostly quite small, some compact and solitary, some forming clumps. Ideal for sunny windows. The flowers are small but generally profusely borne near the top, often in a ring or rings. *M. bombycina, M. candida,* and *M. elegans* are good pink-flowered species; *M. zeilmanniana,* deep rose; *M. elongata* and *M. bocasana* have yellow flowers.

Notocactus. Grown for their colorful bristly spines on small ball-shaped or cylindrical plants. *N. apricus, N. mammulosus,* and *N. ottonis* are species with glowing yellow flowers. *N. graessneri* and *N. leninghausii* are patterned with yellow hairy spines and have exquisite yellowish flowers. Give *Notocactus* one-third more leaf mold than other desert cacti.

Opuntia. A widespread genus that includes a few species native to Canada and along our northeastern coast, but most are subtropical. They are easily grown spiny flat-padded plants with orange to yellow flowers. *O. aciculata* has red spines; *O. fuscoatra,* golden flowers; *O. microdasys* has decorative joined pads of dark green patterned with hairy yellow tufts, or white in variety *alba.*

Paramount hybrids. These combine *Chamaecereus, Echinopsis,* and *Lobivia* in adaptable compact hybrids with flowers in pastel blends or rich red, orange, yellow, or pink.

Parodia. Small spherical plants with colorful white to yellow spines, and flowers in spring. *P. aureispina* has golden flowers; *P. sanguiniflora,* deep red.

Rebutia. These South American species grow as clusters of four- to six-inch delicately spined globes, often covered with abundant flowers—scarlet and borne in spring on *R. minuscula,* and rose-violet in late winter on *R. violaciflora.*

Jungle Cacti

Epiphyllum and Rhipsalis

Epiphyllum and its hybrids are called orchid cacti. They are derived from crosses of epiphyllum species and some outcrosses with the genera *Aporocactus, Heliocereus,* and *Nopalxochia.* Flowers have many petals, are from two to eight inches across, and come in all colors except blue. Semiupright flattened and semileaflike stems reach out to one foot or more. Usually they tend to cascade downward; hence these plants are often grown in baskets. Some lovely kinds are:

E. ackermannii. Probably the best known, easy to grow. Flowers large, carmine inside, scarlet outside, freely borne in summer. Called also Nopalxochia.
    'Discovery'. Yellow hybrid.
    'Hermosissimus'. Free-blooming, tricolored flower; violet, orange, crimson.

'Luminosa'. Compact hybrid, three-inch rose-colored flowers, easy to grow.
'Marina Special'. Giant white hybrid.

E. oxypetalum. Fragrant white night-flowering species, to six feet.
'Sequoia'. Giant orange-flowered hybrid.

Epiphytic *Rhipsalis* is a compact but pendulous jungle cactus, excellent in hanging baskets or raised pots. Green stems have small quarter- to one-inch white, cream, to orange flowers, then often white berries. There are many species, all thriving in light shade and humus-rich rapidly draining soil. *R. cassutha* (*R. baccifera*) resembles mistletoe. *R. mesembryanthemoides* has small white flowers followed by pearl-white berries.

Fragrant white-and-gold-flowered *Pseudorhipsalis macrantha* looks like a dwarf epiphyllum and produces one- to two-inch flowers from October through January. I grow it in a basket with columneas, planted in a humus-rich mix diluted with 25 percent fine fir or redwood bark. Morning sunlight intensifies the flowers' fragrance.

CULTURE

Pot epiphyllums and related cacti in relatively small containers with extra-good drainage of crocks, charcoal chunks, and pea gravel. Pot these epiphytic cacti in the standard succulent mix (Chapter 3) diluted 50-50 with a commercial semiterrestrial orchid mix (McLellan's Wonderbark mix, for example) or, second best, with 25 percent fine-grade-redwood bark and enough chopped sphagnum moss to keep the soil porous. Some commercial growers pot in equal parts of chopped sphagnum and sandy soil and add a sprinkle of granulated charcoal.

Maintain roots lightly moist as new growth is made, then slightly drier and cooler (to 50° nights), never bone-dry at the roots even when they are resting. Avoid direct summer sun, but give full winter light in temperate zones. In late fall through winter keep resting plants in a bright cool place, under 65°. Increase watering as new growth appears in late winter. It is natural for a few buds on epiphyllums to blast, especially on recently potted plants. Propagate these cacti by stem cuttings, layering, or seed (Chapter 5).

Schlumbergera and Zygocactus

These are the favorite Christmas and Thanksgiving cacti. They thrive in the epiphyllum mix, kept somewhat more moist when they are active. The jungle cactus known botanically as *Rhipsalidopsis* blooms near Easter. Growers are now offering cultivars that flower twice a year, fall and spring, like *Zygocactus* 'Electra' and *Rhipsalidopsis* 'Crimson Giant'. *R.* 'Rosea' and 'André' are spring-blooming hybrids.

SPRING OR EASTER SEASON

'André'. Red flowers.

'China Pink'. 1½- to 2-inch flowers.

'Crimson Giant'. Vigorous Johnson hybrid with 3-inch red flowers in April, often again in September.

FALL OR THANKSGIVING SEASON

'Mme. Ganna Walska'. Toothed green leaf pads called crab's-claws, red flowers from late November to February.

'W. Freuden'. Compact plants, buff-orange flowers.

Zygocactus bicolor. Many-forked stems and abundant red, white-centered flowers.

Z. truncatus. Traditional species, flowers in October–November.

WINTER OR CHRISTMAS SEASON

'Amelia Manda'. Large crimson flowers.

'Pink Perfection'. Clear soft-pink flowers.

Schlumbergera bridgesii. Traditional species, carmine-red flowers.

S. russelliana. Upright or pendent; the stems rounded below, flattened above. Flowers red, with orange blush.

These cacti grow as epiphytes or semiterrestrials in Mexico, Central America, and Brazil, usually at higher elevations where night temperatures drop to 40° or 50°. Plant them in humus-rich soil as recommended for epiphyllums, and keep them lightly moist when they are growing. Every two weeks, from late spring through August, fertilize alternately with half-strength chemical fertilizer and an organic product like fish emulsion. In early fall let them go somewhat longer between waterings, cut out all fertilizing, and continue to give them bright light but no hot sun. Leave them outdoors until there is danger from frost, or let them stay on a cool porch with nights in the 40's.

FLOWERS

To bloom abundantly these cacti require cool nights when they are setting buds after a summer of growth. Night temperatures above 65° inhibit maximum bloom. Day length also must be short. Tests show that to set buds on Christmas cacti, the plant needs short days (less than twelve hours) from October to early December or, as an alternative to short days, night temperatures of 45° to 50°. Similar periods of darkness or cool nights are required to bloom all species of Easter, Thanksgiving, and Christmas cacti.

I have success when these plants are left outside until early October, then brought into a sunny window in the basement where nights drop to 65° and the naturally short days of fall are not extended by artificial light. Other growers put plants in a closet every evening before six o'clock, then return the cacti to a sunny window in the morning. This sounds like a nuisance to me, but if you can't provide cool temperatures, it's one way to get quantities of blooms.

City dwellers can leave plants outside on a fire escape. A cool sun porch, pantry, or bay window are other favorable fall locations.

PROPAGATION

Jointed cacti are best propagated by layering or stem cuttings, left to form a callus for a day if any have open wounds. See Chapter 5 for details. For a bushy effect fast, plant five or six small rooted stem cuttings together in a six-inch pot. *Schlumbergera* is sometimes grafted onto the stem of a *Peireskia* plant, an unusual cactus that looks like a vine and actually has leaves. This technique permits the *Schlumbergera* to produce an attractive billow of pendent branches, held several feet above the strong roots of *Peireskia*, and the flowers hang like Christmas-tree ornaments. Succulent specialists sell such grafted plants, but they are more expensive than jungle cacti on their own roots.

Other Succulents

Like jungle cacti, the gasterias, haworthias, hoyas, and sansevierias will accept less than six hours of direct sun each day and still grow with vigor. They are fine plants for the average home or office. In a sunny window striking agaves, majestic euphorbias, and creeping sedums can provide beauty with a minimum of care.

Aeonium

Aeonium plants may resemble hardy sempervivums, the hen and chicks most of us have in the garden, or, as with *A. arboreum atropurpureum,* they may eventually reach two to three feet while still in a rosette form. The flowers of this genus are small but produced in panicles on a ten- to fifteen-inch stalk. *A. haworthii* and *A. tabulaeforme* are yellow-flowered, more compact rosettes. Give them bright-diffuse light, less water in winter during their rest.

Agave

Agaves are a romantic genus, famous for the belief (associated particularly with *A. americana*) that they bloom only once every century, although it really takes less than ten years for most agaves to mature. After blooming they produce many offsets, then die. Hardly a ship sails the sea without a reminder of *A. sisalina* or *A. fourcroydes* on board, as sisal rope from either of these Mexican henequen species. Potent tequila is distilled from fermented leaves of *A. tequilana*, and beerlike pulque is honey water fermented in the center of the living *A. atrovirens*.

I call agaves hemoglobin plants for all the blood drawn by their sharp terminal spines when my window was graced with several symmetrical species. In mature specimens the wicked black leaf-spears will reach two to three inches; don't grow agaves in tight quarters or near a path! They are excellent as accents in sunny planter beds. Mature *A. fourcroydes* I saw in Yucatán were four feet around, but small offsets or young seedlings can be grown indoors for many years before they approach overpowering proportions.

Smaller species, *A. horrida, A. potatorum (verschaffeltii), A. pumila,* and *A. victoriae-reginae* are carefree sorts for sunny windows and bring years of pleasure with very little care.

Aloe

You will see an aloe, "sábila," hanging as a talisman in shops and homes all around Latin America. Deep-green *Aloe vera*, more practical than beautiful, was introduced by conquistadores for its medicinal sap, a possible explanation for the belief that *Aloe vera* brings good luck and prosperity. When I was producing programs for Colombian National Television, I hung a sábila over our natural science set. Its plump rosette brought us good luck for months, until our television teacher burned her hand doing a chemistry experiment.

As revenge, we broke off a leaf and rubbed its clear sap over the burn. In a few minutes pain had gone, and we resumed taping. So powerful is this aloe juice that several drug firms sell an ointment made from aloe leaves. Here is a medicine that you can keep on your windowsill instead of in a bathroom cabinet.

Other aloes are grown for handsome leaves and abundant flowers. In South Africa and Zambia I found aloes grown everywhere in full sun. Rhodesians in Salisbury cultivate several species in street divider beds where compact two- to three-foot plants bloom with abandon. Your captive aloes will do likewise when they are given direct sun for five or six hours a day; but aloes in dimmer light are still attractive for their foliage, which gets longer with less light intensity.

Some fine species are *A. arborescens* with huge recurred blue-green leaves to fifteen feet eventually but good as a small plant; *A. aristata*, dwarf, white-spotted leaves in dense rosettes; *A. brevifolia*, silver-green leaves, three inches long, also in a variegated form; and *A. variegata*, symmetrical three-sided leaves, deep green, barred white. Propagate aloes from basal offsets. If you don't like the dangerous spines of agaves, the aloes are a logical substitute.

Ceropegia

Ceropegia, an odd slender vine, has potatolike tubers along stringy stems. It is nice in small hanging containers or strawberry jars in bright light. Flowers are small, curiously shaped, and usually greenish-yellow, among veined foliage. *C. barkleyi* has green foliage marked silver; *C. caffrorum*, arrowhead-shaped leaves; *C. woodii*, the rosary vine, has heart-shaped silver-gray leaves and trailing stems to thirty inches.

Cotyledon

Cotyledons, African members of the Crassula family, are grown for their metallic gray-green to white-powdered foliage in loose rosette form, not so neat as echeverias. Attractive species for a sunny window are *C. barbeyi* with thick shovel-shaped leaves coated powdery white; silver-white, red-edged, twelve-inch-tall *C. orbiculata*; and the silver-gray orange-flavored *C. undulata* with crinkle-margined wedge-shaped foliage. The curious leaves of these various species mark easily if touched, so be careful in planting them.

Crassula

Crassula argentea, or jade plant, long admired for its classic Oriental appearance and adaptibility, is the best-known member of this versatile genus. Slow-growing crassulae will endure under low light, but it is wise to give them a few hours of direct sun every day to bring out their best coloring and shape. *C. argentea* will eventually reach three to four feet, but small plants are commonly used in dish gardens with other succulents; they take many years to get out of scale in most windows. The starlike flowers are rarely produced on plants indoors.

Other nice species are *C. cornuta* with clusters of plump glaucous-silver leaves; *C. dregeana* hybrids with gray leaves and clusters of red flowers; *C. falcata*, scarlet-flowered and gray-green-leaved; *C. 'Morgan's Pink'* with balls of pink flowers on top of neat leaf towers; *C. perfossa* with symmetrical necklacelike growth; and mat-forming *C. schmidtii*, which has clusters of rose-red flowers on two- to three-inch stems.

Echeveria

Echeverias, forming orderly metallic-tinted rosettes, are perfect small- to medium-size succulents for bright locations or culture under at least two forty-watt wide-spectrum growth lamps. Bright light brings out the best leaf color. Keeping them on the dry side with controlled watering will avoid root rot. Propagate by offsets or seed. This is a large genus, chiefly Mexican. The best kinds for indoor planting are the compact species or hybrids.

E. derenbergii is a small rosette of green leaves suffused with glaucous silver-blue, red-tipped in bright light, the flowers golden to orange. *E.* 'Imbricata' has robust blue-gray leaves in a rosette to eight inches across and deep-orange flowers. *E.* 'Doris Taylor' has a four- to five-inch rosette of deep-green red-tipped leaves delightfully covered with white fuzz. *E. elegans* forms a neat three- to six-inch circle of glaucous fleshy leaves and has pink flowers. *E. glauca pumila* is stemless, compact, gray-blue. *E. pulvinata* has velvety, green foliage flushed red in bright light and orange-yellow bell-shaped flowers in spikes in winter. *E. setosa* grows in a very tight rosette of deep-green, red-tipped, and white-hairy foliage and produces red flowers. Larger kinds are often grown outdoors in warm climates, but most of them look like cabbages.

Edithcolea

Edithcolea grandis is a four- to six-inch creeping member of the milkweed family, of East Africa, and something of a horticultural challenge. Grow it dry, in full sun, and you may have success. It's available from a few succulent-plant specialists.

Euphorbia

The most famous euphorbia is not a true succulent but a thin-leaved Mexican species, *E. pulcherrima*, the poinsettia. By far the greater number of species in this fascinating and protean genus are, however, cactuslike or water-storing plants of arid tropical places. My strongest memory of East African flora is of tall tree-form euphorbias clinging to steep slopes around Ngorongoro Crater—*E. candelabrum* and *E. nyikae*—far too large to fit into our modern homes or small greenhouses.

Some spiny euphorbias suitable for home growing are *E. caerulescens,* upright blue-green stems; *E. grandicornis* as a young plant, having apple-green stems with triangular wings; and *E. lactea*, normally upright three- to four-angled dark-green stems with spines and a lighter band down the center, but also available in a monstrous or crested 'Elkhorn' type. *E.*

mammillaris has stems that look like corncobs. *E. obesa* closely resembles a baseball. *E. polygona* has deeply furrowed dark-green stems decorated with small spines.

Red-flowered spiny-stemmed leaf-bearing euphorbias, known as crown of thorns, include the species *E. splendens*, the hybrid *E.* X *keysii*, which flowers for me all year long if given at least three hours of direct sun per day, and the selected dwarf dark-red-flowered form 'Bojeri'. True flowers on euphorbias are tiny yellow-green clusters surrounded by the colorful (pink, red, yellow, or rarely white) bracts we call "flowers."

Gasteria

The South African genus *Gasteria* and its hybrids with *Haworthia*, the X Gasterhaworthias, are orderly plants for bright-diffuse light, not hot sun at midday. *Gasteria caespitosa* forms a four- to six-inch clump; *G. liliputana,* a dwarf, has mottled green leaves; *G. maculata* is a sturdy grower with red flowers; *G. verrucosa* is a controlled "stack of tongues"; X Gasterhaworthia 'Royal Highness' is an adaptable dwarf rosette, deep green, pebbled white, nice in a desert dish garden.

Graptopetalum

Graptopetalum species are very much like dwarf echeverias and can be treated the same. An excellent species forming blue-gray rosettes is the Mexican *G. paraguayense*.

Haworthia

Haworthias, South African members of the lily family, thrive in bright-diffuse light with moderate watering. Many species are small and are easily planted several together in dish gardens or miniature pots; I like to mulch them with rustic stones or pastel seashells. Some excellent species are: *H. attenuata*, rosette of dark-green leaves with white tubercles in transverse lines; *H. fasciata,* making a clump with offsets, leaves banded white; *H. reinwardtii*, an upright column to about six inches, and *H. subfasciata*, with dark-green leaves crossed white.

Hoya

Hoya vines are frequently listed in succulent-plant catalogs, since they require less water than other flowering vines thanks to wax-coated fleshy leaves. Bright-diffuse light is required if you expect abundant bloom, but direct sun may burn the leaves. See Chapter 7.

Huernia

Huernia is often confused with *Stapelia*, its close relatives. *Huernia* species have yellow scentless flowers marked purple and are smaller plants. *H. macrocarpa* and *H. zebrina* are two delightful and rather different species with four- to eight-inch five-angled stems, quite at home in a sunny window or even under fluorescent lights. *Stapelia* and *Huernia* plants are grown lightly moist when active, but kept on the dry side during their winter rest. Night temperatures around 65° and bright-diffuse light satisfy my plants.

Kalanchoe

Kalanchoes are best known for *K. blossfeldiana* hybrids, favorite winter holiday gifts. Rivaling them for decoration is *K. tomentosa*, the teddy-bear plant, with beautiful gray-green foliage tipped and edged dark brown. Other interesting species are: *K. daigremontiana, K. pinnata,* and *K. tubiflora,* which sprout plantlets on their leaf margins; low-growing brown and yellow *K. marmorata*; and *K. uniflora*, a flowering trailer.

Lithops

Lithops look so much like the pebbles of their South African habitat that they escape notice except by experienced plant hunters. The squat flat-topped plants are seldom larger than chestnuts; a number of them will fit comfortably in a six-inch bulb pan of sharply drained sandy soil. Their flowers resemble sea anemones of white, yellow, or orange, from ¾ inch to 1¾ inches across.

Related living stones are species in about twenty genera, of which *Argyroderma, Conophytum, Dinteranthus, Lapidaria, Pleiospilos,* and a few others are to be found in botanical and private greenhouses and are available from a few succulent-plant nurseries. *Lithops* and *Conophytum* are probably the best known.

Pot these and related genera in the standard cactus-succulent mix, mulch them with gravel, and water very sparingly from December to May (and thereafter only lightly until growth is quite evident). Let the plants dry between waterings, even when they are active, use no fertilizer, and provide bright light, plenty of fresh air, and winter temperatures to 50° at night.

Pachyphytum

Pachyphytum are adaptable thick-leaved Mexican members of the Crassula family. *P. compactum* makes a dense mound of cylindrical leaves touched brown and silver. *P. oviferum* has leaves resembling birds' eggs, of silvery white, blushing pink in bright light. The little bellflowers of both species are red, in racemes.

Pedilanthus

Pedilanthus tithymaloides can grace a dim hall and remain attractive there for several months, but it thrives in bright light when making new growth; I keep mine in a south window where the zigzag stems look nice in silhouette. The thin white-splashed leaves turn reddish in strong sun.

Sansevieria

Sansevieria comprises about fifty species, mostly African, of interesting and easily cared for plants, from four- to six-inch *S. trifasciata* 'Hahnii' to *S. zanzibarica*, a five- to six-foot giant. Some cultivars are called snake plants for the mottled pattern on their foliage and the stiff yet sinuous upright growth. They are justifiably popular for extreme durability.

Snake plants will endure shade to full sun, coolness to heat. Species I studied in East Africa grew in almost full sun, rambling around under tall shrubs, the roots in well-drained sandy soil. In Zambia I noticed that fiber-producing *S. thyrsiflora* grew in shade or in full sun with equal abandon. Sansevierias thrive when kept on the dry side. Wash leaves, or wipe with a moist cloth to keep free of dust. Propagate from offsets or rooted leaf cuttings.

Sedum

Sedums are represented in temperate gardens by cold-hardy species, but many of the tropical varieties can be enjoyed indoors. A favorite for hanging baskets is silver-gray *S. morganianum*, or burro's tail, which cascades two to three feet when given a bright place and careful watering. Any of the plump one-inch leaves that are knocked off the pendent stems will root in moist sand or a propagating mix. I've even had them root in orchid pots of tree-fern compost. *S. pachyphyllum* has tiny banana-shaped leaves and grows happily with companion succulents. Its miniature tree form appears to advantage in a shallow dish garden. *Sedum stahlii*, looking like a stack of jelly beans, grows to about eight inches high, its leaves turning red when exposed to bright sun.

Let sedums dry out between waterings, give as much sun as possible, fertilize once a month when they are growing, and provide night temperatures between 50° and 68° (although they will tolerate nights into the low 40's).

Stapelia

Stapelia gigantea has the largest flowers, ten to twelve inches across, of many species. All have short, squarish, tooth-edged stems, no leaves, and flowers suggesting exotic starfish, in purple-brown, orchid-yellow, or green-yellow, banded or spotted with other colors, and often velvety-hairy or ciliate-margined. Freshly opened flowers smell like dead meat, a useful olfactory adaptation to insure pollination by flies. Don't let this stop you from growing stapelias, since flowers are not really offensive unless you make an effort to smell them at close range. A blooming plant can always be enjoyed by an open window or on the terrace, and even without flowers the spineless plants are interesting.

Yucca

Yucca elephantipes is sometimes used as a decorative indoor plant, since it is a warm-growing species. Many other species are cold-hardy to varying degrees and not satisfactory indoors. As a young specimen, *Y. elephantipes* looks like a stiff *Draceana marginata* but will eventually reach more than thirty feet. Central American *Y. filifera*, or izote, also makes a dramatic pot plant when young and may even produce its one-foot spire of globe-shaped waxy white flowers when given enough bright sun.

General Comments

Ordering Succulents

Get your succulents from nurseries that raise them from seed or vegetative propagation rather than collect them constantly from the wild. Nursery-grown plants have healthy roots and less chance of being infested with pests. New hybrids are available only as nursery-grown plants or sometimes as unrooted cuttings. Insist on getting correctly labeled plants so that you will be able to look up the culture and history of your specimens. This is a good rule for all tropicals and especially cactus, many of which are harder to identify than most plants.

Basic Culture

Pot succulents in the mixture described in Chapter 3 or in sandy succulent or cactus soils available in garden stores (Swiss Farms Cactus Soil, etc.). Keep plants in relatively small containers. Water only when plants really need moisture. Some plants from South Africa, normally dormant there in our summer, will change their growth pattern when cultivated in the Northern Hemisphere, but other plants will not, so study individual plant behavior.

Pest Control

Mealybugs, nematodes, and scale are the most frequently encountered pests on succulents. Controls are discussed in Chapter 18. Remember that Malathion often injures succulents, may kill kalanchoes, so use Black Leaf-40 or a similar nicotine-sulfate spray. Pot only in sterilized soil to avoid nematodes, and follow other recommendations for keeping your indoor plants pestfree. Alfred Byrd Graf reports that Cygon, diluted one teaspoon per gallon of water, is used to kill root mealybugs, which may suck sap from the roots of succulents. I have used Cygon 2E at that same strength for many bulbs, but fortunately I have not had to try it on succulents yet. If you find mealybugs, give the plants a drench as suggested; mealybugs are quite damaging to pot plants.

Mammillaria geminispina, grown mainly for its clustering beautifully spined stems, bears bright-red blooms when given strong light.

Varied shapes and colors make an interesting collection of succulents from around the world. At left foreground, large plant is *Pachypodium lamerei* of southern Africa.

Desert cacti in most genera have flowers similar to those of *Opuntia compressa*, an unusually hardy member of a generally tropical family. This plant grows in a rock crevice filled with humus in my southern New York garden.

Slow-growing succulents closely planted in a well-drained dish garden remain attractive for a year or more if given bright light and careful watering. Here *Opuntia microdasys alba* with dots of white glochids, *Crassula argentea* in small-rooted sections with oval foliage, *Sedum pachyphyllum* looking like clusters of beans, and a low *Echeveria* grow happily together in porous shallow containers molded to resemble rocks.

Heliocereus speciosus, with diurnal scarlet flowers, clambers into a low tree in Yucatán. Its roots were in humus at the base of the tree, and several sections of cactus stem had also rooted in rotted leaves caught between branches.

Aeonium, related to crassulae and echeverias, has silvery-blue symmetrical foliage, here well displayed against a plain wall in Châteauneuf-du-Pape near Avignon.

Pendent *Schlumbergera*, or Christmas cactus, shows to best advantage in hanging pot or basket.

Agaves, New World members of the amaryllis family, vary appreciably in size, but all have leaves in a basic rosette and mostly spiny-tipped.

Aloe species at the Paris Botanical Gardens are sunk in outdoor gravel beds for a summer in full sun.

Aloes blooming in an attractive street mall at Salisbury, Rhodesia

Succulent *Euphorbia lactea* from India and Ceylon is good in strong light.

Euphorbia X *keysii* has stiff, woody, spine-covered stems, small leaves, and bright-pink flowers, seen in a New York City window.

Gasteria verrucosa, a South African member of the lily family

Graptopetalum paraguayense

Haworthia and *gasteria* are crossed to produce Gasterhaworthia. Aloes are hybridized with gasterias to make X Gastrolea (Gaster-aloe). The succulents here are all miniature or dwarf species or hybrids of these genera.

Kalanchoe tomentosa, a fuzzy gray-green succulent of Madagascar

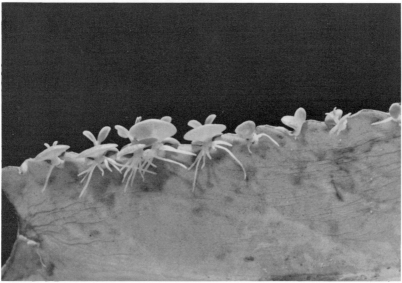

Kalanchoe daigremontiana sprouts tiny plantlets on margins of mature leaves. Each plantlet can be rooted.

Sansevieria ehrenbergii shares its habitat with a hyrax in Seronera, Tanzania.

A kalanchoe (formerly Bryo-
phyllum) and a Mexican sedum
growing in hollowed-out lava
rock

Stapelia gigantea in author's
collection

16

Miniatures–Delights in Many Genera

DIMINUTIVE PLANTS ARE EASILY OVERLOOKED in tangled tropical jungles, and I suppose that in struggling through steamy thickets around the world I must have trod on countless little treasures. But in one historical area some delightful small gems stood out in verdant display. I was climbing Mayan ruins in Yucatán, enormous structures of gray building blocks held together with coral cement and ingenious stone cutting. In cracks, widened by centuries of pounding rains and a broiling sun, grew dwarf maidenhair ferns, their tiny fronds sparkling like emeralds against crumbling carvings. In another, more humid forest along the Amazon River, I discovered creeping episcias and tiny *Caladium humboldtii* nestled in rich humus accumulations under towering vine-covered trees.

Smaller tropicals are practical in limited growing areas or when you want many different plants without worry that some may take over the whole window. Under fluorescent lights dwarf to miniature species in any genus are, almost necessarily, the ones to choose.

Miniature *Saintpaulia* can be grown to blooming maturity in 2½-inch pots, whereas a miniature cymbidium hybrid will reach from twelve to fifteen inches in a 6-inch pot before flowers can be expected. In the gesneriads are so many truly tiny plants that you can fill a window with a collection of species and hybrids. For the smaller geraniums and begonias see Chapters 9 and 10.

Some standard-size tropicals can be used in terrariums while they are seedlings. Palms, for example, will stay under twelve inches for a year or more. Smaller aloes, haworthias, and cacti are nice in a miniature desert landscape, which will retain its minute character for several years.

Faster-growing kinds of begonias, ferns, and gesneriads will have to be divided or moved on to larger containers more often. Culture for true miniatures is generally the same as for other members of a given genus. For example, miniature gesneriads require the same humus-rich soil and high humidity as their larger relatives. Some of the smaller *Sinningia* do best with higher humidity, which keeps small pots from drying out too rapidly. Miniatures require fertilizer and water, but in quantities that fit their stature.

Kinds to Grow

Ground Covers and Small Trailers

Here are some low-growing trailers and creepers suitable for planting around larger tropicals, or to cover the soil in terrariums:

Cyanotis kewensis. Small fuzzy brown leaves, purple beneath. Best in bright somewhat dry situations.

Episcia dianthiflora. Green velvety leaves, dainty white flowers, for warm, humid place with bright-diffuse light. I found it easy to raise from seed.

Helxine soleirolii. Sometimes called baby's tears. Makes a close-growing moss-like mat of small green leaves. Minimum night temperature of 50° acceptable.

Peperomia rotundifolia. I saw this tiny round-leaved succulent growing on moss-covered tree limbs in close company with epiphytic orchids. Grow peperomia miniatures with diffuse light, humidity above 40 percent but not too much moisture at the roots. Another good one, *P.* 'San Salvador' (Logee's), may be a form of this species.

Pilea cadierei 'Minima', *P. nummulariaefolia, P. repens.* Each species of *Pilea* gives a different color. You can have a tapesty of species in the same terrarium. *P. cadierei* 'Minima' is marked silver. *P. nummulariaefolia* has red-toned branches with quilted light-green foliage. *P. repens* has dark-bronze foliage. These need filtered sun, humidity above 50 percent, lightly moist humus-rich soil, nights at 60° to 65°.

Plectranthus oertendahlii. Easy to grow from seed or stem cuttings. Fleshy bronze-green creeper. Bright-diffuse light for best bloom.

Selaginella caulescens, S. emmeliana, S. kraussiana, S. uncinata. These creeping plants, much like the club mosses, do well with high humidity, humus-rich soil, nights at 60° to 65°. Lacy foliage forms a fine background for taller terrarium plants.

Tradescantia multiflora (Gibasis geniculata). Plain tiny green leaves, many white flowers. Easy in a basket or airy terrarium, on dry side at roots.

Compact Ferns for Miniature Landscapes

Adiantum bellum, A. hispidulum. Maidenhair. Add dolomite limestone to humus-rich soil.

Doryopteris pedata. Light-green deeply serrated fronds, eight to fifteen inches tall on wiry black stems.

Nephrolepis exaltata 'Verona'. This and other compact forms of the Boston fern are good backgrounds in terrariums and small dish gardens.

Pteris ensiformis 'Victoriae'. Small-growing table ferns are easy in a humid place with diffuse light. 'Victoriae' has dark-green fronds variegated with silver.

Begonias

Any of the miniature hybrids derived from *B. boweri* are delightful in a terrarium or windowsill collection. Small-leaved *B. cubensis* and *B. foliosa* give a delicate compact effect, very fine on chunks of Featherock, somewhat higher than the other plants around them.

Bromeliads

Low-growing *Cryptanthus* species and hybrids are excellent dwarf foliage plants. The best miniature epiphytic bromeliad is *Tillandsia ionantha*, which will thrive on a slab of tree-fern fiber in bright light. *Cryptanthus bivittatus minor* is good in terrariums.

Bulbs and Tubers

The most charming tuberous miniature I can imagine is green and white *Caladium humboldtii*. Mine is a clump, hardly six inches tall, of a beautiful color and shape, and thrives in a 1½-inch pot in a warm humid place. Other small-growing tropical bulbs are hard to find, but some amaryllis hybrids, like

'Christmas Joy' and the species *A. striata* (*Hippeastrum striatum*), stay under twelve inches tall and do well in a 4- to 5-inch pot.

Geraniums

See Chapter 9 for a list of some charming miniature geranium hybrids. These must have good light and air circulation; they are not terrarium material.

Gesneriads

Tiny *Sinningia pusilla* is the smallest gesneriad, but it grows from a tuber just as do the giant gloxinias; at least ten plants of *S. pusilla* can fit into a single normal gloxinia flower. Hybrids derived from *S. pusilla* include *S.* 'Pink Petite', a salmon trumpet-flowered two- to four-inch plant.

Sinningia 'Bright Eyes' is a long-blooming hybrid with lavender-pink trumpets. Hybridizer Ruth Katzenberger introduced *S.* 'Dollbaby', a very popular clone that thrives in a 2½- to 3-inch pot, best under fluorescents in my collection. It reaches four to six inches tall, propagates by leaf cuttings or seed, but the seedlings are not identical and of course are not called *S.* 'Dollbaby'. *S.* 'White Sprite' is a cultivar of *S. pusilla* which comes true from seed. I always grow several plants together in a 2-inch pot.

The Buells of Eastford, Connecticut, gave me an exciting preview of some improved miniature Sinningia plants that are even easier to grow, more floriferous, and different in color from those now available. So keep on the lookout in gesneriad catalogs for new treasures.

S. 'Freckles' is a *S. concinna* hybrid with purple-toned foliage and three-quarter-inch blue-lavender flowers. Each bloom is delicately spotted deep violet over a broad white lip. Flowers are abundant, each on a one- to two-inch stalk, and side lighting brings out the silver hairs all over the plant. *S. concinna* itself has white flowers heavily marked with purple-blue stripes on top and a bordering of purple around the open front. Underneath and inside are spots that 'Freckles' has inherited. A mature plant does well for me in a 2½-inch plastic pot of humus-rich soil.

True miniature African-violets three to six inches in diameter are available in several colors. They are at home in 2½-inch pots until they make a clump of secondary plants. When this happens, they are ready to divide. Remove side shoots with a sharp pair of scissors to keep the miniature in a single pot longer, or grow them as multicrown specimens in 3-inch containers.

Lyndon Lyon's 'Tiny Blue' and 'Snow In' flower well for me under fluorescent lights. The smallest one I've seen is 'Edith's Toy', but I find it difficult to grow well.

Saintpaulia shumensis, from the West Usambara Mountains, inland from Tanga, Tanzania, is adapted to live under somewhat drier conditions than other species. Since it comes from more than five thousand feet above sea level, it is also used to night temperatures in the 50's.

The most popular *Saintpaulia* miniatures have this species in their backgrounds, as can be seen by flower shape in some and by small very succulent foliage with erect hairs on most. If you experience any difficulty with miniature African-violets, grow them somewhat cooler and drier than your standard-size ones. Miniatures, especially those with *S. shumensis* in their backgrounds, produce many suckers or offshoots around the main crown.

These additional crowns are perfect starts for new plants, so remove them two or three times each year, and treat them as directed for secondary gloxinia stems in Chapter 5. Many miniatures look nicer when repotted at least once a year and kept to single crowns. If an older plant continues to look poorly in spite of grooming and repotting, break off some leaves, and grow a new batch of plantlets, which will produce symmetrical growth. To groom miniature violets, I like to use cuticle scissors; cut off the older bottom leaves that turn yellow, and snip out old faded flowers.

A classification for semiminiature African-violets covers hybrids that mature at six to eight inches. Flowers and foliage are larger than true minatures but still much smaller than giant forms of *Saintpaulia* frequently grown for show. Semiminiatures look good in large brandy snifters or in light-cart displays where space is always limited. If you are planting a terrarium display of *Saintpaulia*, keep semiminiatures in the background, putting the true miniatures up front.

Gloxinias come in small-growing strains and clones that have quite large flowers in relation to the short three- or four-inch-high plants. These grow best under fluorescent lamps where bright light keeps them compact. Some nice ones are: 'Tom Thumb', a red flower edged white (matures in a 2½- to 3-inch pot); 'Slipper Time', a slipper-form red cultivar; and the dwarf seed-grown strains offered in several catalogs.

Episcia dianthiflora, a true miniature creeper with one-inch white flowers deeply fringed around the outer edge, is one that I have grown from seed, but it is also available as stem cuttings or layers. Some of my plants are rooted around the base of a standard gloxinia plant where they trail over the pot.

Orchids

The smallest orchids are also the ones with flowers so minute that you need a ten-power glass to see them, but there are some species that grow less than ten inches high yet produce flowers of respectable size. Some good hybrids are *Ascocentrum* interspecific crosses or, for even larger flowers, the ascocendas, which are crosses with *Vanda* and produce sprays of flowers in orange, red, yellow, and even purple shades on plants under a foot tall.

Among the cattleya type of hybrids are dwarf to miniature plants that are easier to grow than straight jungle species. Fred A. Stewart Company devotes a section of its catalog to miniatures, and other specialists have miniature orchids in many genera. With cattleya-alliance hybrids you will find that those with *Brassavola nodosa, B. glauca, Cattleya aurantiaca, C. luteola, C. walkeriana, Laelia rubescens, Broughtonia* species, and *Sophronitis* species as one parent may be expected to produce compact plants, even when the other parent is a large-flowered cattleya.

Compact epidendrums, like *E. tampense*, crossed with cattleyas will make dwarf hybrids which have sprays of flowers intermediate in size between the two parents. Epicattleya Rose Beauty is a good example of these. Crosses between miniature fan-shaped oncidiums (many by Goodale Moir and released through William Kirch Orchids) are so small that they can be grown on croton or coffee-tree branches in a bright window. The long-lasting white, yellow, lavender, or reddish flowers are produced on five- to ten-inch sprays several times taller than the plants.

Species expand the list of true miniature orchids that are adaptable enough to grow indoors. *Oncidium henekenii* is a two- to three-inch fleshy fan of bronze-green foliage with flowers that look like bumblebees; *O. cheiriphorum* has sprays of fragrant yellow flowers; *O. longipes* is a four-inch plant from Brazil and produces tiny spikes of deep-yellow flowers; *O. triquetrum* forms a three-inch fan of red-spotted leaves and a spray of quarter-inch white flowers marked red, purple, and green. *Oncidium pusillum* is less than three inches high, looks like a single miniature palm leaf, and is dwarfed by its inch-wide yellow flowers.

Ornithocephalus bicornus has sprays of quarter-inch downy green flowers from a two-inch-high fan of foliage. *Leptotes* bicolor looks like a tiny *Brassavola nodosa*, has a succulent cluster of two-inch leaves and fragrant white flowers marked magenta. A delightful miniature for its vanilla fragrance is white-flowered *Neofinetia (Angraecum) falcata*, long a favorite in its native Japan. Recent hybrids have blended this species with *Vanda* (Vandofinetia) and *Ascocentrum* (Ascofinetia) to get colored flowers on dwarf plants. Hybrids containing all three of these monopodial species are called Nakamotoara.

Under eight inches are *Sophronitis* species, used to bring glowing orange to red colors into cattleya-alliance hybrids. The species may succeed under your care if given high humidity and bright-diffuse light, but the hybrids with *Sophronitis* are more adaptable. One fine compact one is Epiphronitis Veitchii (*E. radicans* X *S. coccinea*).

These miniatures are easy to find in orchid catalogs. If you love tiny orchids, you can discover many more by a little searching. If you are considering "miniature" cymbidiums, recall that although the flowers and plants are smaller than standard hybrids, they will still grow to two feet high, so they are not for terrariums or small light-cart gardens.

Succulents

Collections of miniature cacti are often sold in tiny plastic pots, sometimes set together in a plastic tray or clear shelf-size greenhouse. Such plants, usually seedlings, eventually reach ten to twelve inches but will remain attractive and in miniature scale for several years. The plants are more charming if you take them out of the individual pots and arrange them in a desert landscape made with a few stones and weathered wood chunks.

All small plants, not just succulents, have an easier time in groups because one- to two-inch pots are difficult to keep correctly watered, whereas several plants in a larger container are not. With succulents, pots must be relatively small and have sharp drainage, even for group plantings. Redwood or cypress boxes are attractive containers for succulent gardens.

Cacti that mature while under six inches include pygmy Paramount hybrids bred by Johnson Cactus Gardens. The parents are species of *Chamaecereus, Echinopsis,* and *Lobivia,* combined to make easy-to-flower spherical spiny plants. I have three clumps growing together in a five-inch pot, mulched with white marble chips. 'White Knight' is a *Lobivia* X *Echinopsis* that has several white flowers about four inches across, on a plant under six inches high.

Rebutia, such as clustering *R. senilis* with flame-colored flowers in spring, and species of *Parodia,* are compact cacti that seldom exceed six inches in height. All require direct sun for sturdy growth.

Aloe albiflora, A. aristata, A. bakeri, A. bellatula, A. haworthioides, and *A. rauhi* will fit easily into a display of miniatures. White-barred *A. variegata* grows a foot high after five years but is a compact species. The choicer small succulents are not at all common, and some hunting is required to locate them. Some can be raised from seed.

Many *aeonium* and echeveria plants are small when young. *E. elegans* makes an attractive clump in a four-inch pot. *Haworthia attenuata* and *H. fasciata* both have white-banded dark-green foliage in little symmetrical clusters, like a tiny agave. The four- to six-inch plants will thrive in less light than cacti need.

Lithops are like big pebbles, and you can fit a whole collection into a six-inch pot. *Sedum stahlii,* called coral beads, makes short stems densely clustered with half-inch shiny thick leaves that turn red in the sun, a good display even in a two-inch pot.

Habitat

Miniatures, especially those that enjoy high humidity, will thrive in glass bowls, empty fish tanks, or even plastic clothes boxes, but it is most important to choose an attractive container that will set off the charming plants. If you select one of the terrarium type that has no drainage provision, begin by setting in a one-inch-deep layer of pebbles, then a sprinkle of granulated charcoal, a thin layer of sphagnum moss, and only then the growing medium.

Peat-lite, commercial humus-rich mixtures, such as Black Magic and New Era, are excellent for terrarium plants. I add a light dusting of dolomite limestone to mixtures that contain more than one-third peat moss. A terrarium soil must remain sweet and fluffy, so avoid soils of high clay content. For a successful planting, concentrate on one habitat.

Two popular habitats are the moist, warm tropical forest for diffuse sunlight, and the dry, warm to cool tropical desert for bright-diffuse light to full sun. Make a basic plan for the terrarium before you begin. Keep plants in scale with each other, choose species that are found in the same habitat. Pick wood, stones, and perhaps a few shells that are found in the area where your plants grow. Avoid manufactured models, bright-colored plastic pools, and any objects not from the habitat to be re-created.

Planting

Clean the container with soap and water. Rinse well, dry, and polish the glass. You can plant in a fish tank, big glass bowl, slant-front terrarium, miniature greenhouse—any container that lets in light but retains humidity. Desert habitats, of course, can be planted in a big ceramic bowl without any covering glass.

Arrange materials.

Tools like spoons, scissors, dull knife, miniature garden fork, and trowel.

Chunks of Featherock or lava rock, driftwood from fresh water, or well-washed beach wood. Rotting log sections with lichens for a forest setting. Cholla cactus wood for a desert display.

Have plants ready in a tray with moist paper towels around roots or in small pots. Trim off all dead foliage.

Set large pieces.

Add gravel, then insert a small aluminum or dark-colored dish if you want a small pool. Put a few pebbles in the dish to hold it steady, fill in around it to get gravel even and to hide sides of dish.

Add large rocks and driftwood or log sections. If you don't want to see bare earth against the glass, put sheet moss, sphagnum, or live moss all around the inside, extending two to three inches higher than the gravel.

Fill in soil. All soil should contain charcoal chips.

For desert plants use a sandy succulent mix; for other plants, a humus-rich medium.

Plant larger species.

Put tallest plants in rear if you are going to view from one side. Otherwise you might want to have one end with higher plants, creating several vistas.

Tuck in small plants.

Give delicate plants room so they won't be swamped by quick growers.

Land snail shells and small animal skulls add an authentic note to terrariums. Water in.

For desert plants mulch with pebbles or rocks. Woodland plantings look best with moss. Living ground covers listed earlier.

Use a gentle sprinkle to settle plants.

Clean off glass, cover forest or woodland terrariums so that a slight bit of moisture condenses on the glass. When many drops cling to inside of cover, lift the cover or move to one side, to ventilate.

Crystal bowl planted with restrained growers: *Saintpaulia* in center, jewel orchid *Haemaria discolor* at left, and creeping *Pellionia pulchra* at right. All thrive with lightly moist roots, high humidity, and diffuse light from window and table lamp.

Allophyton mexicanum, seldom over five inches tall, does best in bright-diffuse light with constantly moist roots. Foliage is dark green; flowers are lavender throughout the year.

Miniature *Sinningia* plants among rounded stones create a woodland effect in a large tank. Hybrid *S.* 'Dollbaby' towers in background; *Helxine soleirolii* at lower right is good miniature ground cover.

Sinningia 'Freckles', a miniature hybrid of *S. concinna* X *S. hirsuta*

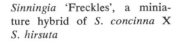

Saintpaulia 'Tiny Pink', in a 1½-inch pot, shows influence of dwarf *S. shumensis* with almost round succulent foliage.

Trichoceros antennifera, called fly orchid, grows well on tree-fern slabs, seldom reaches more than five inches, and has fascinating flowers in ten- to twelve-inch inflorescences.

Dwarf *Aloe haworthioides* complements Rhodesian soapstone chameleon.

17

Plants for Public Buildings

ODAY IN PUBLIC BUILDINGS, tropical plants are favorite finishing decorations. Architects increasingly include provisions for living plants in banks, offices, hotel lounges, hospital foyers, entrance halls, and waiting rooms of many kinds. Large built-in planters, sunken garden areas, pools, sometimes a fountain, have become elements of the initial design of such places. The exhibition and maintenance of exotic plants is a most practical and relatively easy means of making these places invitingly attractive, because climate-control systems, bright artificial lighting, and large windows help to create a suitable healthful environment, especially for strikingly beautiful foliage plants. In air terminals and other places of public passage, vigorous green plants add cheer and interest. Clever placement will soften harsh architectural lines and create smaller intimate sanctuaries within expansive waiting rooms.

Less favorable environments, in old buildings, usually have enough window light for an aspidistra, an *Aglaonema* plant, or a healthy philodendron. During a visit to the offices of a major television network I found otherwise sterile surroundings modified by almost every secretary, who had a pot of philodendron, trailing pothos, even a carefully tended dracaena at her desk, often with no more than an overhead spot lamp to furnish light.

Dark lobbies lit by fluorescent tubes can be decorated with low planters of *Dracaena fragrans massangeana* and *D. deremensis* from tropical Africa or with cultivars of similar shade-tolerant species. Dracaenas alone, in their varied forms, can create a most pleasing, easy-to-maintain display in dim-light locations.

Plants Reliably Adapted to Dim Light

Aechmea fasciata. Once it has formed bloom spike (needs brighter light until then).

Aglaonema. Tough elliptic or narrow pointed foliage, white spathes.

Aspidistra. The truly cast-iron plant.

Calathea. Jungle-floor plants four to fifteen inches high, many species.

Chamaedorea elegans 'Bella'. A dwarf form of an excellent palm.

Dracaena. Several species. See above.

Ficus species. Small tropical fig trees for tubs.

Howeia belmoreana, H. forsteriana. The Kentia palms.

Philodendrons. Wide variety of forms, shades of green, climb or clump.

Rhapidophora aurea (syn. *Scindapsus*) or *Pothos*. Gold-marked leaves, trailing stems.

Sansevieria species and cultivars. Low, medium, or tall.

Spathiphyllum floribundum. Compact foliage, white spathes.

S. 'Mauna Loa'. Large spathes. *Spathiphyllum* prefers warm moist area.

Culture

Plants in public buildings have the same requirements for life that they do in a house or greenhouse: different types needing varying intensities of light, different soil mixtures, different humidity, and different amounts of water and fertilizer. A brief review of the chapters on various plants and studying the photographs will direct you to those species most suited to any particular location.

Some special problems to be met are:

Constant dust.	Wash leaves with warm-water mist.
Lack of humidity.	Install fountains; mist; adjust building humidity control for 40 to 50 percent relative humidity.
Extreme dryness with very hot sun.	Select succulents that tolerate these conditions. Note that not all of them can.
Low light level.	Supplement main light source with spots and fluorescents; extend day length; choose species with low-light tolerance; rotate plants.

Small Offices

Any office or suite, no matter how small, will be aesthetically improved by appropriate living plants. A carefully chosen, healthy, and well-tended collection of windowsill plants has transformed many an indifferent private office. A single well-placed orange tree (*Citrus aurantium myrtifolia*) or a deeply lobed, large-leaved *Philodendron* X *fosterianum* has made a small reception room charming and hospitable. In a bookshelf horticultural fluorescent tubes above a tray of moist gravel will create a good microclimate for a little indoor garden. On a desk top a Sun Bowl or Ripe-N-Grow circular fixture with a twenty-two-watt wide-spectrum Gro-Lux tube is perfect for African-violets or haworthias. Self-watering containers and devices covered in Chapter 4 are designed to solve watering problems over weekends and holidays.

For a small office you or any person seriously interested can take on the pleasure of selecting locations for plants and choosing how they are to be used and which kinds of plants are preferable. With a limited number of plants one person can purchase materials, place the plants, and care for them day to day. The information offered in this book is intended to assure your success.

Larger Areas

Interior landscaping for places where many people come and go or congregate—large corridors and entrance halls, hotel foyers, banks, high-ceilinged waiting rooms and the like—is a job for professionals. It demands an extensive knowledge of special plant materials, sound horticultural know-how including plant pathology, and, on the other hand, a sure sense of design coupled with imagination and taste. Fortunately there are a number of firms that offer complete design and maintenance contracts. As one example, a firm in the New York City area has issued a folder filled with illustrations indicating how they may use plants in public buildings (and private places, too). Various plants are shown in groups, according to size and suitability for various situations. Species and hybrids are listed with exact botanical names and notes on the light range preferred by each. After one or several conferences with the client, this firm submits designs and cost estimates. Similar services and the all-important follow-through for maintenance are offered by other concerns and by individual designers in or near the larger cities of this country. Such firms and designers are normally recommended by architects in the locality and are also listed in some classified directories.

The following photographs illustrate how a variety of plants can be used for indoor decoration, some for smaller places, others for large-scale interiors.

Dramatic use of plants of varied habits and foliage color. An attractive stone mulch turns this lobby display into a work of art, especially striking when viewed from above.

Dracaena marginata, from drier regions of Madagascar, endures low humidity and dim light and is often a perfect choice for an office plant. This specimen is kept lightly moist by a Plantender, an automatic watering device. (*Plantamation, Inc.*)

Bold planting of *Dracaena deremensis* and its variety *warneckii* in a Westchester mall is appreciated at eye level or seen from above through a second-story well. This species endures low light and low humidity; soil is kept evenly moist.

Fluorescent lights in Phytarium chamber by Environment One Corporation furnish illumination for plants in case. Simple hung fixture provides light for plants on shelf underneath. The Phytarium case has glass front, controls for light, air circulation, and supplementary carbon dioxide. Plants below are set on moist gravel. They decorate a reading room of the Horticultural Society of New York.

Indoor greenhouse in a large public room at a Westchester nature center was filled with donated plants, which I arranged to resemble a tropical forest but to require only minimum maintenance. Light is furnished by fluorescents above plants; humidity is retained by all-glass enclosure, but windows provide ventilation. Base is peat-moss–perlite mixture over coarse gravel and hardwood charcoal; large rocks and gravel are used as mulch. *Osmanthus* shrubs at right are planted free; most other plants in sunken pots.

Schefflera actinophylla towering above shiny-leaved camellias and low-growing *Spathyphyllum* (lower left) in a shopping mall. Design and planting by Alan Lawrence of Interior Gardens, Inc.

273

New Ford Foundation building in New York City includes extensive greenhouse-lobby in its center well with glass roof and sides and provides view of plants to interior offices on all floors. Design by Kevin Roche, John Dinkeloo & Associates, and office of Dan Kiley, with plantings by Everett Conklin and Company.

Interior of Ford Foundation giant lobby-greenhouse features permanent plantings of semi-tropical magnolias, camellias, Norfolk Island pines. Ground covers include philodendrons, *Rhoeo discolor*, and ferns. Seasonal color is added with interspersed azaleas and poinsettias. Daily sprinkling and the interior pool furnish humidity.

Ficus retusa from Asian tropics is a sturdy species for training as a small tree.

Circular Wide Spectrum Gro-Lux tube in a desk planter provides sufficient light for healthy growth and blooming of many gesneriads, such as this dwarf *Sinningia* hybrid.

18

Keeping Your
Plants Healthy

Houseplants grown in the correct environment, soil, and container will be more resistant to disease than those weakened by poor culture and unfavorable surroundings. With proper air circulation most fungus will find it difficult to get a start. The same is true when foliage and flowers are dry at night. Fungus troubles begin most frequently at night, when moisture is present on plants in a close atmosphere.

Pests, in contrast, will just as soon attack a healthy plant as a poorly grown one. Insects sometimes infest houseplants so healthy that you won't notice the pests until damage is extensive unless you follow the wise practice of looking for pests before trouble is widespread. Health is dependent not only on environment and culture, but also on vigilant care.

Introduce a new plant into your collection only after it has been isolated for several weeks and fully inspected for signs of insects or fungus troubles. Look for mealybugs in new growth or around roots, check undersides of foliage for red spiders, search for white flies, scales, snails, and rot. In addition to this visual inspection, give each new plant a spray of insecticide, put the plant in a separate saucer or tray, and keep it away from your established plants until you are sure the newcomer has no troubles that might spread.

Isolation

For the best protection, isolate plants completely. I find that a fluorescent fixture in the basement, away from my window and greenhouse plants, is a convenient place to quarantine new arrivals. (Chapter 2 has details on fluorescent lights.) Place pots of new plants on perlite or gravel in a shallow tray. Pour in a cup of insecticide so that any pests traveling outside of the pots will be killed. If new plants have any sort of rot, cut out the infected tissue, dust with Fermate, and mist surface of pots and soil with a solution of Dexon (Olin Mathieson Corporation) or Benlate fungicide (DuPont benomyl).

Insecticides and Fungicides

Agricultural science continues to devise new chemical compounds and forms of natural materials that have value in preserving the health of ornamental plants. Every year new formulas produce medicines and pesticides of improved effectiveness, more specific action, and—most importantly—greater safety for us and other animals. For the latest information on which insecticides and fungicides are best and legal to apply in your area, consult your state agricultural extension service, conservation environmental protection agency, or the nearest botanical garden. Many formerly sanctioned pesticides are now strictly controlled by legislation, and some are illegal to use at all.

Some insecticides are safe to use when applied according to manufacturer's recommendations. Others are dangerous even when used as directed, and these are available only to professional nurserymen, who are supposed to use them with special masks and garments. Still another group of chemicals is relatively safe for you to apply but with continued use cause such damage to ecosystems that they should not be used, even if you can get them. DDT and related persistent chlorinated hydrocarbons wreak havoc after several years of application. These chemicals accumulate in water, soil, plants, and bodies of animals. Restrict your use of insecticides to those products that are known to be degradable in the environment.

Some insecticides are derivatives of plants—nicotine sulfate (Black Leaf-40) and pyrethrum, for example. Chemical insecticides like Malathion and Cygon, organic phosphates, are effective against red spiders, bulb flies, and other common pests, but the chemicals gradually degrade upon exposure to the open air. They do not accumulate in soil or water. Danger to you still exists if the insecticides are not used with caution.

Insurance Spray

A good insurance spray for most new plants is a mixture of Cythion (premium-grade Malathion) or Kelthane, with ferbam (Fermate) or the newer Benlate. Mix according to container directions for indoor plants. The soluble powder Malathion is less harsh than the liquid, hence better for sensitive plants, but the emulsified liquid has caused no trouble for me on tropicals that will accept Malathion at all. Most succulents are injured by Malathion. I used it on healthy established *Euphorbia splendens* to kill red spiders, and the plants came through fine. Under the same treatment a stapelia and a kalanchoe almost died. Anthuriums also are injured by Malathion. Nicotine sulfate is generally safe for succulents, and Cygon has been used for root mealybugs on succulents without reported injury.

Kelthane, a miticide, is preferable to Malathion for orchids, such as *Phalaenopsis*, which may be attacked by false spider mites. Spray imported orchids with the Kelthane and Fermate combination; it will take care of pests that may have escaped the plant quarantine inspectors.

Broughtonia orchids are very sensitive to Cygon 2E, and I have had them set back by Malathion, so don't spray them with such chemicals. Buy plants in person so that you can check for pests, or order from reliable mail-order firms that guarantee clean stock. Mail back anything that arrives with pests on it.

Safety

If you live where it is impractical to apply insecticide sprays outdoors, place a large plastic bag over the plants. Stick the spray nozzle through the top and thus restrict the insecticide to plants. It is important to keep insecticides from accumulating on rugs, furniture, and cement. Even noncumulative insecticides are dangerous to the liver and nervous system.

Systemics

Systemic insecticides are applied to the soil, and roots absorb them for distribution to all parts of the plant. Sucking or chewing insects will die from the poison when they attack a treated plant. I use Ortho Isotox granular systemic and a similar Plantabbs product according to label directions. A few overhead sprays also have a systemic action as they are absorbed through the leaves. For overhead spray solutions I add a few drops of fish emulsion to make the chemicals stick fast.

Apply overhead sprays on plants away from the sun. Maximum efficiency is reached between 70° and 80°. Granular systemics can be applied to the soil at any time. If a pest infestation is found, spray all plants in that area.

Clean mealybugs and scales off plants with a toothbrush and a solution of mild soapy water. Check roots and center of new growths for both of these troubles.

Basic Treatment for Major Pests

Pest	Treatment
Aphids. Green, brown, or black sucking insects, usually on new growth and buds.	Wash off out of doors or in bathtub. Spray with all-purpose plant bomb or Malathion. Systemic in soil is good prevention.
Cyclamen mite. Almost microscopic pest, sucks juices from tender center leaves, mainly gesneriads, causes very stunted growth, hairy leaves.	Spray with Kelthane, repeat in three days, again in ten days. Alternate with Malathion if pests persist. Discard replaceable common plants. One teaspoon in two quarts of Kelthane liquid is safe for gesneriads.
Mealybugs. White cottony sucking insects, often in new growth of orchids, leaf junctions of coleuses.	Remove visible bugs with cotton Q-Tips soaked in rubbing alcohol. Spray with Black Leaf-40 or Malathion (Cythion) according to package directions. Spray again in ten days. For soil mealybugs apply systemic granules or liquid Cygon 2E.
Nematodes. Root-sucking microscopic round worms, cause swellings and distortions of roots. Check when repotting.	Soak soil with a nemacide. More importantly, use only pasteurized soils to avoid this destructive pest.
Scales. Flat firmly attached sucking insects, common on palms, jungle orchids.	Wash off with soapy water, spray with Malathion (or nicotine sulfate on succulents). Repeat treatment in two weeks. Discard severely infested plant.
Red spider mites. Tiny sucking pests, almost invisible. They begin on undersides of thin foliage, eventually make fine webs.	These don't like moist conditions; mist undersides of foliage to keep them in check; also apply systemic poisons to soil as protection. Spray infested plants with Malathion alternated in several days with Kelthane, covering underside of foliage with spray.
White flies. Not too common but hard to get rid of. Sucking pests, rest on foliage, fly off in cloud when bothered.	Aerosol insecticides or freshly mixed Malathion are effective; repeat in eight to ten days. On ferns use nicotine sulfate three-quarter teaspoon per quart of warm soapy water.

Fungus Troubles

If you keep plants dry on top and the air circulating, your plants will avoid most fungus troubles. Continue the clean culture by picking off dead flowers and leaves that may harbor fungus. Fungicides I have found effective are Fermate to rub as dry powder on cuts or when dividing plants and Dexon and Benlate as sprays used according to the package directions. Benlate (DuPont) is a rather new product but has a wide-spectrum effectiveness against many common fungus and rot pathogens.

Seedlings are susceptible to a fungus that causes rapid death, usually first as a rot where stems meet soil. Sowing seed on milled sphagnum moss or mixtures of milled sphagnum with perlite and vermiculite will largely eliminate damping off. As a preventative, treat sowing flats with one of the good fungicides like Dexon. There are other products, such as Panodrench, which are made for this use, but they may be taken off the market in some states. Good light and air and no overwatering help to control damping-off fungus without chemicals. I have no problem when I sow seeds on sphagnum.

Air Pollution

Polluted air damages and sometimes kills plants. In large cities the air is frequently filled with harmful products of combustion and industrial processes. Soot, sulfur dioxide, and ethylene are all destructive to living organisms. Orchid flowers may close after a few days of exposure to polluted air, although under clean atmospheric conditions they last in perfection a month or more. Those that don't close may be disfigured by sepal wilt.

Some West Coast orchid growers are already breeding orchids for smog-resistant qualities, and these new hybrids are listed in their current catalogs. Even these genetically resistant types can't thrive where air pollution is severe. If pollution is serious, unopened flower buds blast or open only partially, with perhaps brown or black tepal wilt. Unfortunately conditions that are best for healthy growth also render the plants most vulnerable to pollutants in the air.

High humidity and moist roots cause leaf stomata to open so gases can enter freely. Drier air and roots sometimes help to prevent damage during air pollution alerts, but this is no guarantee of protection. The best remedy, before we finally clean up the environment, is to filter the outside air before it reaches your plants.

Air conditioners, if not blowing directly on plants, are helpful but will lower humidity. Some sun-rooms may be equipped with wet-pad air filters that lower the temperature, furnish humidity, and help to remove many of the harmful pollutants, but these wet-pad coolers are not practical for living rooms. So long as plant pots are on moist gravel or the room has a humidifier, a standard air conditioner is a safe way to filter air before it enters your rooms. Without the aid of air filters some city gardeners could grow little more than tough sansevierias and aspidistras.

Sunburn

Check Chapter 2 for details on selecting the correct light intensity for specific plants. Thin curtains are adequate protection for some plants from very hot sun. To treat burned leaves on plants with long-lasting foliage, like orchids, cut away any badly burned tissue, dust the wound with Fermate, and keep it dry until it heals. A burned spot can be left on but looks unsightly and may last for several years.

Cuts, scrapes, and smashed tissues invite infection. Cut away any rotting sections a quarter to a half inch into sound tissue, keep the area dry, and dust the wounds with a fungicide powder like Fermate. Healthy broken-off leaves and branches can often be rooted as described in Chapter 5.

An infestation of red spiders looks like this. Droplets of sap are usually present; minute webs are woven by the tiny brown to reddish-green mites, difficult to see without a magnifying glass. Thin-leaved plants are most often attacked.

Aphids on a gynura shoot. Sucking insects like aphids often prefer buds and tender new growth.

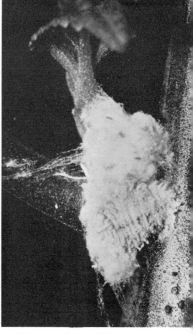

A cluster of mealybugs on a coleus stem. White cottony material holds eggs; adult is seen at lower portion of sticky mass.

Scale insects on a palm frond

A heavy infestation of scales on an epidendrum orchid

Sophrolaeliocattleya hybrid suffering from sepal wilt caused by air pollution

Amaryllis bulb partially eaten by bulb-fly grub. Drenching soil with Cygon will protect bulbs from this pest.

Helpful Lists

Calendar of Flowers

Plants marked with an asterisk (*) include cultivars that can be almost everblooming under optimum cultural conditions. These same types can provide a succession of flowers if plants of different ages are grown.

Spring (March–June)

Amaryllis
Cattleya mendelii, C. mossiae, and hybrids
*Columnea**
*Crossandra**
Eucomis
Euphorbia splendens and its varieties and hybrids, notably *E.* X *keysii**
*Gloxinia**
Miltonia, warm-growing hybrids with Brazilian species
*Phalaenopsis**
Rhipsalidopsis
Smithiantha
*Streptocarpus**

Summer (July–September)

Allamanda
*Begonia semperflorens**

Brassia species and hybrids
Cattleya dowiana hybrids
Episcia
Epiphyllum hybrids
*Geranium**
Hoya
*Passiflora alato-caerulea**
*Saintpaulia**
Sprekelia

Fall (September–November)

*Anthurium**
Beloperone guttata
*Brassavola nodosa**
Bromeliads
Cattleya bowringiana, C. labiata, and many hybrids
Dendrobium phalaenopsis hybrids
Hoya
Oncidium varicosum and hybrids
Zygocactus and hybrids

Winter (December–February)

Aeschynanthus
Angraecum sesquipedale and hybrids
Begonia 'Dresden Gold', and many cane types
Cattleya trianaei and many hybrids
Dendrobium nobile and hybrids
Narcissus, paper-whites and 'Soleil d'Or'
Oncidium splendidum
Paphiopedalum
*Phalaenopsis**
Renanthopsis
Rechsteinera cardinalis
*Saintpaulia**
Schlumbergera and hybrids
Smithiantha
Veltheimia

Plants for Cool Locations (to 50° winter nights)

Begonias

Angel wing, Christmas, and semperflorens hybrids

Bromeliads

Dyckia
Tillandsia, Central America and Florida species

Bulbs

Cyclamen
Lachenalia
Narcissus
Scilla
Veltheimia

Foliage

Agave
Araucaria heterophylla
Chamaerops excelsa
Citrus trees
Fatshedera and *Fatsia*
Hedera helix cultivars
Monstera deliciosa
Philodendrons (most sorts)
Podocarpus

Geraniums

All cultivars and especially *Pelargonium* X *domesticum* hybrids

Orchids

Mature *Cattleya* and *Laeliocattleya* hybrids
Cymbidium
High-altitude species in many genera, as of Andean. *Odontoglossum* and
   hybrids
Laelia anceps hybrids
   Cool-preference *Paphiopedilum* (usually plain-leaved)

Succulents

Agave
Cacti (except jungle types in active growth)
Lithops

Plant Societies

African-Violet Society of America, Inc.   Monthly magazine
P.O. Box 1326
Knoxville, Tenn. 37901

American Begonia Society   Monthly magazine
10331 S. Colima Road
Whittier, Calif. 90604

American Fern Society   *American Fern Journal*, quarterly
Department of Botany
University of Tennessee
Knoxville, Tenn. 37916

American Gesneriad Society   *Gesneriad Saintpaulia News*, six
Box 91192   issues per year
Los Angeles, Calif. 90009

American Gloxinia and Gesneriad Society   *The Gloxinian and the Other Ges-*
c/o Mrs. Diantha Buell, Secretary   *neriads*, six issues per year
Eastford, Conn. 06242

American Orchid Society   Monthly *Bulletin*. Worldwide affili-
Botanical Museum of Harvard University   ated societies.
Cambridge, Mass. 02138

American Plant Life Society   Yearly publication devoted mainly
Box 150   to bulbs
La Jolla, Calif. 92037

Bromeliad Society   *Bromeliad Bulletin*, six issues per
1811 Edgecliff Drive   year
Los Angeles, Calif. 90026

Cactus and Succulent Society of America   *Journal*, six issues per year
Box 167
Reseda, Calif. 91335

Indoor Light Gardening Society of America   *The News*, bimonthly, about grow-
4 Wildwood Road   ing plants under lights
Greenville, S.C. 29607

International Geranium Society
1413 Shoreline Drive
Santa Barbara, Calif. 93105

Geraniums, four issues per year

Los Angeles International Fern Society
13715 Corday Avenue
Hawthorne, Calif. 90250

Monthly fern lessons and year book

Saintpaulia International Society
Box 10604
Knoxville, Tenn. 37919

Shares *Gesneriad Saintpaula News* with American Gesneriad Society

Sources of Plants and Supplies

Alberts and Merkel Bros., Inc.
P.O. Box 537
Boynton Beach, Fla. 33435

Color catalog, rare tropicals, many genera of bromeliads, foliage species, orchids. Catalog: 50¢.

Alnap Co., Inc.
66 Reade Street
New York, N.Y. 10007

Supplies, including growing mediums for epiphytes. Free lists.

Atlas Fish Emulsion Co.
1015 O'Brien Drive
Menlo Park, Calif. 94025

Fertilizers. Free culture leaflet on African-violets and orchids.

Beahm Gardens
2686 Paloma Street
Pasadena, Calif. 91107

Epiphyllums, haworthias, hoyas

Bermas Plastic Co., Inc.
Box 534
Bardonia, N.Y. 10954

Aquamatic planters

Buell's Greenhouses
Eastford, Conn. 06242

Most cultivated gesneriads, unusual gloxinias, new miniatures. Catalog and color booklet: $1.00.

W. Atlee Burpee Co.
Philadelphia, Pa. 19132

Some seed and plants of tropical houseplants plus growing supplies. Free catalog.

J. T. Dimmick Forest Co.
Garberville, Calif. 95440

Redwood bark products, direct shipment anywhere. Free list.

Edelweiss Gardens
54 Robbinsville-Allentown Road
Robbinsville, N.J. 08691

Wide assortment of begonias, bromeliads, orchids, succulents, other tropicals. List: 35¢. Visitors welcome.

Encap Products Co.
P.O. Box 278
Mt. Prospect, Ill. 60056

Green-Garde iron and insecticides

Fennell Orchid Co.
26715 S.W. 157th Avenue
Homestead, Fla. 33030

Orchids and growing supplies. Free current listing. Visitors welcome to outdoor orchid display.

Fischer Greenhouse
Linwood, N.J. 08221

Many African-violets, some other gesneriads, supplies. Plant catalog: 15¢.

Floralite Co.
4124 East Oakwood Road
Oak Creek, Wis. 53154

Fluorescent light fixtures, tubes, plant stands. Free list.

Arthur Freed Orchids, Inc.
5731 South Bonsall Drive
Malibu, Calif. 90265

Phalaenopsis, many miniatures, and related orchids. Free color catalog. Visitors welcome.

Bernard D. Greeson
3548 N. Cramer Street
Milwaukee, Wis. 53211

Growing supplies, some *Saintpaulia*. List: 10¢.

Gubler Orchids
9441 East Broadway
Temple City, Calif. 91780

Orchids, especially cattleya-type hybrids and a few unusuals. Free catalog.

The House Plant Corner
P.O. Box 810
Oxford, Md. 21654

Some gesneriads and orchids. Complete illustrated catalog of supplies: 25¢.

Hyponex Co.
Copley, Ohio 44321

Chemical fertilizers, supplies, Wik-Fed pots. Free list.

P. de Jager & Sons, Inc.
188 Ashbury Street
South Hamilton, Mass. 01982
or
132 Dinnick Crescent
Toronto, Canada

Quality bulbs. Free catalog.

Johnson Cactus Gardens
2735 Olive Hill Road
Fallbrook, Calif. 92028

Complete cactus and succulent catalog, color illustrated: 25¢.

Jones and Scully, Inc.
2200 N.W. 33rd Avenue
Miami, Fla. 33142

Orchid specialists. Free color illustrated catalog. Visitors welcome.

Kartuz Greenhouses
92 Chestnut Street
Wilmington, Mass. 01887

Gesneriads, begonias, assorted other tropicals for home growing. Catalog: 25¢.

William Kirch Orchids Ltd.
2630 Waiomao Road
Honolulu, Hawaii 96816

Free catalog of unusual orchids includes hybrids of many genera. Air-mail shipping anywhere.

Lager and Hurrell
426 Morris Avenue
Summit, N.J. 07901

Orchids and supplies. Culture book-catalog: $2.00. Visitors welcome.

Laviga Horticultural Corp.
184 Lighthouse Beach Road
Hilton, N.Y. 14468

Growing medium for gesneriads

Logee's Greenhouses
Danielson, Conn. 06239

Illustrated catalog, $1.00, has many color illustrations, long listing of rare tropicals, especially begonias, geraniums. Visitors welcome.

Paul P. Lowe
23045 S.W. 123rd Road
Goulds, Fla. 33170

Free mimeographed listing of begonias and bromeliads

Lyndon Lyon
Dolgeville, N.Y. 13329

New African-violet hybrids including miniatures. Send stamp for catalog.

Rod McLellan Co.
1450 El Camino Real
South San Francisco, Calif. 94080

Free color catalog of unusual orchids, many supplies, Wonderbark Mix. Visitors welcome at greenhouses.

Merry Gardens
Camden, Maine 04843

Some supplies. Culture booklet-catalog: $1.00. Free list of unusual tropicals.

Nature's Way Products
3505 Mozart Avenue
Cincinnati, Ohio 45211

Free list of organic fertilizers

George W. Park Seed Co., Inc.
Greenwood, S.C. 29646

Excellent color catalog includes tropical plants, seeds, culture data, many supplies.

Robert B. Peters Co.
2833 Pennsylvania Street
Allentown, Pa. 18104

Chemical fertilizers, soil testing service. Free catalog.

Plantamation, Inc.
340 E. 57th Street
New York, N.Y. 10022

Plantender automatic watering devices. Free folder.

Plantation Garden Products
P.O. Box 127
Boynton Beach, Fla. 33435

Catalog of supplies, many for orchids: 20¢. Free chart on insecticides.

Roehrs Exotic Nurseries
RFD 2, Box 144
Farmingdale, N.J. 07727

Complete tropical plant selection. Booklet *Decorative Plants for Interiors*: $1.50. Basic lists free. Visitors welcome.

John Scheepers, Inc.
63 Wall Street
New York, N.Y. 10005

Flower bulb specialists. Free catalog contains some tropical bulbs, some supplies.

Seaborn Del Dios Nursery
Box 455
Escondido, Calif. 92025

Bromeliads, cycads, palms. Free lists. Visitors welcome.

Shaffer's Tropical Gardens
1220 41st Avenue
Santa Cruz, Calif. 95060

Phalaenopsis specialists. Free color catalog includes some supplies, plant growth chambers.

Shoplite Co., Inc.
650 Franklin Avenue
Nutley, N.J. 07110

Free catalog of fluorescent light equipment. Booklet on growing under lights: 25¢.

Spaeth
25-16 12th Street
Long Island City, N.Y. 11102

Containers, prefab waterfalls.

Fred A. Stewart Co.
1212 E. Las Tunas Drive
San Gabriel, Calif. 91778

Free color catalog of orchids includes section on miniatures, many unusual hybrids, supplies.

Stim-U-Plant Laboratories, Inc.
2077 Parkwood Avenue
Columbus, Ohio 43219

Planting mix, fertilizers, and insecticides. Free culture leaflets and supply list.

Tinari Greenhouses
2325 Valley Road
Huntingdon Valley, Pa. 19006

Color catalog of African-violets, companion gesneriads and supplies: 15¢. Visitors welcome.

Wayside Gardens
Mentor, Ohio 44060

Many unusual bulbs and tubers. Catalog: $2.00, refundable with order.

West Coast Gesneriads
2179 44th Avenue
San Francisco, Calif. 94116

Gesneriads. Many new things. Catalog: 10¢.

Weyerhaeuser Co.
Tacoma, Washington 98401

Fir bark products. Free folders on growing orchids in bark.

Whistling Hill
Box 27
Hamburg, N.Y. 14075

Unusual gesneriads, no African-violets. List: 15¢.

Wilson Brothers
Roachdale, Ind. 46172

Geranium specialists. Free catalog includes some other tropicals, a few supplies. Visitors welcome at greenhouse.

Zink's Greenhouses
P.O. Box 1676
Vista, Calif. 92083

Succulent specialists. Catalog with many black-and-white photos: 25¢.

Bibliography

American Begonia Society. *The Begonian*. Long Beach, Calif. Monthly magazine.

American Gloxinia and Gesneriad Society. *The Gloxinian*. Old Greenwich, Conn. Monthly magazine.

American Horticultural Society. *Cultivated Palms*. Special issue of *American Horticultural Society Magazine*. Washington, D.C., 1961.

American Orchid Society. *Bulletin*. Cambridge, Mass. Monthly magazine.

———. *Handbook on Orchid Nomenclature and Registration*. Cambridge, Mass., 1969.

Arbelaez, E. P. *Plantas Utiles de Colombia*. Madrid: Sucesores de Rivadeneyra, 1956.

Aubert de la Rue, E., Bourliere, F., and Harroy, J. *The Tropics*. New York: Alfred A. Knopf, 1957.

Bromeliad Society. *Bulletin*. Los Angeles. Monthly magazine.

Gesneriad Saintpaulia News. Knoxville, Tenn.: Indoor Gardener Publishing Co., Inc. Semimonthly magazine.

Graf, Alfred B. *Exotica 3*. New Jersey: Julius Roehrs Co., 1970.

———. *Exotic Plant Manual*. New Jersey: Julius Roehrs Co., 1970.

Hawkes, A. D. *Encyclopaedia of Cultivated Orchids*. London: Faber and Faber, Ltd., 1965.

Menninger, Edwin A. *Flowering Vines of the World*. New York: Hearthside Press, Inc., 1970.

Moore, Harold E., Jr. *African-Violets, Gloxinias and Their Relatives*. New York: The Macmillan Company, 1957.

Pirone, P. P. *Diseases and Pests of Ornamental Plants.* 4th ed. New York: The Ronald Press Company, 1970.

Traub, H. P. *The Amaryllis Manual.* New York: The Macmillan Company, 1958.

Wilson, Helen Van Pelt. *Helen Van Pelt Wilson's African-Violet Book.* New York: Hawthorn Books, Inc., 1970.

———. *The Joy of Geraniums.* New York: M. Barrows & Co., 1965.

Withner, Carl L., ed. *The Orchids: A Scientific Study.* New York: The Ronald Press Company, 1959.

Index

DATE DUE
